Strategies for Survival

The Psychology of Cultural Resilience in Ethnic Minorities

Peter Elsass

Translated by
Fran Hopenwasser

New York University Press
NEW YORK AND LONDON

NEW YORK UNIVERSITY PRESS
New York and London

Library of Congress Cataloging-in-Publication Data
Elsass, Peter.
[Jordan er vores mor. English]
Strategies for survival : the psychology of cultural resilience in ethnic minorities / Peter Elsass ; translated by Fran Hopenwasser.
p. cm.
Translation of: Jorden er vores mor.
Includes bibliographical references (p. 239) and index.
ISBN 0-8147-2188-5
1. Motilon Indians—Cultural assimilation. 2. Arhuaco Indians—Cultural assimilation. 3. Acculturation—South America. 4. Resilience (Psychology)—Cross-cultural studies. 5. Minorities—South America—Psychology. I. Title. II. Title: Cultural resilience in ethnic minorities.
F2319.2.M6E37 1992 91-45886
305.898'3—dc20 CIP

New York University Press books are printed on acid-free paper, and their binding materials are chosen for strength and durability.

Manufactured in the United States of America

c 10 9 8 7 6 5 4 3 2 1

All photographs are by Peter Elsass, except for those on pp. xvii and 23 by Morten Bruus, and on p. 99 by Guillermo Padilla.

Contents

Preface

Why does one society survive, while others perish? How do exploitation, violence, and terror arise?

The psychology of survival is best understood when it is examined in many different cultural contexts and in a broad variety of social situations.

The following chapters are a series of descriptions of Indians and descendants of slaves in Latin America, all of whom have attempted to survive with their traditional culture intact. However, they have encountered different kinds of violence and terror. Some have survived; others have disappeared.

Since 1973 I have followed the Arhuaco Indians in Colombia and the Motilon Indians in Venezuela. Returning twelve times to the same places and the same families, I have followed them in their development or decline. I have visited descendants of slaves in inner Surinam, and spent a few days in the Jonestown colony in Guyana, ten days before it committed collective suicide. All of these small societies are characterized by living apart from the mainstream society, like "floating islands," struggling in different ways for independence and autonomy.

In the beginning, my visits to the Indians had a clear goal: to document their oppression. I traveled around with a tape recorder, and Indians spoke into it about their struggles for survival. Afterwards, I went into the dominant white society and played the Indian tapes for officials, government people, missionaries, and landowners. I recorded their responses on tape, which I later played back for the Indians. By going back and forth across the borders, I was able to gather concrete material on the oppression of the Indians. I later handed all this material over to the Indians without imposing my own interpretations or explanations upon it.

After I had visited the Indians a couple of times, I wrote the book *Indianerliv* (Indian Life) (Elsass 1977). It was a great success and received good reviews in my own country, Denmark. But the Indians received it in a different way. For example, I wrote about the Arhuaco Indians as a people who lived in harmony with nature and within the group. Later, when I read my book aloud for the Indians, they made themselves comfortable before the campfire and asked me to read it for them one more time. Their response was that *Indianerliv* was interesting to listen to, but that it was more about me and my dreams than about them and their daily life.

Now that I know them better, their story has become harder to tell. I know some of them so well now that I no longer can talk about them in a simple or coherent way. On the other hand, this closeness has allowed me to gain insight into the underlying structures that presuppose their survival, and to arrive at some notion of why violence and terror have penetrated their community.

My personal presence, on location and living with the people, has been important. At times, my stays have been brief, as my interest was to travel on in order to do comparative studies before my impressions faded away. Thus, my work diverges from that of the anthropologist's monographic studies, based on long stays at a limited number of fieldwork locations. In contrast, I have visited many places for the purpose of comparison. It is my professional background in psychology that distinguishes my interpretations from improvised guesswork.

In the final chapter, written with Kirsten Hastrup, some reflections on the concept of advocacy have been propounded from a more distinctly anthropological point of view. Even though we are somewhat ambivalent about the notion of anthropological advocacy, we believe that these reflections provide a starting point for a discussion of how to translate concern about the survival of ethnic minorities into action.

The general aim of this book has been to combine anthropology and psychology. On the basis of an examination of different examples of the development and decline of isolated societies, I offer some general considerations on the survival of Indians and the descendants of slaves. Furthermore, on a higher level of abstraction, I attempt to gather general characteristics of a psychology of survival. This has not turned into a single, unified theory, simply because it would be far too ambitious to believe this to be possible. On the contrary, it has proved to be important to juxtapose incompatible material, at times creating confusion in order to attain new insight. In an area as emotionally charged as terror, oppression, and population decimation, a one-dimensional understanding falls short.

Or as the Maroons in Surinam say: "If you don't stir up a hole, you won't find out what's inside."

Acknowledgments

Many persons have contributed to this book.

To benefit from the lengthier sojourns in the field, I have sought out anthropologists who have spent long periods of time in the places I have been. The works of Alicia and Gerardo Reichel-Dolmatoff, Roberto Lizarralde, Robert Jaulin, Sally and Richard Price, and Nathan Irving Huggins have been a source of inspiration, and at times I quote extensively from them.

I have received much help from persons with local knowledge, including Ana-Maria Echevvery, Kike Reichel-Dolmatoff, Martin Hildebrandt, Orlando Jaramillo Gomez, Jim Douglas, Chris Healy, and Guillermo Padilla.

I have especially appreciated the friendship and cooperation of Morten Bruus, Hanne Mortensen, and Niels Pagh Andersen in making the film *The Earth Is Our Mother*. Eugenio Barba and the Odin Theater have inspired me to understand asociality and separation from the larger society as necessary prerequisites for survival, regardless of whether one is dealing with group theater or Indians. Søren Hvalkoff read an earlier draft of the work and gave relevant suggestions for change. Thanks to Kirsten Rode for her painstaking secretarial assistance and to Fran Hopenwasser, not only for her translation, but also for her corrections to the content of the text. I also wish to express my gratitude to Leo Goldberger for his ardent scholarly stimulation and interest in the realization of this book.

Cooperation with other professionals and friends has been greatly rewarding, but it is the Indian people who have given me the final courage to break with my psychological profession and introduce other ways of thinking into my work.

Finally, thanks to Kirsten Hastrup for her unremitting inspiration and stamina, and to Rasmus, Simon, Anders, and Frida, who have given me back my faith in wildness and have been indulgent even when things have gotten out of hand.

My work has been supported by the Research Council for Development Research, Danida, the Humanities Research Council, and the Carlsberg Foundation.

Strategies for Survival

Nabucimaque, August 9, 1986

I have arrived with a film crew at the Arhuaco Indians' sacred village, Nabucimaque. Before we get permission to enter into the village, I have to promise the Indians that we will discuss all aspects of the film with them. It is my ninth visit to the Arhuaco Indians, but nevertheless they keep asking why I have come and what my purpose is. We wait and wait, and over and over again we answer their questions about why we are making this film.

The days go by without our gaining permission. We are getting desperate about time passing and our having to repeat the same explanations day after day. After a while we, ourselves, begin to doubt if the trip is worth the trouble, and at some point I utter in despair that I do not know why we are making this blasted film. Only when the Indians have heard me say this do they permit us to start filming. Apparently, one has to acknowledge doubt in order to come into the Indians' sacred village.

PART ONE *Indians*

1. *Motilon*

In Columbus's time, European civilization was characterized by such enormous internal struggle that its only hope for survival was to conquer another continent and create the New World. The eradication of Indian cultures was the basis for European rebirth in Latin America.

The annihilation and massacre of Indians stems from a long and rich cultural tradition. Western culture has always had metamorphic pictures of evil, like Homer, Virgil, and Dante's devils in the underworld. However, only with the European conquest and colonization of the New World did this underland become concrete reality. The Indians took on the roles of the evil devils who were to be eradicated or converted.

Today missionaries are continuing this crusade. They go out to the isolated Indians, preaching order and control. In return, the Indians attempt to survive by creating disorder and chaos in the European world-view.

The Mission Los Angeles del Tucuco To come to the Motilon Indians, one has to go beyond the last outpost of Western civilization. It is a whole day's drive in a Land Rover over an inhospitable no man's land, where hour by hour the distance between houses and cabins gets greater. Then the road begins to improve, the scattered houses are no longer so far apart, and one arrives at the entrance to Indian country.

The Perijá Mountains in the western part of Venezuela, on the border with Colombia, are the land of the Motilon Indians. It is impossible to come into contact with the Indians without going through the mission Los Angeles del Tucuco, which is situated in a bottleneck between the high mountain ridges. All traffic to and from Motilon country passes through Tucuco's buildings.

Tucuco is, in fact, an Indian name for a supernatural being that inhabits a river. The Indians normally call the river itself Canóapa, however, and are careful not to take the name of a higher power in vain. When the Catholic Capuchin monks named the mission after the heathen mountain god it was probably by mistake, a wrong since remedied by renaming the place Los Angeles del Tucuco—Tucuco's Angels (Persson 1971, 55).

At Los Angeles del Tucuco everything seems to be in proper order. The first thing you see when you drive up to it is the church, flanked on either side by square, fortress-like buildings, which are the dormitories where girls and boys are reared. Some two hundred children live in this compound, where parents are urged to let them stay for three to four years without seeing their families in the meantime.

Santa Ana and San Francisco, two small towns that lie near the mission, have become the slum area and garbage dump of the mission station.

The Tucuco mission and four smaller missions are dotted over the whole Motilon area of the Perijá Mountains. In many cases the missions have defended the Indian cause against the white landowners who have unjustifiably appropriated Indian land. Venezuelan hacienda-owners, however, accuse the missionaries of having a double standard. With its 735 square kilometers, Los Angeles del Tucuco is the largest landowner in Zulia district. The mission justifies its position with the argument that the large expenditures involved in protecting the Indians and rearing them in the Catholic faith have necessitated the maintenance of a large estate run by a cheap Indian work force.

Schooling and Childrearing In the preface of a schoolbook, it says, "In Sierra de Perijá, the Catholic Capuchin Order's mission is to introduce the Motilon Indians into our civilization."

However, there is a practical problem in teaching: none of the Catholic nuns and monks have learned to speak the language of the Indians. Attempts have been made to overcome this difficulty by using Indian children who have been able to learn Spanish quickly. These children often stay at the mission for several years and gain the status of prefects. In some cases, they even take over the teaching and rearing of the smallest children until they no longer need the help of translators. This solution has proved to be greatly advantageous for the mission because the children are more quickly introduced into civilization when one of their own paves the way.

The pedagogical method lets the children repeat what the teacher says. Schoolbooks are so sparse that pupils must make copies of what few books the mission has in its possession. In practice, the teacher usually reads the question out loud, after which the pupils repeat it loudly in unison, often many times. The answer is read aloud and committed to memory in the same way. Afterwards, the pupil writes the question and answer in his or her notebook. Most of the pupils' school-days go by according to this method of repetition, and one constantly hears children, sounding like parrots, repeating what the missionaries have said.

This kind of teaching has led to a number of errors in the Indians' schoolbooks. The following examples are taken from a Motilon Indian's notebook:

The Natural Sciences.

How does a rabbit reproduce?—Directly.

How does a bee sleep?—Standing up.

What are the fins of a fish for?—To ascend, to descend and to keep itself horizontal in the water.

History

What kind of people lived in Venezuela before Columbus?—A people who had no knowledge of comforts.

How did Simon Bolivar die?—Naked, as he was born.

What pushed Columbus' ships forward?—An eastern wind.

What is a monarchy?—A kind of government that does not exist in civilized countries.

What is a human being created for?—To live in society.

Neither teachers nor pupils get these misunderstandings corrected, nor is there a chance to make the textual material more meaningful. There is a general belief that two kinds of knowledge exist: the empirical kind, which one acquires in daily life, and the abstract kind, which one learns in school.

Knowledge gets reduced to a set of ready questions and answers that are invariable. School knowledge consists of being able to answer standard questions in a precise and stereotypical way. Thus one learns to avoid asking ambiguous questions, because a missing answer lowers one's prestige.

Schooling often ends when the child gets confirmed within the Catholic church. The mission's archives contain class pictures of confirmands in suits and summer dresses, Indian children in the guise of Western civilization. The clothing, though, is identical from picture to picture, borrowed for the occasion from the mission.

Deculturization and the Murder of a People After the period at the mission, most children attempt to move back to their villages, but problems usually arise. The stay at Los Angeles del Tucuco has gotten them to leave their traditional lifestyle behind without their having been able to acquire a new one.

An evening at the Tucuco mission illustrates how Motilon Indians are left in a cultural vacuum with a ballast consisting only of the reprimands of the Capuchin father and good advice. Approximately seventy-five Indians came to the station to bring their children home after an internment of a few years. The father gathered the parents together and started by saying,

> You must try to teach your children to work in the village. They ought not strut about like tourists or good-for-nothings. They ought not lie about in hammocks in shady corners, while the older generation, their parents, work for them like slaves. . . .
>
> You must try to sow something or other, banana plants, corn or coffee, whatever, so you are not dependent on the mission taking care of all of you. You cannot always count on getting work here at the station, because you are often not strong enough. And if you do not sow and cultivate something, or if you do not want to leave the mission, what will happen then? Either you will starve or steal or get sick. . . .

As soon as the mission has broken down the cultural identity of the Motilon Indians so they no longer can be considered *salvaje,* or "savages," it loses interest in them. The Indians get only superficial instruction in the economic and social problems that await them outside Los Angeles del Tucuco. At precisely the point at which the mission could have a useful role to fulfill, the Indians leave it and have to manage on their own as proletarians in a cultural no man's land. They have now become pariahs, accepted neither in their own villages nor in the so-called civilized world.

The Motilons have gravitated toward the whites, many of them moving to the slums surrounding the big cities and perishing in a hopeless dream of becoming one of the real *civilizados*. However, the Capuchin monks have not built up any missions in the shanty towns, where they could have found a sizable target area for anyone who wished to fight sin and decay.

The general goal of "spreading the teachings of Christ among the Motilon Indians" has had some clear consequences. In the space of the forty years the mission has existed in the Perijá Mountains, several of the Motilon Indian villages have disappeared. Of the four thousand Indians living today in the mountains, approximately two thousand five hundred are Yupa and one thousand five hundred are Bari Indians.

The anthropologist Roberto Jaulin (1973) claims that fifty years ago, four times as many Indians lived in the area. At that time they were divided up into small societies with separate names, for example, Macóa, Aponcito, Monostára, Chaké, and Dobokubi. But today the Motilon Indians only have two names, Yupa and Bari.

Lizarralde and Beckerman (1982) write that approximately six hundred Indians died of epidemic diseases when the mission first came into contact with them forty years ago.

The story of the Motilon Indians is a story about our insatiable need for unexploited resources. The Motilon Indians inhabit an area that has a rich supply of oil and minerals. The anthropologists Lars Persson (1971, 1972a, 1972b) and Roberto Jaulin (1973) have revealed their findings, showing that Indians along the Colombian-Venezuelan border were persecuted and killed in large numbers at the end of the 1930s, when the oil company Texaco found oil in Indian land. It is estimated that 550 Indians were slaughtered either in an air attack or through private raids when they resisted white penetration. The last massacre took place in 1964; eighty Indians were shot when they tried to prevent Shell from coming into their country and constructing a landing field (Jaulin 1973, 28).

There was, of course, a law saying that no one was allowed to claim property rights to the land inhabited by the Indians. However, this legal protection led the colonists either to drive the Indians off their land or to kill them off, so they could say to the officials that the land was no longer occupied by the Indians. In 1974, the borders of the reservation were established, so that no one could any longer justify settling on Indian territory. Nonetheless, settlers continue to steal land from the Indians, and even though the Indians today have the law on their side, they rarely get any help from the authorities.

Love without Concern The missionaries in the Motilon area have often been there on the pretext of protecting the Indians from attacks. However, regardless of their declared intentions, they have paved the way for transgressions. They have not been able to repress their unconscious need to destroy the Indians.

Bruce Olson, an American missionary, according to Jaulin (1973) is one example. Some years ago he created his own apocalyptic world, with Motilon Indians as participants. He declared that he would "deliver the Indians from evil in the outer world" (Olson 1973, 23). Bruce Olson received Texaco's support for his project, and one of the things he did was to establish a small hospital à la Albert Schweitzer in the middle of the jungle. However, Olson was not educated as a doctor, and the hospital had catastrophic consequences. Working with some Colombian doctors, the anthropologist Roberto Jaulin lodged a complaint with the authorities that the hospital functioned as a source of contagion (Jaulin 1973, 93, 114). The Indians were admitted with minor ailments, stayed awhile, and returned to their homes with far more serious epidemic illnesses. In the area in which the hospital was located, there had been about two hundred Indians in 1964, but when the hospital opened epidemics broke out, reducing the Indian population to 37 in 1967 (Jaulin 1973, 93).

Jaulin wrote that extermination of this kind corresponded to what happened in Europe during the plague. Then, too, missionaries gathered all the crisis victims in churches to pray to God in fellowship and in the name of love. However, instead of their achieving eternal salvation, infections spread and they died in large numbers (Jaulin 1973, 109).

The result is the same every time one sets out to save a people. There is a symbolic suspension of the distinction between "love" and "concern," so that love can only be conveyed to the Indians when it is detached from consideration. On the other hand, one can also claim that the missionaries' display of concern is without love, because their work among the Indians in so many cases results in more land, oil, and minerals going to the whites. The missionaries would probably claim that this was not their intention. Nonetheless, the apparent result has been profit.

An example of concern without love can be seen in the case of the oil company Texaco, which built up an enterprise in the vicinity of the hospital a few years after its establishment. Regardless of Olson's motives, he had in practice paved the way for the oil people.

The Swedish anthropologist Lars Persson brought this story with him to Denmark, and it became a contributing factor to the establishment of the IWGIA (International Work Group for Indigenous Affairs) headquartered in Copenhagen in 1968. Texaco immediately attempted to camouflage its role as perpetrator of the extermination of Motilon Indians, placing a full-page ad in the Danish newspaper *Politiken* on September 5, 1968:

> For the Motilon Indians, who live in the jungles of Colombia, Texaco is on the side of the "good spirits." One of Texaco's daughter companies, Colombian Petroleum Company, supplies the tribe with vaccines, penicillin, food and medicine—and in fact, we have rescued the Motilon from extinction. We live by selling heating oil to millions of homes all over the world, but our sense of responsibility reaches far beyond this: we feel obligated to help mankind wherever we work. We are convinced as well that you, too, appreciate the way in which we work. . . .

In all fairness, it should be mentioned that since then, Olson has admitted he committed errors in his missionary work (Küng 1981, 80). Olson has become one of the very few who have acquired a close relationship with the Motilon. Since 1968, he has lived for years on end in their isolated long houses and is the only foreigner who has succeeded in learning their language.

As time passes, Olson has become more and more reticent about spreading the message of Christianity. In 1988 he remarked that instead of him converting the Motilon, they had converted him. His attitude today is that many of the Indians know the basic values of the gospel in their own way, and therefore, there is no reason to build churches and preach for them. Several missionaries have distanced themselves from Bruce Olson because he has done less and less missionizing in more recent years (Küng 1981, 90), and the Catholic missionaries criticize Olson on the basis of his old mistakes. At the same time, some of his earlier critics among anthropologists and journalists have begun to praise his efforts in supporting the Motilon (Küng 1981, 174; Lizarralde and Beckerman 1982).

Today Bruce Olson works among Motilon Indians in Colombia and has among other things gotten them organized into the Asociación Comunidad Motilon Bari de Colombia. On the outside it looks exclusively like an Indian organization that fights for Motilon independence, but on the inside, Olson is the anchorman.

The Mission as an Outpost of Civilization The Motilon were an entity for hundreds of years before the Spanish colonization. They constituted an independent civilization consisting of extended families in which the members supported each other, took care of educating the young, and assumed social responsibilities. All of them had spiritual lives involving gods and shrines, embedded in religious systems accounting for life and death, and moral concepts about good and evil. Even though the Indians have not participated in Western technological development, they have all had a highly structured spiritual life with abstract ideas and codes of such complexity that the term "primitive" is clearly inapplicable. Even the smallest and most isolated groups of Indians have a history that is at least as long as ours.

Today, however, there are no Motilon Indians who have been able to avoid influence from the modern world. Especially in the places where the Catholic missionaries have worked, the result has been that the Indians end up at the very bottom of the social scale.

Spreading the message of Christianity cannot be done in isolation, but rather in a cultural context consisting of major parts of Western technological society. The missionaries transmit not only the teachings of Christ, but a whole culture as well.

Father Felix de Vegamian at the Tucuco mission has said, "Missionary work takes place exclusively among non-civilized peoples with the aim of spreading knowledge of true civilization, that is, of the material and spiritual values that improve human nature. Man can improve more and more in civilization, and it is the aim of the mission to improve ourselves" (Elsass 1977, 52).

However, even though the Capuchin monks wish to achieve goal-oriented cultural change, they have rarely studied the Indians, lived among them, tried to understand their culture, or learned their language.

Even when they want to change something, they have not investigated beforehand the object they wish to change. There are a few exceptions, for example, Father Felix de Vegamian, who wrote a dictionary of the Yupa Indian language (1978). However, even though the Yupa Indian language resembles that of the Motilon Indians, none of the missionaries have made use of it in their attempts at making contact with the Motilon. This lack of interest in anthropology is characteristic of many missionaries. No missionaries among the Motilons or other ethnic groups in Colombia or Venezuela have published scholarly studies documenting the severe survival problems of the Indians.

As a rule, the efforts of the missionaries produce results that are decidedly more material than spiritual. Influence is registered primarily in three areas: changes in dress, in living arrangements, and in geographic placement.

That the Motilon are encouraged to wear dresses or shirts and pants leads to a number of changes. First of all, Western-style clothing gives access to the status of being "civilized," and getting new clothes often creates the need to earn money. However, since the Indians do not know how to dress in the Western mode, they often appear as a concrete manifestation of a tattered proletariat.

Indians have been encouraged to give up their usual living arrangement in big common houses and to move instead into one-family houses, the aim being to reduce promiscuity. However, no Indian society has ever been described as promiscuous by anyone other than the missionaries. Polygamy can occur, but normally has clearly delineated rules. The disintegration of the long houses, on the other hand, has led to an increase in promiscuity, because collective responsibility has been destroyed. Families have lost their original boundaries and individuals seek comfort in promiscuity.

The disappearance of the long houses has led to the creation of new settlements. However, since the missionaries usually assist in the building process, offering aid, for example, in laying electrical lines and water mains, the villages often end up being placed close to the mission and to the roads on which construction materials can be transported. Thus, the newly erected villages are the first step on the way toward the deculturization of the Indians.

Many of the Motilon do not believe in Jesus, despite the fact that during the last twenty years they have participated several times each month in a Catholic mass. That the Indians continue to avow the cultivation of their own gods can of course be seen as an expression of resistance to the missionaries. In another sense, however, it can be claimed that the Christian message has not at all been central to their conversion. The fact that contact between missionaries and Indians has been possible at a particular time and place indicates the marking of a new era and the need for a new code, for Indians as well as missionaries. Religion was the wild card that set off the gradual changes allowing the Indians to slip into the Western world-view. The founding of Los Angeles del Tucuco was symptomatic of the ability of Western expansion to maintain its foothold in Indian country; a new period had begun. When the Motilon were converted, the break between two histories, two world-views, was given a name. It was Christianity.

The History of Tucuco The Motilon first attacked the white man in 1499. The Indians and the missionaries kept each other in check throughout the following centuries. In our time, however, there has been a decisive change in power relations (Bonilla 1972).

In 1945, the mission, Los Angeles del Tucuco, was founded. The history of the mission has been printed in a small selection of yearbooks which are kept at Tucuco (de Vegamian 1972). If one gets on good terms with the missionaries, permission can be granted to look through the books and write down some quotations:

1945: Los Angeles del Tucuco is founded in dense jungle about nine days' journey from the closest town, Machiques. Father Clemente de Viduerne writes in his diary:

> One must have an enormous will to be a missionary. It is a kind of heroic feat, and one must feel like a conquistador if one is to stay here and keep the jungle at a distance in this obtrusive mission. We are alone and isolated from the world around us, without aid, without privacy and without comfort.

1950: September 14: Father Marcos de Udego's diary:

> I was awakened at 4:00 A.M. by the constant barking of our dogs. I got up to see what was wrong, and with a flashlight in hand, I went in to wake Father Clemente. We were the only ones living at Tucuco that week. I followed after the dogs with my flashlight, and on the path I see Father Clemente lying on the ground with an arrow in his breast.
>
> "Oh my God, they've shot me. Jesus, what an infliction. I'm going to die,"

wailed Father Clemente. I was two meters away from him, but turned immediately around and tried to escape. I was terrified and about to lose my mind, when two arrows zipped past me, one fell to the ground right in front of me and the other brushed right past my head. The wounded man managed to get on his feet and in great pain wobbled back to our house. When he came inside, he himself broke off the piece of arrow that stuck out of his chest.

1956: The first Indian couple gets married in the church at Tucuco.

1960: July 22: Some Motilon Indians had been continually shooting all the whites who penetrated their area. However, Father Rumualdo succeeded in establishing peaceful contact with them. He had gotten the military to help the mission for a few months by throwing *Bombas de Paz*—"peace bombs" over the long houses of the Indians. They consisted of sugar, flour, salt, knives, machetes and axes, all packed in monk's clothing. Furthermore, there was a picture of a Capuchin monk patting an Indian on the shoulder, so the Motilon would be able to visualize the benevolent givers. After that, Father Rumualdo succeeded in landing a helicopter and holding the first mass.

The Venezuelan newspaper cleared the front page and showed a picture of some Motilon Indians that had been flown back to the capital of the province, where they were driven around in open trucks to show that they were quite harmless. The headline read, "Love was victorious in the jungle."

The mission wrote in its journal:

> Shell was interested in examining the area, especially around Valle Motilonia, fifteen kilometers south of the mission. They wanted to be certain that there was oil in the area, as some of the air photographs indicated. The mission gave them all the help they wanted with the greatest of pleasure. (de Vegamian 1972, 568)

1964: Los Angeles del Tucuco gains contact with the last group of Indians, the Japreria people:

> We succeeded in convincing all the Indians to follow us into civilization. We gave them new clothes and threw out their dirty old barkcloth clothing.

1965: Venezuelan TV selects a Motilon Indian to be *reina por una día* —"queen for a day."

1970: The mission celebrates its twenty-fifth anniversary. Since its foundation, 139 marriages have been entered into and 578 children have been recruited into the mission compound, 26 of whom function as teachers in the villages in the jungle. Catholicism is preached for the Indians at least once a month.

1986: Twenty-five years after Los Angeles del Tucuco established the first peaceful contact with the Motilon Indians, the mission declares that all Indians have been baptized.

Tucuco's historical development runs parallel to Venezuela's history of oil and land.

Due to the Second World War, Venezuela was in serious economic crisis at the time the mission was established in 1945. With the aim of repairing the national economy, multinational companies were given a free hand to extract and remove resources from the country. Therefore, they openly approved of the mission paving the way into new oil fields.

In 1959, when the mission started a campaign to pacify the Motilon Indians, the Cuban Revolution had just taken place. The United States was afraid of similar revolutions occurring in other parts of South America and therefore increased its aid to Venezuela. After his election, President John F. Kennedy started the Alliance for Progress initiative, which was supposed to strengthen the partnership between North and South America and insure stable development. Unrest among the peasants was to be quieted. New areas were to be cultivated and colonized. Everyone (except the Indians) was to have as much land as he or she wanted, and the land the Indians lived on was confiscated in the name of the Alliance for Progress.

In later years it has become clear that Venezuela is not capable of adequately supplying itself with food, in part because the structure of agriculture is such that landowners have turned their production more and more toward export. Intensive cattle breeding has become one of the major sources of income, but since the acquisition of land has not expanded on a par with the increase in cattle herds, exhaustion of the earth results from using it to produce as much fodder as possible. Even though the Indians have to a large degree been able to keep their land peaceful during the last few years, the problem of erosion has arisen, because the surrounding hacienda owners suck all the water out of the mountains by felling trees and clearing the earth for their fields and cattle.

The Psychology of the Mission There are no clear, rational explanations for the mission's motives in committing cultural murder against the Indians. The terror against the Indians is of course historically connected with the Western pursuit of profit and the need to control the labor force. However, underlying this premise is an abstract pattern of broadly based unconscious cultural forms, in which missionaries become the exponents of the fracture, breakdown, and rehabilitation of Western civilization. Pure and orderly, they speak of the devil as evil in their Bibles. As exponents of their own society's wildness, they go into the jungle to convert the intractable Indians who live like animals in their primitive, chaotic societies. Thus they go out in order to subdue the evil in themselves, in their own society, and in their own times. Ultimately, the missionaries become exponents of Western civilization's ongoing struggle with chaos, purity, and danger (Douglas 1984).

One can find this attitude concretely reflected in the way in which the missionaries talk about the Motilon. For example, the Capuchin monks often use the expressions, *los pobrecitos* "poor little ones" or *eso no sirve,* "it doesn't work." The anthropologists Alicia and Gerardo Reichel-Dolmatoff, who have traveled widely in Colombia and Venezuela studying missionary work, say that they have never met a missionary who did not use these expressions when dealing with the Indians (Reichel-Dolmatoff and Reichel-Dolmatoff 1977, 421).

The Indians literally die from their encounter with missionaries, but ironically, the sphere of death, their annihilation, is an eminent point of departure for the missionaries' revelations. From grief therapy we know that, paradoxically, the closer we come to the experience of death, the more alive we feel. Through fear we may experience a growth in consciousness. As in Dante's *Divine Comedy,* one travels through an underworld of horrors and torments, slowly descending through good and evil, harmony and chaos, ending in the dark woods. Eventually one reaches paradise, but first one must touch bottom and ride the back of a wild, primitive being. The same holds true of the missionaries. Western civilization forces them to go out into the wild jungle in order to inscribe unpredictability in themselves (Taussig 1987, 312).

Psychologically speaking, the missionaries encountered a reality full of contradictions when they went out on their expeditions among the last of the "wild" Motilon Indians. The missionaries were studious young people from Spain, often the youngest children of peasant families who could not provide them with support. These children had little prospect of taking over the family trade, and were sent to convent schools as the last option. Here the dormitory protected them from their prior poverty, while they earned a living by studying and praying. Young, studious, and cowled, they were sent out on outer missions after several years.

The sphere of foreignness was an obtrusive hell, where the processes of growth and decay created a state of chaos, whose only goal was survival. For the missionaries the jungle was a country that God had created in anger, where creation had not yet been completed and was therefore still split up into thousands of contradictions—harmony and chaos, love and hate.

When Werner Herzog was making his film *Fitzcarraldo* he described the jungle that the missionaries had encountered:

> There is some kind of harmony. It is the harmony of overwhelming and collective murder. And we in comparison to the articulate vileness and baseness and obscenity of all this jungle.
>
> . . . In comparison to that enormous articulation, we only sound and look like badly pronounced and half-finished sentences out of a stupid suburban novel, a cheap novel. . . .
>
> And we have to become humble in front of this overwhelming misery and overwhelming lack of order. Even the stars up here in the sky look a mess. There is no harmony in the universe. We have to get acquainted to this idea that there is no real harmony as we have conceived it. But when I say this, I say this all full of admiration for the jungle. It is not that I hate it. I love it. I love it very much. But I love it against my better judgement. (Herzog 1984, 57)

The missionaries were left in the grips of this chaos and this uncontrolled wildness. In the jungle, their fears, aversions, and hatred could multiply and be projected into whatever they saw around them. They saw traces of disorder, chaos, and their feelings of guilt everywhere in the wilderness. In order to redeem themselves and the civilization they represented, they set out to redeem the Indians.

The First Contact Father Rumualdo was the first one to come into contact with the last group of "wild" Motilon Indians, who lived in extreme isolation and used bows and arrows to shoot at any white person approaching their territory. On Friday, July 22, 1960, he wrote in his diary:

> 11:10 A.M.: I arrive by helicopter and step forth in the direction of a large house, which is their living quarters. The Motilon Indians are greatly shocked when

they discover that a foreigner has come to visit them. They all run away and hide, except for one man, an elderly leper, who could not run. I embrace him. When the other Indians see this, they come one after the other out of their house and out of the jungle.

11:15 A.M.: The next helicopter lands. Joyousness, embracing, gifts, rejoicing. Everyone makes signs that we should stay. The pilot is frightened. The others fly off again. Father Vicente and I are the only ones who stay behind. We eat. Distribute sugar and toffee. The women will not receive us. The men and children do.

5:15 P.M.: Fifteen new Indians arrive, all equipped with bows and arrows. They are accompanied by women and children. They look at us with anger and surprise and begin to talk excitedly to each other. We pretend nothing is wrong, but we're scared. We offer them crackers and candy. The women take them, while the leader gives us glowering looks. When I step forward in order to embrace him, he pushes me away angrily and holds his bow and arrow up as a shield between us. Shaking with fear I go back to Father Vicente, who says, "Let's try to get away. Let's make believe we are going down to the river to get some water to drink and then we can run away." Nonetheless, we agree to stay and try to stay calm. We begin our evening prayer, the Rosario, which we think will be our last prayer on earth. We pray together loudly, and thank God, the Indians begin to listen to our prayers. A few begin to make signs indicating they want some of our clothes. We give them a little of our baggage and in that way become good friends. An old woman hugs me several times, while the other Indians laugh out loud.

8:00 P.M.: The Indians begin to go to sleep in their hammocks. We lie down on the ground and try to sleep, but we can't fall asleep. (Rumualdo 1987, 151)

The next morning the helicopter flew out to them with all the necessary accoutrements for a Catholic mass, and the first church service was held among the Motilon Indians. Everyone kissed the crucifix, and from that day the missionaries figured that with God's help the Indians had been pacified.

In 1976 I met the Motilon Indian, Alucie, who had been present the day Father Rumualdo landed among them and recorded his remarks:

We ate together and were together. My father was there. The women and children were there, but most of the men were off hunting. The rest of us sat like this, close together. The Father was very close by, and suddenly we see him. We yell, "A white man is coming with his men," and we all ran screaming out of the long house. The Father and his men ran after us and caught hold of some of us. He grabbed us by our loincloths or hair and shouted, "No, no, no. Bari is good. Bari is good." But we did not understand what he said, even though he tried to say it in our language. The whites all yelled a lot. But we understood nothing.

Apparently, what Father Rumualdo describes in his journal as an embrace is experienced by the Motilon Indians as an entrapment. Despite an atmosphere of fear, chaos, and confusion, the two parties find each other. There are pictures from this first contact where one sees missionaries and Indians smiling with their arms around each others' shoulders, in mutual trust and devotion. The Motilon Indians invited the missionaries into their long houses with the same enthusiasm and hospitality that the missionaries showed later on when they invited the Motilon to stay at the mission station.

The two parties became human in each others' eyes, thus creating the background against which each one could reflect on the state of wildness. Victim and victimizer became the best of friends.

Taussig has noted that the relationship between Indians and missionaries resembles that of the victim-victimizer, resting on a sense of humanity, but whose components are objectification and incomprehensibility. It was only because the Indians were human that they were able to serve as a labor force and as subjects of torture; for "it is not the victim as animal that gratifies the torturer, but the fact that the victim is human, thus enabling the torturer to become the savage" (Taussig 1987, 83).

The extinction of a whole people entails several phases, the first of which is built upon humanity and sympathy (Timerman 1982). Later this phase is replaced by a state of reciprocity, where life is created through violence and chaos. Finally, the Indians become objectified, which enables the transgressor to exercise true terror and eradication without being affected by it himself. Thus a whole people can disappear in silence, without anyone discovering it.

The first phase of destruction of the Indians occurred when the missionaries threw pictures down over the long houses, before they made contact with them. Each of these so-called peace bombs contained a picture of a missionary laying a hand on the shoulder of a Motilon Indian. The purpose was to acquaint the Indians with the missionaries before they landed in their helicopter. In another sense, it was a way of gaining control over the situation. The missionaries worked like scientists: their goal was to observe, to come closer to their object, and subsequently, to be able to control it and distance themselves from it. Similarly, the pictures were a precursor to the arrival of the missionaries, enabling both parties to create a distance as soon as they came into close contact with each other. The basis for the first contact had been established. However, the wildness of the Motilon Indians vanished when the peace pictures were showered over them, comparable to the way in which photography captures reality, but always leads to the irretrievable loss of the rendered object (Sontag 1977).

The next phase in the program of terror arose when the peace mass was held. In an indomitable rhythm of year after year, the missionary experienced the mass as the scene of the revelation that sent him out into the jungle to convert the Indians. The first time he preached for the Indians, he experienced that the Christian message gained in holiness when held up before the wild tribes. Through personal inspection, he could see devil's play among the Motilon. He defied his fear of the Indians and became attracted to them, because they gave him the opportunity to define Christianity, civilization, and himself.

The Indians Imitate the Magic of the Missionaries The magic of the Indians provoked the missionaries more than anything else. In contrast, however, in the case of Los Angeles del Tucuco, there are several examples of the Indians perceiving the missionaries as full of magic:

The anthropologist Lars Persson tells how the Indians at the beginning of the 1950s parodied the missionaries by painting figures on wooden boards, which they attached to poles and carried around in the villages like Catholic saints (Persson 1971, 49). They called these figures *tiot tiot,* which probably comes from the Spanish *Dios Dios*—"God God." Gradually, the figures changed and became stylized symbols, drawn on paper or strips of cloth. This process took place concurrently with the intensification of the teaching of reading and writing at the mission. Through their children, the older generations were able to see how letters and numbers were formed. They began to imitate the missionaries by sitting and mumbling over drawings of simple signs with right angles, which they made on strips of bark or cloth.

This observation led the French-Venezuelan anthropologist José Cruxent to believe at the end of the 1950s that the Indians communicated by means of pictographic writing. His observation caused a great sensation, and theories were proposed that these isolated and so-called primitive Indians had a written language passed down from ancient high cultures, whose writing had certain similarities to that of Easter Island (Wilbert

1961). However, the more material that was gathered, the harder it was to interpret the writing.

Despite the fact that Motilon Indians were a homogeneous people linguistically as well as culturally, the written language had not spread to all villages. In fact, it only appeared among the Indians who had had close contact with the missionaries. The Tucuco mission began its work in the years after the Second World War, and the anthropologists who had been in contact with the Motilon before this time, for example, Alexander Clark, had never mentioned a word about any written language (Wilbert 1961).

The written language was also called *wesyekepú,* which means "a piece of wood for one who goes in front on the path." This corresponds to the function of a written language: a message one writes on a piece of wood and sends with someone who goes from one place to another. By pointing at each of the signs, the "writer" told what they meant. The messenger was instructed to repeat the message until he knew it by heart and was then sent off.

Tiot tiot is an example of a mnemotechnical system that arose under the influence of the missionaries. The Indians have taken over our idea of a written language and adapted it to their own needs.

Our cultural traits change character, adapt, and are given new expression when the Indians take them into their possession. They copy the missionaries, listen to their subtext, and surround it with magic, in order to get their religious message to function.

Many of the Indians express the feeling that it is easier to talk to a saint than to Jesus. The reason, they say, is that God's Son is up in heaven, far too far away from everyday life to be understood and taken seriously. The saints, in contrast, are nearly like people, who appear in various ways around the mission station. The Indians say that when the missionaries burn candles for the saints, pray to them, and give them gifts, it must be because they perceive them as immature, lazy, and forgetful. The Motilon have gone even further, punishing the saints as they would other children. Once, when St. Francis refused to produce rain, some of the Motilon reversed the picture of him hanging in the church, so he hung with his face turned in toward the wall.

Thus, the Indians sense the hidden message and make the magic of the missionaries into their reality. By taking the missionaries' message completely literally, the Indians make it clear that in a sense the missionaries, themselves, believe in the witchcraft they forbid others to practice.

The Indians get caught in the field of tension between good and evil, Christian and heathen, civilized and barbarian. However, the contrasts vary, and what one sees in others is perhaps a part of oneself. The quantity of projections is unclear, and the boundaries between Western European civilization and Indian culture are fluid. The consequence is that wildness, grotesque and dramatic, prevails against that which is beneficial. Not only does wildness become a characteristic of the Indians, but in a more general sense, of a whole other order of thinking than the European, a means of bringing the establishment out of balance, a form of disorder and dis-ease.

Nonetheless, the disquietude between the opposing elements creates liveliness and movement. By making a parody of us and laughing at us, the Indians make their wildness visible and become capable of surviving.

The Destruction of the Long Houses: Cementing of the Earthen Floors

Before Los Angeles del Tucuco came into contact with the Motilon Indians, the Indians lived in big long houses, called *bohios,* where eight to a hundred people lived under the same roof. These houses were shaped like the hulls of ships, lying with their bottoms turned up, isolated in the dense jungle. The roof was made of palm leaves that reached down to the earth. Here and there in the hull there were small entrances, so low that one had to bend over and crawl in order to get in.

The Indians started by felling trees of a certain height, so the sun could freely shine in on the underbrush. In the course of a few months, the sun had scorched the vegetation away so that the Indians had a big open area, where nothing grew. The Indians built their bohios on these islands in the dense jungle.

Inside, the houses were divided up by heavy poles that supported the roof. The round area in the middle was the kitchen. There was a row of hearths, which the different families shared. The hammocks hung criss-crossed, over and under each other, between the kitchen area and the outer walls. The children slept right above their parents, in such close proximity that a mother or father could just reach up and rock the child to sleep. Each family had an area in the long house where they kept their possessions. Placement was based on a complex kinship pattern, which

Campigne, October 21, 1983

Father Felix is eighty-two years old and does not hear well. A couple of times a month he comes out to the Motilon Indians in Campigne in order to hold mass. The Indians love him, and his masses are well attended. After the mass, there are usually a half-dozen Indians who want to confess. However, when Father Felix holds the mass, confession becomes a public event, as one must speak so loudly that anyone can hear what is said. As the Indians have never truly understood what confession is all about, they shout one nonsensical story after another in his ear. Meanwhile, the others sit and listen and laugh. Father Felix is very popular in Campigne.

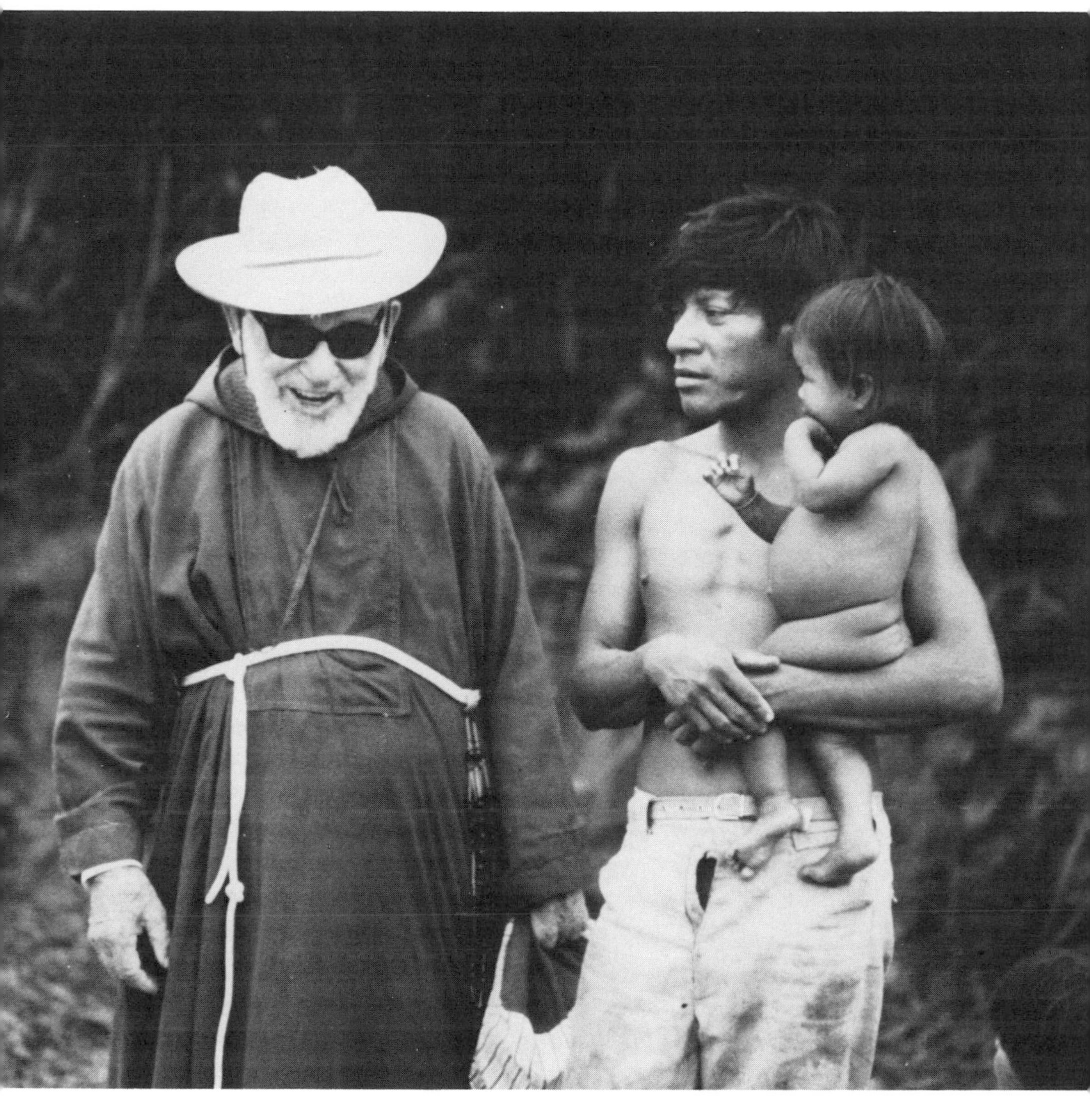

also determined where the children could play and the parents could sleep. Even though the many inhabitants lived close together in the long houses, there was an inner organization which circumscribed the boundaries of privacy for each individual.

The palm roof served both to insulate against the sun and to muffle noise, rendering the interior of the long house a cool space where one could rest and escape from the green lushness of the jungle, whose sunlight and many sounds could be much too obtrusive.

When the missionaries saw these common houses, they were disturbed by the fact that so many people lived together in one and the same dark room. The earthen floor and the palm roof seemed to them to be unsanitary. The Indians spat on the floor and used a part of the kitchen areas as their toilet and garbage dumps. The missionaries returned from the long houses and said that they had seen kitchen utensils in baskets, dead animals, old pieces of meat and fried fruits hanging from the ceiling in long strings, and vermin from the palm roof falling into the hammocks. Social life in the dark seemed chaotic and primitive. One could not tell how many people there were and what they were doing. To the missionaries, it appeared that the Indians crossed family boundaries when they sought each other out in the hammocks, making love indiscriminately.

Thus, the mission got the Indians to move into small, light, one-family houses with cement floors and tin roofs, with toilets and kitchens placed outside.

The first thing the missionaries did was to transport sacks of cement to the furthest corners of the jungle, in order to cement the earthen floors. This had catastrophic consequences.

When the children had relieved themselves inside the house, the Indians had the custom of cleaning the floor by using a machete to scrape up the dirty earth onto a palm leaf. The feces were carried outside and thrown onto designated garbage heaps. The Motilon Indians were accustomed to cleaning the kitchen region several times a day by scraping the earthen floor and throwing it outside. When the cement floors were introduced, the Indians did not change their old habits. They continued to throw garbage on the floor, and the children continued to relieve themselves in the middle of the house. The adults continued to scrape the floors with palm leaves and machetes instead of sweeping and washing. In the course of a few weeks, the floors got slimy and unsanitary with dirt and feces, becoming infectious sources of contagion.

The introduction of cement floors had other consequences as well. The women used to use a loin-loom, which they fixed between two poles that were hammered into the ground. However, the women had to abandon this weaving technique, as they could not hammer the poles into hardened cement floors. The women used to weave while taking care of their small children and keeping an eye on the cooking and the hearth. It was out of the question, however, that they should sit outside their houses, in part because this would have put them at a remove from their social roles and in part because it was too hot in the sun. The result was that the Indians stopped weaving their own traditional clothes. European clothes had been used on occasion before, but with the introduction of cement floors, the last original loincloths and kirtles disappeared (Jaulin 1973, 53).

The Indians began to wear "decent" clothes, but out in the isolated habitations they found it hard to get enough sturdy clothing, partly because it was a long way to the nearest shop, and partly because they could not afford it. As a consequence, many of the Indians were given the missionaries' old, discarded clothes, so they came to look like vagabonds in rags. Besides the fact that poor clothing lowered their self-esteem, it also became a factor of illness. The Swedish anthropologist, Lars Persson, has said that "there was no moral difference between giving an Indian a pair of pants and tearing a pair of pants off a white man (Persson 1971, 141). In practice there was a difference, though, in that a pair of pants for an Indian could cause the spread of disease. The German anthropologist, Johannes Wilbert, who studied the Motilon throughout the 1950s, wrote that when they went around in the damp and dense underbush, their pants would always be wet and clammy, thus reducing their resistance to cold and flus. The result could mean death for Indians, given the difference in their immune defenses. Furthermore, some of the Indians had advanced stages of venereal diseases. An infection, of course, should not be enclosed in the same clammy pants weeks on end, but should rather be exposed to the sun and air in order to dry out (Wilbert 1961, 10).

The introduction of the corrugated tin roof also had drastic consequences. Even though the traditional palm-leaf roofs often leaked and had to be repaired, they had the advantage of insulating from the hot, burning rays of the sun. Although the introduction of iron for roofing produced a cleaner and sturdier roof, the result was that the huts became unbearably hot in the middle of the day. Social life came to a standstill, and the Indians had to seek the shade of a tree in order to get through the midday heat.

For sanitary purposes, the missionaries introduced kitchen houses, which were placed outside. Consequently social life became divided. Families, no longer having their own hearth, had to sit outside their houses when food was to be prepared.

Moving the hearths outside also brought about changes in food products. The Indians had been accustomed to smoking fish and deer meat by hanging them above the hearth. Not only did the smoke have a preservative function, it deposited a layer of tar on the inside of the roof and on utensils, hammocks, and clothes. This layer of tar somewhat prevented cockroaches, bedbugs and insects from getting into the Indians' possessions. When the hearths were placed outside the houses, the Indians no longer had smoke as a means of prevention against vermin and as a preservative of meat.

The missionaries insisted on the houses being smaller and better lit. The roof was lifted off the ground and put on palisade walls, and the entrance doors were made larger. In this manner, more light came in, but with the light came great quantities of insects. The old bohios had kept the insects outside, but in the new houses they made their way into the half-shady areas, and in places made the houses unsuitable for habitation. Anopheles mosquitoes began to swarm around the Indians' living spaces, giving rise to a malaria epidemic at the end of the 1950s.

Lizarralde and Beckerman (1982) have documented that approximately six hundred Motilon died as a result of the destruction of the long houses.

A Society of Leisure Becomes a Consumer Society The missionaries considered the long houses proof that the Indians lived in a state of deprivation. Indian society was primitive and stateless, without a history or markets of sale, and with an economy that was subsistence-level. The point of departure for the missionaries was a view of history in which culture evolved from a primitive state through various stages, ending in civilization. The final stage and apex was the formation of the state with all its power structures.

However, rather than revealing a deficiency, a close analysis of Motilon culture reveals complex structures, which secure the Indians a position in relation to nature and their surroundings that is adapted to their needs. In the jungle, there were no a priori assumptions: special technologies had been developed with a know-how that resembled that of a modern-day computer. The aim was to use a minimum of energy to fulfill the needs of the members of the society. For many Indian groups this meant they had a very short work day. Lizot writes, "The Yanomani Indians' disdain for work and their total lack of interest in the technological process as such is evident. They do not work more than three hours a day" (Lizot 1973, 140). Arcand (1972) says that the Cuiva Indians often spend sixteen out of twenty-four hours lying in their hammocks.

Formerly, the Motilon had a "society of leisure," in which they sought with minimal effort to reap a sufficient supply of food from nature, so they had time to enjoy life and devote themselves to cultural pursuits. However, this seeming state of indolence is gone by now. One reason is that the surrounding natural environment has become impoverished of animal life. Furthermore, Western civilization has presented the Indians with new, technically more advanced tools, or development which, paradoxically, has increased rather than decreased their workload.

The Indians have not been able to resist the implicit logic lying behind our technological conquests, that is, an increase in work tempo and output. There is an ecological explanation for this: the Indians used to be hunters, and their bows and arrows, being made from nature, had the practical advantage of being cheap. A rifle is considerably more efficient, hitting targets more precisely and at greater distances. Today the Motilon prefer rifles, even though rifle shots scare away the game. Furthermore, the very efficiency of rifles has contributed to the impoverishment of animal life. At the same time, the Indians have become dependent on the larger society around them in order to buy cartridges. Similarly, other technological discoveries have led to increased productivity, extending beyond the Indians' former necessities. Their economy has become a "political economy" (Clastres 1977, 166). While they formerly produced in accordance with nature's possibilities and the needs of the group, the new technological advances have thrust the Indians into producing for a society that lies outside their own limits.

Life for its own sake has been transformed into working for the sake of others. No longer is the rule of equality and bartering in an egalitarian exchange system the social code. Productivity aims rather at satisfying others' needs. Indirect exchanges, where the interconnections with the larger society are delayed, have increased the possibilities of being cheated and misled.

Leisure time costs money. One must pay back what one owes, and the landowner demands that the Indians pay for their indolence. Thus begins the division of Indian society into rich and poor. Timelessness has been replaced by a sense of historical time, and Indian culture has evolved from a subsistence to a market economy. Hunters and gatherers have become farmers, their first outlet for sale being the mission station and then nearby towns. The objects of trade are the Indian work force in exchange for trivial luxury items of modern technology like digital watches and transistor radios.

The Long House as the Microcosm of Indian Culture The original bohios of the Motilon Indians were sophisticated communal systems, designed to promote survival in the difficult jungle. In more ways than one, the great common houses of the Indians were not mechanically and trivially built up, stone upon stone, like Western cities. Rather they were tied, intertwined and woven, reparative and restorative in reciprocity with nature (Meunier and Savarin 1970).

As a reflection of this construction, the Motilon Indians established themselves in complicated family systems with complex incest taboos. The arrangement of the bohio interior was the key to this system, and since the Indians did not have a written language, the house functioned as a church and county register with its rules about how each individual should live.

Space and kinship were conjoined in the long house. The large cool room was divided so that each family had its own area. The oval ground plan could be divided into a square, and in the middle there was a common area with hearths. Each hearth had a family group, but the space was so limited that the families ate in turns, according to their positioning in the house. This placing also determined the order in which they walked when they made forays into the jungle. The Indians fished collectively. Men, women, and children left their homesites and gathered along the river in particular groupings, some to make dams and spread plant poison in the water, others to fish, and still others to prepare the fish. The division of labor was connected with their position in the long house.

Besides the horizontal division, there was also a vertical division. The height that the hammocks hung over the ground bespoke kinship relations. Husbands and wives had their hammocks close to the ground, and the older they got, the closer they moved toward one of the two main entranceways, though they always remained within their family area. The younger one was, the higher one's hammock hung, and the hammocks of young unmarried men hung the highest.

Nature outside the long house was named in accordance with its relation to the quadrants in the house. The animals were given names that described how high they moved over the ground, using the same adjectives that described the vertical position of the hammocks.

The social system, which might appear to a stranger to be provocatively anarchic, was in reality a well-structured house. There was a spokesman inside the house, a *nyatubay,* and one outside the house, an *isdora.* The spokesman's function was always divided between two or more men, who together represented all the different family groups living in the bohio. The Indians distinguished between social relations, which were either *sagdodyira,* "blood relations," or *obdyibara,* "work relations." The incest taboo forbade marriage or sexual intercourse between sagdodyira. In addition, there were other complex kinship relations, which kept the group dynamic and protected against endogamy and the formation of cliques.

The bohio of the Motilon Indians was like a commune with room for innumerable functions. There were family rooms, kitchen, work places, space for animals, pantries for food, nursery school, daycare centers, and recreational areas, just like the centers of Western cities with their cinemas, hotels, and restaurants.

The long house was like a microcosm of Indian society. It functioned as a symbolic mediator among its inhabitants and between its inhabitants and the outside world. It gave its inhabitants a point of reference and a relationship to history, not only to their ongoing history, but to the history of their origins and myths. The house and the myths referred to each other, and one could not be realized without the other. The common house contained a key not only to social organization, but to a world-view as well (Pinton 1965).

When the missionaries transformed these oval common houses into villages with rows of small, square, individual houses, the paradise of the Indians was laid to waste.

The Indians had to go from house to house to visit each other, in an attempt to maintain the old structures. The Capuchin monks introduced the social pattern they knew from their cloister, with common kitchen and eating facilities, and individuals having their own separate chambers. Lighting counteracted promiscuity and improved conditions for reading, intellectual work, and prayer.

The missionaries attempted to get men and women to enter into Catholic marriages, which created a great deal of confusion, as two individuals who had been married at the mission could, according to their old traditions, have children with others. Children belonged to the bohio, and when Los Angeles del Tucuco convinced parents to let their children stay at the mission for a few years, the children lost a fundamental sense of belonging to their own group.

The relationship between time, space, and motion was broken down. The Indians still actually use the old terms, nyatubay and isdora, but they no longer have the traditional meaning for the arrangement of spokesmen. The nyatubay today is a person who has been at the mission station, has been converted, and has learned to read and write. He is regarded as the chief of the village and is the one to whom foreigners address themselves. Power has become concentrated. Provocative anarchy has been dissolved, and the whites have achieved a system that they know and can control.

The Vulnerability of the Indians: A Collective System without Leaders

The Motilon Indians have generally not shown much resistance in withstanding the influence of the missionaries. A few groups have, in fact, shot at all intruders with their bows and arrows, but the Motilon on the whole have never been able to organize themselves and put up resistance.

One of the reasons for this split is that the Motilon from different long houses simply did not know each other. They had the sufficient and necessary number of points of reference in their own houses. Each long house was self-sufficient: it was complete and contained so many people that they did not need to travel to other houses to fulfill their social needs.

The Indians' vulnerability stems as well from the fact that their society rarely embraced conflicts. In the big group, they were so close to each other that there was no room for open disagreements. Arguing was rare, and if a disagreement arose between two people in the same long house, the conflict would usually be resolved by one of them moving to another long house. The Indians have transferred this resolution pattern to their relationship with whites. When foreigners have imposed themselves upon the Indians and stolen their land, they have reacted by withdrawing to more inaccessible parts of their region.

Both the missionaries and the pioneers are performance-oriented, measuring their activities, production, and records. The missionaries are proud of their progress, and their yearbooks are full of accounts of how many have been converted and married. Similarly, the white pioneers measure their viability by the number of hectares they have conquered and cultivated.

The Motilon Indians do not have the same ambitions and cannot demonstrate the same results. Their personal property is quite limited. They do not have an ownership relationship to the earth and cannot point out what is theirs.

Participation is more important in their social activities than winning, with results that have at times been bizarre, as when they undertake Western sports, like soccer and volleyball. Ball-playing is completely new to them, and they rarely split up into two teams, but rather run around in a big group, laughing and chasing the ball. When they have been at the mission for a year, they begin to understand that they have to split into two groups and play against each other.

The Motilon truly differ from the missionaries and the settlers by showing a completely different sense of respect for life. Their many dogs are a concrete example of the difference.

The Motilon knew nothing about dogs until the missionaries gave them some. In the course of the next few years, these dogs reproduced in such great numbers that today it is a problem for the Indians. The dogs are allowed to go where they want and do what they want, like licking pots and plates. The Indians will not exterminate the dogs, even though the animals have become a plague for them.

The dogs exemplify the unfortunate consequences of the Indians' generosity and respect for life when the whites place their own cultural elements within the limits of Indian culture.

The encounter with the white man is a confrontation between totally different social and psychological structures. In some ways, the encounter with white colonists is easier than with missionaries. Some of the Indians leave their homes and work for a few months as guest workers at adjacent haciendas. Most of these work relationships run smoothly as a rule (Jaramillo 1983). However, the encounter with missionaries always brings changes in its wake, first and foremost being the destruction of the *causa perpetua* of their culture—the long house.

The surrender of the Indians to missionary influence cannot be explained by calling them anti-aggressive, gentle, or naive. On the contrary, the Motilon have shot with bows and arrows at all foreigners approaching their land. Their outwardly-directed defense mechanisms have, in fact, been characterized by unmasked aggression. However, when the missionaries succeeded in placing themselves within the Indians' own boundaries, as a part of their sociality, the battle was lost. The only survival strategy to which the Indians had recourse was the same one they used in their own context: moving away when conflicts and disagreements arose. The Indians reacted against the missionaries by turning their backs and moving to remote regions where they could not be reached. However, this method of escape functioned as a survival mechanism only as long as large areas of virgin forest remained. With the expansion of colonists and missionaries to even the most inaccessible areas, the Indians have had to give up escape as a strategy for survival.

Earlier, a long house with about eighty people occupied a territory of four hundred to a thousand square kilometers. Today, the Motilon live on just one-eighth of the land they owned fifty years ago (Lizarralde and Beckerman 1982).

Today, there are only two long houses left. They lie in isolated areas of the jungle on the Colombian side of the border, several days' travel from the nearest pioneer village. A few families live there. They are the last two remaining places where the Indians still have sufficient amounts of land to be able to be themselves.

The Motilon as a Counterculture Motilon Indian society can be seen as a negation of Western society. When I visited one of the last of the long houses, the Indians took pride in demonstrating that they did not obey my commands, that my concept of time was different from theirs, and that their power counteracted mine. The concrete expression of this is that I have never been able to rely on any of the agreements or appointments I have made with them. In certain situations, I have not even been able to get them to give me a helping hand, even when I was about to lose my life. Once when I got into trouble crossing a racing river, they did not throw me a rope. And, when one of their mules crossed right in front of me, kicking out at me, I could not get the Indians to take it by its muzzle and lead it away. The Motilon Indians simply do not understand loud voices and direct commands, and as a result I was almost washed away in the river a couple of times and once suffered a broken leg when a mule kicked me.

However, in more recent years I have experienced their collective helpfulness, when they have made everything and anything available and daily life and expeditions have taken on a certain cheerfulness. Life in the long house consisted of long days that melted into nights where we talked and babbled, ate and slept in a flow of time that lasted until I got a backache from lying in the same hammock for days.

Only now, after getting to know the Indians better, can I see how we have always been each others' invisible opponents. Either they have refused to come to my aid, or they have given me so much attention that I literally got a backache. Even though I have attempted to discard my European power games, they have transfixed me just as I have transfixed them in my film and books.

The premise for this reciprocity, this dialectical counter-play, is the Motilons' exposure to white civilization over a period of several hundred years, even though some of them have lived in great isolation. There have always been violent clashes between the whites and them. It has mainly been the whites who have terrorized the Indians, but the opposite has also been true. Thus, both parties have power in the political sense of the word, because violence, the prerequisite of power, has been present for several centuries.

Instead of calling the Motilon a society without power, it is rather a society with "powerless power" (Clastres 1977, 14). It is a form of invisible counterculture that has arisen in contrast to Western culture, which is characterized by its historicity and focus on development and renewal. On the other hand, Motilon culture is based on informality and equality. It is ahistorical, its concept of time is circular, and its people live isolated from larger society, in a sought-after balance with nature.

These cultural traits stand in sharp contrast to Western culture, not perhaps a conscious, willed contrast, but from a European point of view, a contrast that can be read as counterculture.

The Indian Leader By characterizing the Motilon Indians as a counterculture, one indicates that they are not weak-willed objects passively allowing themselves to submit to missionaries and colonists. However, in order to understand Motilon opposition, one has to suspend assumptions and see how power and political institutions come into play in places where they seemingly do not exist.

The *nyatubay* is the personified illustration of Motilon Indian counterculture. He is a peacemaker, whose task it is to be the moderator, one who evens out differences and mediates in conflicts (Clastres 1977, 23). He is a good speaker, expressing and formulating the unexpressed needs of the group. His greatest responsibility is to secure peace and harmony in the group, not by power, but with the aid of knowledge and powers of judgment, honesty, and verbal abilities. He is like an arbitrator, who attempts to mediate and persuade. He must be generous with regard to his possessions and, for example, cannot oppose the demands of people who are placed under his administration. In some Indian societies, the chief is the one who owns the fewest possessions of all. The extent of his generosity determines his popularity, and his authority and power are dependent on the goodwill of the group.

The nyatubay is a paradoxical metaphor for the Motilon's need for political power. By refraining from the concentration of power in one person, they all take part in, and come closer to, the execution of power. Thus, the Indian leader is not an indicator that Indians avoid and neglect conflicts. On the contrary, the nyatubay function makes it essential that everyone participates in the political life of the society. When one minimizes the concentration of power, aiming for generosity with possessions and words, power has a way paradoxically of emerging through its seeming impotence.

The nyatubay is often a person to whom one does not listen. He communicates with the group at dawn and at sundown, often tossing out a few formal remarks that have no direct relation to daily life itself.

For example, he sits at the hearth or lies in his hammock and without anyone directly showing that he or she is listening to him, he speaks in so low a voice that it is difficult to hear what he says. Everyone attends to his or her business as if nothing has happened, in any event not showing openly that attention is directed toward what he says. If something important turns up, a few people may gather around him, but they will often be occupied with some domestic chore while they chat, and will not turn their faces toward him and listen. The chief has a role similar to that of a group therapist. His most significant function is to carry out a ritual which conveys the group's tradition, and to do so in such a way as to conceal the fact that he is the seat of power.

A Society of Equality Perhaps it is an overstatement to call the longhouse culture of the Motilon a political organization and even define it as a counterculture, an egalitarian power system that opposes Western hierarchical institutions of power. Are not the Indians simply a group of people who have gradually been forced further and further into the jungle, a group of people just doing their best at surviving?

On quiet days of fieldwork, I slip into seeing the Indians as being naive and uncivilized. Stripped of culture and visible rituals, clothed in our discarded garments, they look like the vagabonds of the jungle, living in broken-down old shacks. However, if every human group is seen as a political organization, engaged in establishing and maintaining internal cohesion and external independence, then the society of the Motilon Indians can be seen as an expression of minimal politics.

There is a revolutionary ring to the word "*egalitarian,*" with its origins in the battle cry *egalité* from the French Revolution. The word signals not just a simple absence of hierarchy, but a call for the end of dominance. Egalitarian societies are described as systems which must in a sense fight for equality (Woodburn 1979). Their members must be constantly aware that no one acquires greater wealth, exercises more power, or demands more status than others. Equality is not a simple state that automatically emerges when powerful leaders are deposed. Even in minor actions, equality must constantly be put into practice and publicly demonstrated as a contrast to all possible forms of inequality latently lurking everywhere (Woodburn 1982).

Equality is then a result of unremitting efforts. The anthropologist Forge, who has worked in Papua New Guinea, writes, "To be equal and

Chirindakaira, December 10, 1985

Alucie was my guide when we went out to one of the last long houses of the Motilon. A wordless reciprocity that I knew from earlier encounters with the Motilon quickly developed between us. Walking in the jungle is very demanding. Instinctually, Alucie always set the tempo at my level of energy, and when I was about to give up, he would prod me on with his shenanigans and make me forget my fatigue.

However, our friendship did get put to the test a few times. One day when we were crossing a river in water up to our waists, I was about to lose my footing. I yelled to him, "Help, hurry up and give me a hand, NOW!" But even though he was right in front of me, he pretended he had not heard what I said. By a miracle, I succeeded in not getting washed away.

The next day was a disaster. He was riding on a mule that kicked people. It crossed my path, and when I raised my voice and yelled, "Hurry up and remove that animal," he again pretended he had not heard me. The result was that the animal kicked me, and broke my leg. It was hard for me to forgive him.

Among the Motilon friendship is based on reciprocity. If one begins to raise one's voice to give commands and orders, it is simply ignored, even if someone is about to lose his life. Equality is more important than life.

stay equal is an extremely onerous task requiring continual vigilance and effort. Keeping up with the leader may be hard work, but keeping up with all other adult males of a community is incomparably harder. The principal mechanism by which equality is maintained is equal exchange of things of the same class or of identical things. Basically all presentations of this type are challenges to prove equality" (Forge 1972, 533).

Thus the egalitarian society contains latent differences and conflicts, but its ability to survive rests on whether it can contain oppositions without destroying and dissolving the group. For example, among the Motilon Indians polygamy exists as an extreme expression of generosity, and furthermore serves the political advantage of surrounding the individual with family more than with acquaintances and possible enemies.

The political strategy of the Motilon is an organization that exists in its demand for non-existence. In order to neutralize the outer political authorities, they establish chiefs based on generosity and the exchange of property, women, and words instead. Power for the Indians appears in hidden ways, masked as a negation of the others' power. The background for this circumscription of power is that mass society, with its decisive economic and technological power, would totally eradicate them if they ever assumed visible power or put emphasis on posing a threat.

Furthermore, the inward-directed egalitarianism of the Motilon has not led to an outward-directed powerlessness. On the contrary, the Motilon have been one of the most feared groups, because they have shot with bows and arrows at any foreigners impinging on their territory. Only when the missionaries came inside their boundaries and gained physical admittance into their long houses could they no longer defend themselves. The group took in a new element that they could not absorb. No one could mediate in the conflict, because there was no longer a common language. Since the missionaries were not attuned to the same form of generosity as the Indians, a disequilibrium arose. The disharmony that could not be harmonized made the Indians regress and long for a more one-dimensional expression of power. They began to accommodate themselves to the missionaries, for example, allowing themselves to be persuaded to cement the floors of the long houses and send their children for a stay at the mission station.

The missionaries reacted to the fact that the Indians did not take orders through a spokesman, and since no one seemed to take responsibility for anyone else, they believed that the society was lawless. Reacting against this lawlessness, they enforced their authority and at the same time declared their love for the Indians in a hypocritical fashion. Thus, they each reacted in their own way to the others' need for order and power.

The Noose Nonetheless, prankishly, the Indians have managed to adapt, so they can survive yet another stretch of time. They may well have ceased to shoot at intruders with bows and arrows, but as an example of their counter-strategy, many Indians wear a little string around their necks. They have heard the missionaries say that suicides cannot be buried in sanctified earth. The Indians say that if they go to heaven when they die, and it turns out not to be a very nice place, they can always slip away by showing off their string and saying that they hanged themselves.

2. *Arhuaco*

The Spanish Conquest of the New World still plays a significant role in the daily life of the Indians. The old images turn up in a montage that governs the Indians' struggle for autonomy today. The memory of the slaying of human lives and of the misfortune and suicide that followed in the wake of the conquest is fixed in their minds. The restless souls of that period still haunt the Earth, and give rise in the utmost sense to the unfavorable winds and evil eyes that visit the Indians. In this way, the history of conquest creates its own witchcraft, and the old people who lived before the Spaniards are still alive. Within the Western, Christian cosmos today, they act as troublemakers for modern conquistadors—the missionaries, oil hunters, pioneers, and big hacienda owners.

The role of the past is expressed concretely in a case where Indians actually gained insight into their own history through shamanistic rituals. This insight could give them the courage to act, for example, to kick the Western missionaries out.

Rejection of Foreigners The Arhuaco Indians are neighbors to the Motilon Indians. They live on the Colombian side of the Venezuelan border.

In contrast to the Motilon, the Arhuaco Indians have been able to reject foreigners, keep their boundaries, and defend their rights to their land. In remote valleys in the Sierra Nevada, they have been able to build their cities a couple of thousand meters above sea level, hidden from Western civilization. Unlike the Motilon, the Arhuaco are hierarchically organized, with leaders and commissaries in precise structures in which the few exercise power and control over the many. The Arhuaco have consciously kept apart from Westerners in order to rid themselves of Western civilization.

In 1973, a young Dane, Jørgen Schou, came to the border town, Donachui:

> Elisabeth and I went up to the table, made our introductions in Spanish, and I presented our request. The situation was not the opulent gift giving we had been imagining in our fantasies. The Indian didn't even look up from his magazine. I repeated our plans and asked him directly if we could pass through. Finally, the Indian looked up. "No," he said curtly and slowly turned the pages of his magazine. Then we came with a lengthy explanation and expressed our willingness to pay the passage fee the Indians demanded. Once again the Indian looked up, and rejecting our request for permission to go further into their territory, he said, "It is not possible, not even for a half an hour." (*Information*, July 23, 1973)

The Arhuaco do not appreciate others coming and trying to understand their culture and their problems. They want to take care of themselves.

Arhuacos call everyone who is not Indian *bunachis,* "whites." They know from experience that the more contact they have had with the whites, the more difficult it is to maintain their regionality and own identity.

Every village has a couple of watchmen who go right up to white travelers, block the road, and order the whites to turn back. If the whites still try to go on, they may get a shove, but the watchmen generally do not resort to violence. It can be perilous, if one goes alone into the mountains and gets lost. The Indians know this, and they tell this to foreigners. Anyone with respect for the mountains does turn around.

A few foreigners have come with fine-looking, official papers on which it is written that they have permission from the Colombian government to travel around in the Sierra Nevada. The Indians have become particularly suspicious of such papers. They want to be the ones to decide who is to be their guest.

Nonetheless, in the course of time quite a few people have gained entry into their country. The Arhuaco Indians themselves tell of the difficulties they have had with foreigners: "They are always asking why we do this and that. They want to buy things and never give gifts. They take photographs of us, which we never get to see. In the city, you can buy postcards with pictures of us. They earn foreign money with them, but we have never gotten any of the profit. They say that they want to study us and help us with one thing or another. But when they leave us, we never hear from them again."

Sogrome, April 2, 1976

I have returned to the Arhuaco Indians in the remote village of Sogrome. This is where I had my longest stay, when I first began visiting the Indians. I got to know some of them so well that I believed we had become good friends. But when I returned some years later and came bouncing into the village filled with joyful anticipation, no one recognized me. Even my best friend said that so many tourists came through the town that it was impossible to distinguish one from another.

Crestfallen, I sat by myself and after a few hours, went over to a family and tried to make myself useful by cleaning some corn. One of them asked offhandedly how much my new backpack had cost and if I still worked at the State Hospital in Denmark. They remembered me well. Among the Arhuaco Indians, one simply does not come bursting into a village throwing daily life off balance with boisterous greetings of "Hello, hello, how are you" and "It's been such a long time."

In 1968, a Japanese mountain-climbing expedition visited the Indians and gained entry into the mountains. The Japanese were fanatical mountain climbers, and the Sierra Nevada have always been famous for their beauty. During this expedition, however, several incidents arose that gave the Arhuaco serious grounds for distrusting foreigners.

Firstly, the Japanese shot some mountain goats, believing them to be wild animals not owned by anyone. The Indians, however, have seldom perceived of any animals as wild. They knew exactly how many animals there were in the area and viewed this hunting of mountain goats as out-and-out robbery.

Secondly, a member of the expedition was killed when they were high up above the snow line. The body was transported out of the mountains to the nearest provincial capital and flown back to Japan. In contrast, when an Arhuacan dies, the deceased is brought from the valley up to the snow, and the actual burial ceremonies take place high up in the mountains.

These two incidents coincided with the occupation of some Indian farmlands by the two biggest landowners in the provincial capital. A few months later, the government built a road up to one of the Indians' holy mountains, on top of which they erected a military radio tower and a small barracks.

To the Indians these events were interconnected, and they decided thereafter to deny all foreigners entry into the mountains. The only ones allowed to enter were poor Colombian tradesmen, who traveled around on mules and bartered, in a way that would earn no one a living.

A year later, Colombian government officials came and offered to help the Indians. They began to travel around in the Sierra Nevada, saying where they came from and acknowledging that the Indians had been treated unfairly and deprived of their land. They distributed countless official papers with stamps and signatures, verifying that the owner of the document was the authorized leader of some agency, such as farming affairs, educational concerns, health care, religious matters, or legal services.

The government thereby relegated power to the isolated society, so that its members could seemingly govern their own affairs, while making it look like the government actually did support the Indians. However, the effect was the opposite. The distinguished-looking papers were incongruent with the Indians' original traditions for decision-making, and the Indians often met to argue about how the official papers should be interpreted. In several cases, two people had been issued identical papers.

As in the case of the Motilon Indians, white society first tried to place itself within the Indians' physical and psychological boundaries and thus disturb their power structure. However, in the case of the Arhuaco, they did not succeed.

The government's masked friendliness did not produce the expected result. The Arhuaco formed their own political organization and are today one of the few Indian peoples who have managed ever since to keep out intruders.

They themselves have financed the education of some of their youth in the provincial capital. Thus the Arhuaco have their own dentists, nurses, and mechanics, and at the moment, there is one person studying law at a university in Bogotá. They have established their own schools with Arhuacos as teachers, and by opening shops here and there in the mountains, they are attempting to build up a network of tradesmen and experts who are themselves Indians. Thus they can maintain independence from white state society.

During a meeting the Indians had with the government, one of the officials fell asleep. The Indians took a picture of him and printed it in the newspaper, *Unidad Indígena,* with the following caption, "While we analyze our problems, the leader of the government Bureau of Indian Affairs takes a nap" (*Unidad Indígena,* no. 4, 1983, 5).

The Ecological Principle: The Earth Is Our Mother Only a few foreigners have been in the Sierra Nevada and given detailed descriptions of the Indians (Isaacs 1983; Lizarralde, Beckerman, and Elsass 1987; Loaiza 1984; Marquez 1978; Reichel-Dolmatoff 1985, 1991). There are in all about six thousand Indians, divided into three groups: the Kogis, the Sancas, and the Arhuacans. The Indians have had contact with Spanish culture since the beginning of the 1600s, but the degree of influence from white culture has varied from group to group, largely dependent on how geographically inaccessible and isolated they have been. The Kogis and the Arhuacos, who are very similar, have been the most successful at preserving their original culture. In recent years, the Sancas have been greatly reduced in number, and today nearly everyone wears Western dress. The differences between the Arhuacas and the Kogis have been described elsewhere (Reichel-Dolmatoff 1991, 97), but in this context their similarities will be emphasized. The following presentation of the Arhuaco to a large extent draws upon the works of Reichel-Dolmatoff (1978, 1984, 1985, 1991).

In many of the outlying places the Arhuaco Indians are self-sufficient, and some of the few things they use from Western culture are car tires and flashlights. The car tires are torn into strips and used as sandals to protect their feet. The flashlights, since it gets dark by 6:00 P.M., are convenient if you need to look for something.

Indian country covers an area of 186,000 hectares (Reichel-Dolmatoff 1984). Most of it is inaccessible and infertile, lying so high up that it is impossible to use for farming. The mountains are snow-covered, in places reaching as high as five thousand seven hundred meters. During the daytime, they stand in glittering sun, while toward evening the snowy peaks get covered by clouds. At night there is no wind, and it is ice cold and quiet.

The Indians are always traveling. Families are seen wandering through rain and wind on steep mountain paths, carrying heavy burdens of crops, fuel, babies, sugar blocks, coffee beans, and such. At first it may strike one as wretched to see these families wandering from place to place in order to find a piece of earth that will yield a little produce. However, a closer acquaintance with the Indians reveals that wandering is a discerning adaptation to European culture.

During the Spanish Conquest, the Indians were forced to leave behind the fertile earth of the valleys and take refuge in the mountains. In order to survive on the barren soil, they had to expand their radius of activity, both horizontally and vertically. Archeological excavations show that in the past the Indians cultivated corn on small terraces, using artificial irrigation systems. Today, however, corn has been replaced by other crops, like bananas, beans, and sugarcane.

Compared with the original methods of cultivation, farming techniques have become simpler and seemingly less advanced. The Indians never plant an area with the same type of crop twice, but take into account the capacity and maintenance of the surroundings by planting over a wide area. Long periods of drought do not have a catastrophic effect, because the Indians emphasize great resource variation, so they always have a place to stop and find food on their eternal wanderings (Reichel-Dolmatoff 1984).

This method of cultivation is a defense against the earth being taken away from them. To the outside world, they protest against the whites' stealing their earth, but among themselves, they may point out areas that do not get utilized. By laying out many small fields, in different places and in different ecological niches, the Indians have built up reserves, not of produce, but of earth that can be taken into use and cultivated in times of want. They do not spend their efforts on overproduction and do not store food for more than a few days. Only in emergencies do they sun-dry produce as a means of preservation. Instead, they wander from place to place, wherever there are crops to harvest. Every family has several houses, and when they need potatoes, for example, they go to the temperate zone where potatoes grow, or if it is bananas they need, they go down to their house in the subtropical zone.

The Indians themselves say the earth is their mother, and that they do not take more from the earth than they can give back (Elsass 1987). Their white neighbors have never understood this premise, interpreting the extensive cultivation of the mountains as a sign of not knowing how to farm, which has been their excuse for taking the earth away from the Indians.

Priesthood and Hierarchy The Arhuaco Indians must constantly seek advice and permission from their own priests in order to organize their daily life according to divine principles. These permissions are often given very concretely, in the form of the priest presenting a small stone, a few seeds, or a little piece of wood, which the Indian then always keeps in his shoulder bag. These talismans, called *sewas,* are presented to the Indians according to given patterns of authority. The number and type of sewas that each individual possesses determines his power over sun, rain, heat or cold, and the fertility of his earth, and thereby his status in society.

The priests have two important functions, one being to keep the population density under the level at which the earth's fertility can provide enough foodstuffs, and the other being to insure that some areas be left barren, so as to constitute a reserve in times of need.

This kind of ecological control of resources presupposes a central government, where a small group with a highly developed social conscience administers the various permissions. The priesthood of the Arhuaco Indians has no external, physical privileges. On the contrary, there are exacting demands on the priests to be everyone else's models of obedience to their sacred law.

The highest-ranking leader of the Arhuacos is called a *mamu,* and is referred to as the person with the greatest spiritual knowledge, the one who can unite the tribe's powers into one common force. Being educated to become a mamu requires many years of daily training in meditation and self-control.

Several times a month, confession takes place, with the Indians coming one at a time to talk to the mamu in his house, or with the Indians gathering together in big common houses, where they step out in front of everyone and confess publicly. The Indians refer to the mamu in Spanish as *un abogado,* "a lawyer," who is placed between the individual and the society or the supernatural. An important prerequisite for the role is that the mamu is *científico,* "scientific," and that he is capable of putting himself at a distance from his own feelings and personal motives for the sake of clarity of vision. The mamu has influence and indisputable authority in just about all details of life. He takes care of his people and is their guarantee that no evil can touch them, as long as he is present.

Besides the mamu, there is a secular, civil authority in most villages, *el comisario,* a kind of sheriff. The whites consider him to be the real leader and the one with whom they have their dealings. To the Indians, however, he is more like a secretary for the mamu, a kind of public relations man who knows the larger society's playing rules.

The land of the Arhuacos is divided into twenty-five districts, each having its own mamu. They meet once a year and select a leader, *el cabildo governador,* who represents the whole Arhuaco society at negotiations with higher governmental authorities in Colombia (Lizarralde, Beckerman, and Elsass 1987).

Society is thus a carefully structured hierarchical system, with the mamu institution as the central unity. Its function is to insure that individual and society live in accordance with "sacred law."

Restrictions and Punishment The lives of the Arhuacos contain many restrictions and more obligations than rights.

There are three important rules of living based on the premises that enable the Indians to run their world. They involve overcoming 1) sensations of hunger, 2) physical aggression, and 3) sexual desire.

In cases of physical aggression the punishment itself is usually physical and always stiff. An often-used method is to crush some ceramic bowls on the floor in the ceremonial house and mix the shards in a pile with some thorny branches. The guilty person is made to strip to the waist, fall down onto this pile and roll around. This method of punishment is considered one of the stiffest. Carrying rocks is a milder form of punishment. The criminal is made to hold a rock with his extended arm. When he lets his arm fall, he gets pushed and maybe even hit. Or, he may be sentenced to spend a few days paving a piece of road in the village. Punishments of this kind will always be public. Before any punishment is carried out, the guilty person is given the chance to speak in his own defense and prove his innocence in front of everyone present, after which the mamu stipulates the penalty.

The anthropologist Gerardo Reichel-Dolmatoff was once attacked by a drunk Indian who, for no apparent reason, threatened him with a knife. A few courageous Indians broke in, and the anthropologist got away with just a few cuts on his arm. The same day another Indian stopped Reichel-Dolmatoff and demanded money of him, because he had slept in one of the village's common houses without asking the mamu for permission.

When the local mamu got word of these two events, he set up a hearing and invited Reichel-Dolmatoff and the two Indians involved. The one who had nearly stabbed the anthropologist to death got a warning, while the other, who had demanded a little money for an innocent overnight stay, was sentenced to cane lashes in the ceremonial house. All the Indians agreed that he should get the stiffer punishment, because he had unlawfully assumed more authority than was his due. According to the rules, only the mamu was regarded as the real keeper of the common house. The penalty was stiff because he had violated the structure of authority of the place. In contrast, the drunk Indian had not attempted to upset the order of society (Reichel-Dolmatoff 1984, 149).

The Greatest Ambition: To Know a Lot If you ask an Arhuaco Indian what his greatest wish or ambition is, he will answer, *saber mucho,* "to know a lot." One of his goals in life is to attain a detailed knowledge of religion, myth, traditions, and kinship history. This acquisition is regarded as a long and difficult path that first brings security and maturity in old age.

Worshipping Guneaka, the Great Mother, in devotion and submission, is mandatory, in order to be born again and then be able to free oneself of her. Guneaka is a symbol of fertility—the earth and its crops. Knowledge of her laws is essential for survival and constitutes the real core of maturity and knowing.

With a certain sense of pride, the Indians regard themselves as poor. Knowledge is their goal, and hunger, frustrations, and suffering are their virtues. Even though they place an opposite sign on the values of Western civilization, the general structure is nonetheless the same.

An example of the Indians' ambitions may be seen among men of the marrying age, who, in all their youthful heat, begin bragging to one another about having the greatest amount of knowledge. They do not say "I am richer than you" or "I am stronger than you." If they get into an argument, they will probably say, "I know more than you." During ceremonial celebrations, young men may begin to compete among themselves. For example, one of them may begin to quote a special song. Before long, one of the others interrupts and says, "What you're singing is wrong. Listen to how it really sounds." A third person may break in and add other comments. A discussion of this sort may develop into an argument, and if any of the participants are drunk, it can end in a regular fight. The older ones, who formally speaking are the ones who know best, intervene and get everyone to calm down. After an episode of this kind, the young men may prepare for the next confrontation by practicing some particularly difficult myths, songs, or dances. At the next such occasion, they may defiantly step forth and say, "Well, let's see if you know this song." After that, they may strut about in self-satisfaction, until someone else presents another difficult song.

These song clashes almost never occur among older men, who have the status of knowing a great deal. They possess a nearly limitless repertoire, and if they begin to clash, it is interpreted as unmasked hostility. They consider it a virtue to converse and to sit together and think. If one asks them what they are doing, they answer, *estamos sentados,* "we are sitting." An individual would say, "I have worked hard and walked far today, and now I am sitting and thinking." "Sitting" is a pleasure and a sign of seriousness and engagement in the problems of life, an expression of devotion to the laws of the Great Mother.

The Indians say that they are the only ones who sit. "The civilized whites sit all day, but what do they do? They do not meditate, they only think about money, cheating each other, and food" (Reichel-Dolmatoff 1985, 271).

Coca and Alcohol The Indians use coca. It is not actually a narcotic, and the effect is not very strong. After a few hours of chewing coca, one feels a pleasant, energetic sense of well-being. Fatigue disappears, thoughts flow more quickly, and memory improves. Another important effect of chewing coca is the suppression of the sensation of hunger. The Indians say that coca is their "gasoline."

The use of coca is largely assigned a religious significance, as a means for acquiring more knowledge and getting better at talking about the old days. However, for most people, hunger is part of daily reality, and the frequent use of coca reflects the stimulating effect that makes one forget hunger.

During the long religious ceremonies, the Indians have to stay awake for several days and thus consume large quantities of coca. They must not eat, and they have to avoid falling asleep, so they can constantly dance, sing, and recite, all of which, as they say, is for the purpose of "talking about the old days."

The older ones claim that chewing coca results in impotence and loss of desire for women. It suppresses everything evil and dangerous, and since sexual acts are regarded as deeds of darkness, coca, like meditation and religious rituals, is helpful in controlling desire.

Connected with the use of coca is a whole series of symbols, which show its sexual significance. When a young man is initiated into the adult world, he gets permission to chew coca for the first time. He is presented with a little gourd, some lime, and a thin, sturdy stick. The lime functions as a kind of catalyzer that releases an active agent in the leaves. By putting the stick into his mouth and placing a little lime dust on the right spots, he can get the leaves to emit a stimulating effect.

To the Indians the gourd represents a woman. During the initiation ceremonies, he uses the thin stick to poke a hole in the gourd and then pours the lime into it, symbolizing the deflowering of the woman's hymen. The stick is a masculine object, and by poking it in and out of the gourd, the Indian shows that the movements of sexual intercourse are a prerequisite for the release of coca's effect, an effect that suppresses sexual desire. Thus, essential needs get controlled and modified by the entwining of inhibition and impulse in circular interdependence.

A protruding stick in a gourd filled with lime represents food, women, and memory of old traditions, all at once. The Indian always has this gourd at hand. He carries it in his shoulder bag with the coca leaves and continually takes it out and touches it, poking the stick up and down, keeping in constant symbolic contact with the essential needs that his culture demands he control and suppress.

The consequence of the suppression of such elementary physiological needs as food and sex means that psychological and social conflicts often simmer under the surface and can erupt at any time, in a combination of sexuality and aggression. The children learn that they must always protect their sex organs in a fight. They are often reminded that the evil forces of darkness are out to castrate them. They often hear warnings, like "Watch out for your penis, for you never know what the hidden forces may wish to eat," or "Keep your legs together, for you never know whether a snake may decide to creep up into your vagina" (Reichel-Dolmatoff 1985, 78).

When the children are about to become adults, the same conflict between sex and anger is expressed as a virulent suppression of women. Woman is regarded as an unpredictable being, who all too easily awakens a sense of insecurity and lack of control in her surroundings. Only as long as she is preoccupied with childrearing and farming does she fulfill the Great Mother's law of controlled reproduction. A woman left to her own devices, without children and earth, becomes a potential temptress and seductress, and thus a challenger to the very abstinence that is the basis of survival for the Indians.

The Arhuacos place reproduction at the core of their life and worldview. The union of male and female elements creates a new principle, which in itself fosters maturity and fertility, not only between man and woman, but also in society and the world as a whole.

However, the closer the contact between white civilization and Indian society, the more the Indians have lost control. Unpredictable factors have impinged upon their society, creating imbalance and depriving them of a sense of perspective. During the last decade, whites have penetrated further and further up into the mountains, transgressing the boundaries of the reservations. But even more destructive is the transgression of the Indians' psychic boundaries.

State society has discovered a sure method for breaking down the Indian way of controlling impulses: alcohol. Bottles of rum have proved to be the best spearhead for penetrating Indian borders. Against the background of a culture that demands abstinence and self-control, Indians have let themselves be provoked all too easily into impulsive clashes with the system, as for example when they drink themselves into a stupor.

In the last few years, the narcotics traffic has made inroads into the area, despite the Indians' opposition to white consumption of their coca. Under the pretext of studying mysticism or doing anthropology, hippies and young tourists have wandered around in the land of the Indians. At times, political agitators have gone into some of the Indians' larger cities in order to recruit votes. In the coal production at Cerrejón, mines have been placed so close to Indian land that they have caused erosion and destruction of the ecological balance. The Colombian government has proposed new energy plans which entail using the water from one of the Indians' sacred lagunas for the power plants. And so forth and so on . . .

Thus the balance inherent in the Indian world-view of not taking more from the earth than can be replaced is disturbed.

The Loom and Its Many Interpretations The Arhuaco mode of thought exists for the purpose of creating order and stability in society. However, the Arhuaco cognitive mode is a counter-image of ours, and if we Westerners try to overtake theirs, we run into distinct problems with our sense of reality. At times, the Arhuaco mode of thought approaches in appearance the thought disorder that typifies our psychotic patients. It is characterized by what a psychiatrist or a clinical psychologist would identify as a tendency of meanings to fluctuate, vagueness, and thinking that tends to be too concrete—traits that place Arhuaco outside the European conception of reality. Nevertheless, precisely this mentality is one of their most important survival mechanisms (Elsass 1986).

Their use of the loom and the way they make clothes illustrate a characteristic principle in the Arhuaco concept of life. The following is derived from anthropologist Reichel-Dolmatoff's studies of the Kogi Indians, who in many ways resemble the Arhuaco Indians (Reichel-Dolmatoff 1978, 1991, 103).

The Indians wear clothes that are woven on a simple, upright loom.

Most of them refuse to wear anything other than what they themselves have made. The men do the weaving, which is considered a serious task requiring a great deal of skill, responsibility, and concentration. Their clothes are not for sale.

The loom consists of a simple rectangular frame made up of four heavy boards. The boards are bound together at each corner with rope, and in order to stabilize the frame even more two sturdy sticks are tied diagonally across the square. The frame, measuring about 1.5 by 1.5 meters, is heavy, robust, and stable in form due to the criss-cross reinforcement. While the weaving is going on, the person sits in front of the loom, which is usually placed outside the house up against an outer wall.

The Indians clothes are based on an extremely simple, elementary weaving technique. The Indians themselves are aware of the technical simplicity of the loom and of their clothes. This elementary simplicity characterizes nearly all of the Indians' material belongings. Their tools, kitchen equipment, and interior arrangements are simple and utilitarian. The Indians themselves say, "Our things may be simple, but they live."

The inner life that the Indians attribute to their material culture and surrounding nature is not an expression of an animistic orientation, which involves the belief that dead things have souls, and so forth. Rather it expresses a complexity where objects and phenomena contain a sum of concentrated information, a wealth of associations and meanings, which make each thing a storehouse of detailed codes. To a certain extent, then, a thing can speak to its owner: answer a question, be a clue to his actions, be his memory, and his point of reference. Such things do not in themselves have a life force and energy, but they are models and mnemonic devices.

The material culture of the Arhuaco Indians is limited. They possess only a few things. However, each thing and each natural phenomenon is an expression of an organizing principle in which one category can be exchanged for another. On one level, a house is a cave, a cave is a belly, a belly can be the heart, the heart can be fire, fire the sun, and so on. This kind of displacement and fluctuation of meaning allows things and phenomena to represent different points in a nonlinear code, in which jumping from one meaning to another is dependent on whom one is with and what context one is in. The Indians know very well that they are dealing with the fluctuation of meaning. They can consciously juggle with the concepts, without losing their "as if-ness."

These are, in brief, the essential principles in the Indian mode of thought. Their myths and traditions are verbal equivalents of their things and of their environment. The myths do not have a "hidden" or "true" meaning, but are messages derived from the material surroundings.

When the Indians refer to the geography of the Sierra Nevada, they say that different locations are placed like the perimeter of a loom. The loom becomes a landscape map. The four corners of the loom are the Colombian cities that surround the mountains. The center of the loom, where the two sticks crisscross each other, represents the mountains, snowy peaks. Once this descriptive framework is established, it is easy to point out the rivers, mountains, and villages in relation to each of the four corners.

It is also possible to make an anatomical interpretation of the loom. The five points where the loom is tied together become the reference points. The uppermost cross on the left side of the loom becomes the left shoulder, and the uppermost cross on the right side, the right shoulder. The point where the sticks crisscross is the heart. Thus a person standing with arms folded across the breast represents a loom.

Furthermore, these five cross points can be identified as the Indians' five most important ceremonial centers. Their precise geographical location in the Sierra Nevada mountains can be pointed out on the frame of a loom. They carry names like Makotama (right shoulder), Kuncaka (left shoulder), Guimelake (right thigh), and Seizua (left thigh).

A loom is thus a practical device for the individual's orientation in relation to himself and his environment. It serves as a visual means for storing information that can be passed on to others.

To Weave Thoughts of Life An Arhuaco sings a special song and melody when he sits down in front of his loom:

> I shall weave the fabric of my life;
> I shall weave it white as a cloud;
> I shall weave some black into it;
> I shall weave dark maize stalks into it;
> I shall weave maize stalks into the white cloth;
> Thus I shall obey divine Law.
> (Reichel-Dolmatoff 1978, 12)

The first line in the song strikes an important theme. The clothes of the Arhuaco Indians contain "the fabric of life," and when a man weaves a piece of cloth, he "weaves his life." By weaving, he symbolically organizes his personal feelings and social existence. The Arhuacos have a metaphor: "A man's thoughts are like threads, and the process of weaving is like thought processes." They explain, "Weaving is thinking. While weaving a thread through the loom, one thinks many thoughts about work, family, neighbors, everything. In a way, the cloth we weave is like our thoughts."

During the process of weaving, these personal themes are put into relationship with the weaver's social network. The Arhuaco Indians take the metaphor a step further: "When the heart thinks, it weaves." "Thoughts produce a piece of clothing." However, the Indians are quick to emphasize that the quality of a piece of clothing may well depend on the quality of the threads and the weaver's skill, but the quality of a man's life depends on his thoughts and the way in which he transforms them into actions. The substance of life is a loom of knowledge and thoughts. "Life's wisdom makes us grow, in the same way a piece of cloth is made."

There are many myths that deal with the origin of weaving. One of them says that the Great Mother, Guneaka, was the only one that knew the art of weaving. She kept this knowledge to herself and forbade everyone to look at her when she was weaving. When the first people saw her clothes, they admired them and asked how she had made them. She kept her knowledge to herself, but one night her son pretended to be sleeping and secretly watched her while she was weaving. The next day, her son tried to imitate her and clumsily made a little piece of cloth. A few days later, when the mother saw the cloth, she exclaimed, "Who has disclosed my secret. I was the only person who knew how to weave." When she realized that her secret had been discovered, she decided to instruct her son, so that he at the very least could weave properly. She gave him two big balls of yarn. Her son and his wife began to weave, but now it was their turn to forbid their children to watch them. However, the latter already knew what was worth knowing. And since that time, people all over the Sierra Nevada have been busy weaving (Reichel-Dolmatoff 1978, 14).

One need not be an inveterate Freudian to interpret this story. The Arhuacos say openly themselves that weaving represents sexual intercourse and that the story of the origin of weaving can also be interpreted as the child's discovery of the sex life of adults. The loom is an anatomical model, and the lower horizontal crossbar is "the part in which the weaving takes place." The loom is a feminine object, and the name of the slide, *Zakwanci Asigi* means "the masculine part of the fabric of life."

Thus, with a few metaphorical twists and associations, the Indians let their thought processes move from a technological process to the human anatomy and physiological reproduction.

The square frame with its crossbeams is the basic element in the architecture of the Arhuacos. When houses and temples are about to crumble, their walls and roofs get reinforced by large frames like those of the looms.

As the loom is the basic element in the Indians' houses, it is also a basic element in their world-view and cosmic visions. The Indians call the earth a giant loom, upon which the sun weaves "the fabric of life." This picture stems from empirical observations:

The upper horizontal supporting beam on this "world loom" is formed by a line that can be drawn between sunrises and sunsets for the summer equinox. In contrast, the lower beam is drawn from the movement of the sun at the winter solstice. The way in which the sun revolves in the course of a whole day makes it weave both a dayside and a nightside of the cloth, representing light and dark, life and death.

The model of the sun weaving on a cosmic loom can be found in many places. The Indians say, "The sun weaves on a loom that encompasses the Sierra Nevada. It weaves among the four ceremonial capitals. It weaves in the temples, and it weaves in people's hearts." Thus, the sun is the sacred weaver, who represents the principle of order and integration.

The temples of the Arhuaco Indians are large structures in the shape of a beehive, with a circular ground plan and a high conical roof. The temples are made of wood and grass. They are simple and unornamented, as a rule containing only a few flat stones placed in a pattern. The roof has a few small holes through which the sun shines. During the day, the sunbeams draw semicircular tracks, from west to east across the temple floor. Seen in relation to the flat stones, these tracks are an expression of the sun weaving "the fabric of life" on the temple floor. The sun begins to weave on the shortest day of the year, June 21, beginning in the lower left corner of the loom. Every day it moves a trifle upwards. When the sun disappears under the horizon, the Indians say that it penetrates the opposite structure of the temple, that is, invisible rays penetrate an invisible, complementary temple, in which black light is expressed as shade. Therefore, the Indians say that every piece of cloth has two sides, an outer side that represents daylight and life, and an inner side that represents darkness and death.

The sun weaves two pieces of cloth a year: one in the summer and one in the winter, one for itself and one for the moon, the sun's wife. At winter solstice and summer equinox, the sun is finished with one piece and about to begin on another. At these times, the Indians hold their big ceremonial celebrations, making the loom ready so life can go on.

The daily life of the Arhuacos is simple, following some of the same rules to which weaving must submit. Weaving a piece of cloth is in essence a moral act. It demands discipline to spin a thread so that it becomes even and strong, and it demands concentration to weave a uniform, solid piece of cloth. A competent weaver is a good person, and a good piece of clothing is an achievement one can be proud of.

There are different opinions as to which character traits the good weaver should possess. Some say that he above all must have the ignorance of a little child. He must be whole, complete, and perfect, as only a little child can be. After that, the person must be purified by the nullification of all his knowledge and power, so that he forgets all previous experience. The third condition is that the person must "feel cold," that is, he must be able to master and control all feelings, go into situations without being affected, without anger or grief. Moreover, there is a long list of precautions and character traits the good weaver ought to possess.

The Arhuaco Indians say "We must have this loom constantly before our eyes. It is to remind us always, everywhere, day and night, of the need to live well, so that our soul will go the right way. We must think of this all the time." Or as the Indians sing during their rituals in the temples: "Alone man weaves the fabric of life."

The frame of the loom can thus be understood and interpreted on many different levels: topographically, anatomically, sexually, architectonically, astronomically, and morally.

Thought Disorders as Survival Mechanisms The material culture of the Arhuaco Indians is limited. They have few things, but each thing and each natural phenomenon is an expression of an organizing principle, in which several categories can be exchanged for one another. Formally speaking, the order of thinking of the Indians is characterized by fusions and fluctuations of meaning, when, for example, they can say "we think well while weaving, so we weave our thoughts. You can see on someone's clothes what thoughts he has." The different topics fuse in the experience of a global topic, and a condensation of speech elements arises, as for example in "weaving the fabric of life." Things and phenomena can thus represent different points in a nonlinear code, in which jumping from one meaning to another is allowed, depending on which person and which context the material world is confronted with.

In a narrow Western context, Indian uses of the loom and metaphorical interpretations have some similarities with a mode of thought that would induce psychosis in our society. The Indians are probably aware that these fluctuations of meaning take place, but rarely can they consciously juggle with these concepts without losing their "as if-ness." They have remarked with firm conviction, for example, that one could "see what someone was thinking by his clothes."

That the Indians can accept these fusions of categories, like weaving, thought, and sun, seemingly without each entity losing its original identity, is in part due to the fact that their daily life is less complex and consists of fewer objects than ours.

In our more complicated part of the world materially speaking, with its greater supply of consumer products, we have given each single object fewer and more specific meanings. Only in the limited areas where we allow ourselves artistic and creative freedom can we make use of a mode of thought characterized by fusions and fluctuations of meaning.

To a certain degree, we make use of the same mode of thought as the Arhuaco Indians. In the old Nordic sagas, it is said that "the Norns spun the thread of life," and today one can hear the expression, "clothes make the man," or if we find exactly the right hat we may say, "That hat is me." However, if we used the Indian mode of thought we would run into problems with our conception of reality. Objects in our surroundings would more easily blend into each other, and our mode of experience would to a larger degree be characterized by the kind of fusions and fluctuations of meaning seen in our psychotic patients.

It should be mentioned that, in a formal sense, the Indian modes of thought described here are not of the same kind as the clinical thought disorders that characterize our psychotic patients. The thought patterns of the Arhuaco Indians constitute a systematic and collective system that all the Indians share and understand. In contrast, our psychotic patients are characterized by an individual system of thought, not shared with the other members of society.

The mode of thought of the Indians must be seen in the context of their social cosmology, and a materialistically simple daily life with few consumer goods. In a broader sense, Indian thinking is a survival mechanism in a complex and problematic natural environment. The sacred earth of the Indians provides far too poor a basis of subsistence for them. Most of it is barren, lying in remote areas with sparse vegetation and a moon-like landscape.

The Arhuaco Indians are at the mercy of the sun and the naked, sterile earth that can only be cultivated with great difficulty. The sun tells the Indians whether rain is on its way to their crops. Thus they observe it, many times a day with great interest, at times with anxiety. Due to the height of the mountains, the Indians are exposed to very cold temperatures at night and burning heat during the day. These changing temperatures make the Indians' weaving of their own clothes necessary.

These natural conditions are the reasons why the Indians are dependent on the sun and the loom, and think of the sun as "the great weaver of the fabric of life." This mode of thought is not particular to their society, but can be found among many tribal peoples all over the world. The prehistoric Egyptians, Greeks, and Sumerians all utilized this conception of the sun and the loom.

For the Arhuaco Indians, it is a way of creating order in their universe and of keeping themselves alive in an infertile environment. Nonetheless, if whites simply utilized the Indians' mode of thought, it would create chaos and disorder in our picture of the civilized world.

The Missionaries Are Thrown Out the Door The same missionaries who broke down the culture of the Motilon Indians have attempted to colonize the Arhuacos.

In 1917, the Capuchin monks founded a mission right next to the Arhuacos' sacred capital, Nabucimaque. It quickly grew into a large trading center, and at the beginning of the 1960s there were about 250 cattle grazing around the sacred village. The mission functioned as a settlement for Indian children, where they were forbidden to speak their own language, and had to have their hair cut and wear Western clothing. Moreover, the missionaries established schools at several places in the Sierra Nevada mountains, where the children learned the catechism, reading, and writing, all in Spanish. Approximately fifteen hundred children have been through this socialization process.

On August 7, 1982, about six hundred Arhuaco Indians met in Nabucimaque for their annual meeting, and decided to throw the missionaries out of their country. Late one night they went to the mission, and the leader of the Indians delivered a letter of protest:

> You have wanted us to forget our Indian traditions, but when it comes right down to it, we are Arhuaco Indians. Those who have gone to your schools have daily seen an authority in priests' clothing and short hair, not an authority in *manta* and long hair. On the radio we hear that universities other places in the world are on strike. Students protest because they cannot get the education they want. Now it is our turn. We want a school and an educational system that defends and preserves our society and its values.
>
> Therefore, we all agree that you must leave us.
> (*YAVI*, no. 19, April 1983, 3)

The leader in charge of the mission answered that he, personally, could not solve the problem: "I do not have the authority to make any decisions and cannot respond to these complaints. The highest executive authority for the mission is the Bishop, and he is in Bogotá. Therefore, I must request that you wait for his and the Colombian government's decision" (Echeverry 1982, 20).

When the answer was translated into Arhuaco language, a storm of protest broke out. The Indians said that they had waited for sixty-six years, and they could not wait any longer.

After a brief exchange of words and a fair amount of hooting and hollering, the six-hundred Indians overtook the mission without violence. They sat down everywhere in the hallways and began singing some of their traditional songs. That got the missionaries to leave the mission.

In the following months, the Indians began to arrange the rooms into classrooms, and on February 15, 1984, the first Indians began receiving their own education in their own school.

The Historical and Political Consciousness of the Indians The Indians say that before they took over the mission, they had had no particular plans. The change had come about after some of the mamus present carried out a shamanistic ritual. Afterward, they came back to the meeting and said that they had come in contact with a situation many hundreds of years ago, where they had had their heads cut off by the missionaries and their temples burnt down. After they spoke of these pictures, they all made the sudden decision to take over the mission. Journalist Ana-Maria Echeverry, who was present, has told me that everyone had been sitting around chatting, prepared to end the meeting, but when the mamus told what they had seen, there was total agreement within a few minutes that the time had come to take over the mission. That was when they went in a group up to the main mission building.

During the shamanistic ritual some images from the time of the Spanish Conquest suddenly fluttered through their consciousness, reminding them that they were again in danger. An understanding of this montage of images is a key to comprehending Arhuaco history and memory, the interweaving of which gave the Indians the insight to know when to put up resistance to the white man.

In these shamanistic images, the historical consciousness of the Indians has little in common with Western civilization's view of the way in which actions are played out linearly and continually over time. The logic of the images is not expressed in the language of historical materialist analysis, but rather more closely resembles a montage of images in which connections emerge from differences, as can be seen in the manifest content of the unconscious. Borrowing an expression from Walter Benjamin, one can say that the mamus' images had the form of sails set in the winds of history. The images were sails; the way in which they were set made them elements for political action (Benjamin 1979).

The example of the Arhuacos, who put the missionaries out on the doorstep, is an illustration of why political movements in the larger society have never really been able to understand the Indians' way of thinking politically. Many of the left-wing movements that have wanted to help the Indians win have naively declared their solidarity with the Indians. Typically, however, even though the Arhuacos have received a string of offers of help from the left wing, they have refused them all. They do not want the whites' political opinions imposed on them and will have nothing to do with political agitators, who have come into their area recruiting votes. One of the Indians complained to me once about the way the whites talk about politics. He used the expression that politics is to the Indians what oil is to machines. "The whites use too many words; one doesn't just go up to a machine and spray it with oil. One adds oil in small amounts to the hidden threads and joints, which one must know about ahead of time."

The skepticism of the Arhuacos toward Western political thinking has led to their development of other forms of mobilization than those we know from our system. In a general sense, the force behind the Indian movement is a collective memory and a reconstruction of history. It is of less importance whether this process is an objective reflection of actual conditions in the past.

This relationship to the past can be illustrated by the fact that in the years before the missionaries were thrown out, the Arhuacos were in fact less tradition-bound than they are today. At that time, more spoke Spanish and wore European clothes, but now they have recaptured tradition, regarding speaking their own language and wearing traditional dress as an honor. In some cases, it appears that what Arhuacos have identified as history is purely fictional. More significant is the consciousness that Indian people have something to share other than what they actually do share.

The attitude of the Arhuacos toward tradition has led them to become opponents of the dominant society's development ideology, which regards the Indians as poor people who need to develop and take in new things. The Indians have often rejected development experts who come into the area, because they do not believe they need to be developed. On the contrary they have stressed that Indian culture is a prerequisite for white civilization.

The view of the experts has been linear: the Indian represented possibilities that needed to be cultivated so they could blossom. The key words have been growth and development. In contrast, the Indian view has been circular: everything is present in the moment as different alternatives, and the key words are "here and now" in a balance between past and future. The result is that the government has, so to say, not been able to fit the Indians into a strategy for development, and even though the many national and international development organizations have had the best intentions of supporting locally based projects in Colombia, they have in reality never supported the Arhuacos. The Indians have applied many times for money to educate their own people and to establish a health station, but have found their applications rejected every time, because they want to administer the money themselves. They want nothing to do with developmental aid experts, because they believe the concept of development imposed upon them makes them invisible.

In Dialogue with the State Not only are the history and geography of the Motilon and Arhuaco Indians divergent, but there are also internal differences between the two groups. The Motilon are characterized by equality, lack of coercion, nonhistorical, nonhierarchical, and anarchic structures in large communal living arrangements. The Arhuacos constitute a hierarchical system with coercion and power, history, and small kinship groups. The difference between them reflects two aspects of political mobilization: the Arhuacos have been capable of throwing the missionaries out, while the Motilon have come more and more under the spell of Los Angeles del Tucuco.

The Arhuacos have developed their own political language, which allowed them to express themselves as a people at the right moment in time. Their ethnic consciousness has injected life force into their mobilization, and they have been able to integrate an understanding of others into their self-understanding.

Like many other tribal peoples, the Motilon rarely enter into a political discourse. They move further and further out into the forest in order to survive, and cannot consciously articulate their status as an ethnic group situated in a colonizing nation. They have not acquired the language needed to present the government with arguments for self-determination and their rights to the land.

The Arhuacos, on the other hand, have become increasingly mobilized the more white society has encroached upon them. For example, they have shifted more and more of their cultivation from intensive to extensive farming to show that they need more land.

The Arhuaco Indians have also established contacts with lawyers and intellectual philanthropists, who lobby for them in government offices. White "helpers" of this type have run court cases for them and formed alliances with other Indian movements.

The Arhuaco Indians have been very efficient about setting up dialogues with the government and understanding the Western way of organizing. However, the more the Indians have tried to learn the rules of the game, the more they have become a part of it.

The first sign of cooptation was that the Indians themselves began to be plagued by bureaucratic processes that delayed and paralyzed decision making. For example, the Arhuacos have accused each other of having too many unnecessary meetings. The next sign was a splitting up into different factions. A few years ago the Arhuacos posted a declaration on a scattering of houses in their villages:

"We are getting split up among different governmental institutions, religions, and political parties. If this continues, we will soon not have a sufficient number of people to supply them all with members" (*Unidad Indígena,* no. 1, 1980, 5).

Thus, the relationship to the government was at first a dialectical one, in which the Indians related to the surrounding society as to an opponent; after a while it changed in character to a symmetrical relationship in which the opposing parties came to resemble each other. After a period of time they faced each other as teammates and opponents with shared elements in a common structure. Both parties established their own chauvinism, with spokesmen and mitigators, experts and offices, that could keep each other in check.

The dialectical relationship is the best one for promoting mutual respect for one's own rights. The parties observe each other closely, each one always trying to contest his adversary. Moreover, systems theory says that symmetrical relations contain possibilities for faulty development, because the parties may end up uncritically seeing their own mirror-image in the other, with considerable risk of repeating the other's mistakes (Bateson 1972; Wilden 1972). In later years, the Arhuacos have gotten into this kind of symmetrical relation to the larger society, and thus have had to escalate their manifestation of power in relation to their opponent, in order to imitate him. Before the Indians knew it, they had become participants in a great political game, which ended in bureaucratization and factions.

The Reconstruction of Identity The survival of the Arhuaco Indians is based on a struggle to protect and maintain their identity. This preservation of identity takes the form of a chauvinism in which all non-

The Nabucimaque Indians, August 8, 1988

It was Sunday in the Arhuacos' sacred village, and very little was going on. The Indians like to "sit," as they say, and let their thoughts wander. Most of them just sat staring out into the air.

Suddenly we heard the sound of a helicopter, and a few minutes later it landed with a small contingent of soldiers just outside the city wall. They were looking for guerrillas.

One of the soldiers asked the mamu, Noberto, if he could buy the poporo *that he used for chewing coca. The mamu replied that it was very old and not for sale. Later Noberto asked the soldier how many shots there were in his pistol and how much such a gun cost. The soldier answered that it was not for sale either. "No," said Noberto, "a man doesn't sell out his weapons."*

Indians are discriminated against and in which they see themselves as a chosen people, as proper Indians and human beings. Ethnic chauvinism of this kind reflects a hatred toward state society and a desperate attempt at regaining one's own identity. It can either take the form of a reconstruction or, if necessary, as a construction of one 's own history, with symbols, heroes, rebel forces, victories, and defeats, all for the purpose of establishing a separate consciousness as a counterforce to the official, national history.

Thus, the Arhuaco Indians do not experience themselves as inhabitants of a remote corner of the world. Even in the most out-of-the-way villages in the mountains, they regard themselves as the center and hearth of all life and civilization. They refer to the surrounding Colombians as *hermanos menores,* "younger sisters and brothers." They believe that Colombians were originally a part of the Arhuaco culture, but through the years have lost the ability to sing and dance according to the old traditions. It is the Indians who take care of the world. *Indio siempre cuidando hermanito,* they say: The Indian will always take care of his younger sisters and brothers." If they do not obey the precepts of the religion and keep up their spiritual knowledge, the world will go awry. The sun will not rise, summer will not follow winter, and it will rain and rain.

The Arhuaco Indians do not allow the technical advances of the whites to confuse their self-awareness. For example, they believe that in reality it was one of their legendary mamus who once constructed the railroad running near the Sierra Nevada mountains. Some Indians stubbornly claim that airplanes, telephones, clocks, and television existed in their society many hundreds of years ago, at the time the Taironas lived before the arrival of the Europeans. The Indians who gò to the provincial capital do not express any particular enthusiasm for what they have seen. For example, the anthropologist Reichel-Dolmatoff tells of a time when he flew with a mamu to the capital, but when they got off the plane, the Indian claimed that he could have gotten there just as fast in his own way (Reichel-Dolmatoff 1985, 294).

The Indians claim that the Catholic religion is in reality a simple derivative of their own religion. They say that many of the Catholic names are ones the Spanish stole from the Indians. The Indians call their ceremonial house, *casa ceremonial,* or *Cansamaria,* which the Catholics have freely translated to Casa de Maria, the Virgin Mary's House. One of the important sons in the Indians' religion is called Sintana, but is often called Xusikungui, which the missionaries have freely translated to Jesucristo (Reichel-Dolmatoff 1985, 355).

The Indians staunchly assert that the whites have imitated them and not the reverse: their culture is the original one, they came first, and they constitute the midpoint of the world. The white culture is just a simple derivative.

In practice, Indian survival takes its point of departure in a lack of confidence in rejection of our civilization. Or, as one of the Arhuaco Indians once put it, when he turned away some anthropologists who had come to help the Indians with their problems:

> "Work a couple years with our white neighbors first, and if we see them improving, you'll be welcome to come back here."

3. *Chemescua*

When colonialism reached its apex at the end of the last century, the great empires slowly began to crumble from their own inner forces. Young intellectuals began to fight against the ideas of authority, responsibility, psychological certainty, hierarchy, power, and evangelism. Society was to choose a future without heroes, without great drama and without one-sided victories. Decolonization had begun.

However, among the Indians, the opposite process took place. Some of them slowly began to move into the cities, distancing themselves from their original culture. The racist oppression they had been exposed to became part of their own potential. They became in a sense prisoners of their own village settlements, defenseless against the advantages and disadvantages of the new technology, and primitivized in their sexuality and ability to make contact with others. They reacted with fatigue, a variety of small illnesses, and depression. Their society became characterized by the same anxiety, brutality , and social control that they faced earlier in their encounter with the colonizers. The old pattern of hegemony began to turn up again among them.

The Road to the Last Village Both Indians and whites live in Chemescua—the name has been chosen to preserve the anonymity of the place. It is the last village one passes through when leaving our civilization to go into Arhuaco Indian territory. For us the journey to Indian country begins here. For the Indians, Chemescua is where they perish. It is here their journey ends.

To get from the capital of the province to Chemescua, one travels by truck down a narrow mountain road, through streams and rivers, jumping more than driving, avoiding rocks and fallen rock slides, far too close to deep holes and abysses. Under way, fellow passengers point out places where trucks have fallen down. One can see by the number of crosses alongside the road that the risk involved in driving here is real. The villagers are relieved, as a rule, when the trip to the capital is over, and in order to keep from worrying about the ride home, they get plastered. The driver is also half-drunk, and to prove that the trip is not so dangerous, he puts his foot on the accelerator at the most dangerous spots. He comes to a standstill just before a curve, guns the motor, and releases the brake, so that the car lurches forward in a death leap. Even before arriving at Chemescua, the foreigner sees signs of the close relationship these people have to self-destruction and death.

Apart from this road, all other roads to Chemescua are narrow mountain paths, which can only be traversed on foot or on the back of a mule. These paths constitute a complicated network of connections that cover the whole valley and most of the surrounding mountains. They fit into the landscape, and the way they rise and fall in relation to the contours of the mountains constitutes the most energy-efficient means of getting from one place to another. Some of the paths are made over rough-hewn rock, and go back to Chibchan culture. One day's walk leads to the nearest white town, and one day's walk in the other direction leads to the Indians. This network of paths contains essential information and is a symbolic illustration of Chemescua's relationship with the world around it.

Most people only move between the village and their fields. Year after year they go to work back and forth across the same paths. Someone asked for directions will probably give a wrong answer, because the Indian only knows *su camino,* "his road." Where other people's paths and roads lead to is none of his business.

Paths and roads have another meaning for those who are a little better off; they are tools for trade and means for visiting friends, family, a doctor, or a priest. For the rich, roads have great significance, and are often discussed regarding their condition and maintenance. When they meet in the evening, the rich talk about their future plans, about the possibility of getting a bridge built, and they criticize the officials of the province for neglecting the city and not supporting its development. A proper road is the means and prerequisite for development, for better economy, for medical help, and better health.

However, small farmers and ordinary people rarely show the same interest. They keep to themselves and walk su camino. For them, the lack of communication is an advantage. It makes it harder for the police to come in, and sales agents, political agitators, priests, and robbers are kept at a distance. In Chemescua, they want to be left in peace. This serves them best. If a proper roadway is built, the village will go down the drain, because bad guys will come and interfere and steal their few possessions, of grain, cattle, poultry, and women.

Poverty and Self-Hatred In Chemescua, everyone wears European clothes, even those who are of Indian origin. Being well dressed is an ambition, and there are examples of people who avoid being seen because they of necessity have to wear old clothes. Thus, there are some ten to fifteen people in Chemescua who for years have seldom passed through the middle of town. They use the back roads and go to and from their houses in the dark, for fear of being ridiculed and humiliated for their poverty. People who work in the fields often take an extra set of clothes with them and change to the nice clothes before returning to their village. People may refuse to speak to foreigners, because they are wearing the wrong clothes. When one approaches them, they turn their backs, walk away, and pretend that nothing has happened. They do not wish to be regarded as being backward, nor to be humiliated and ridiculed. Thus they look down on those who wear Indian clothes, regarding them as the enemies of progress.

Everyday life used to be simple and healthy. There were possibilities for maintaining an ecological balance in which earth, air, and water were unpolluted, and one could enjoy the fruits of nature without any precautions. This attitude still leads many people to relate to their surroundings without regard for the fact that the small society has grown so much larger that it pollutes nature with its refuse.

Water is fetched near the houses, right next to the place where the farm animals graze. A pail of water, which can cover the daily needs of a family, is used as drinking water, for cooking purposes, washing dishes, bathing children, rinsing fruit, soaking beans, and, finally, for the pigs and dogs.

Personal hygiene is limited. People do not consider dirt and excrement to be spreaders of illness. Cleanliness is evaluated more by how one smells than how one looks. Therefore, there is a large consumption of various perfumes.

The population of Chemescua gives itself up unconditionally to trash, shit, and animals. It is as if these people have been pushed so far over their Indian borders, away from the center of civilization, that as time goes by their defense mechanisms have broken down.

Chemescua is a picture of what happens when white European civilization clashes with the civilization of the Indian. One finds here the remains of the societies of the Spanish conquistadors and the original Indians, all clad now in so-called modern civilization.

The two ethnic groups, Indian and white, have been mixed in every way over the past two centuries, so that not one single individual exists today whom a geneticist would call a "pure phenotype." However, the mixtures have taken place with so much violence and oppression that discrimination and prejudice is still connected with particular appearances.

First and foremost, one distinguishes between *indios* and *civilisados* —"Indian" and "civilized" people, terms also implying poor and rich, old and young, ugly and beautiful. The words seldom refer to racial origins, but always to social connections. Since Indians are found at the lowest level of the community in Chemescua, the word indio is a curse-word.

Even though Chemescua consists of many different populations, each with its own status, most people in the provincial capital consider it an Indian town, whereas the Indians up in the mountains regard it as an exclusively white town.

It is this being in limbo, neither white nor Indian, that leads the inhabitants to destroy themselves through self-hatred.

The Pattern of Illness: Symptoms of Depression The average age of people in Chemescua is low. The primary cause of death is gastrointestinal diseases due to parasites and various deficiencies. In only a few cases do people reach ages advanced enough to die of cancer, heart disease and other illnesses characteristic of our civilization.

During the last ten years, a doctor has come a few times a month from the provincial capital to consult with the inhabitants of Chemescua. According to his information, most of the inhabitants show symptoms of depression, regardless of their somatic condition. They are characterized by fatigue, feelings of insurmountability, lack of energy, and loss of appetite. They often stay in bed for days on end, without

Chemescua, May 20, 1983

If I asked too many questions of people in Chemescua, their reaction was that I should rather ask people in the provincial capital, Valledupar, where they are more accustomed to dealing with preguntones—*"inquisitiveness." When asked who this preguntones applied to, they answered, "People like you—the tax collector, the police and the priest."*

knowing what is wrong. They list "fever" and "headache" as the cause and lie about listlessly. They often draw attention to and dramatize their infirmities, and spend a lot of money on painkillers.

Many suffer from seizures, called "*ataques,*" "fainting spells," during which they fall on the floor or the bed with eyes rolled back, and cramps. Frequently, they describe in graphic detail how a depressive feeling, involving pain in the diaphragm, forces its way up to the head, ending in an attack. As a rule, women are the ones who have these attacks, the trigger often being a marital argument. Both parties know that such attacks are played out in order to make an impression and scare each other.

In this borderline area, where health and illness clash and where one is very close to giving oneself up to nature, impulses are let loose and total immersion in seizure is an acceptable mode of behavior. People allow each other to be dramatic and attention-seeking.

There is no reason to romanticize Chemescua. Daily life here lacks the so-called nicety of civilization, so that one dies too soon after a life filled with days of listlessness, depression, and malaise.

The people of Chemescua have a conception of human beings as being born evil: the innate part of the personality is destructive, while the acquired part, upbringing and education, tries to suppress the evil tendencies. One does not reproach parents for having an unmanageable child, as such children are seen as having been born with characteristics so wicked that they are beyond their parents' and their own control. This view leaves little room for feelings of guilt or a belief in sin and morals. Life is short and must be lived as well as possible.

A birth only slightly alters the family's routine. If a boy is born, the father buys a bottle of rum and shares it with some friends. If it is a girl, no celebration is held.

Giving birth is an obligation for a woman, a service she renders for the man she lives with, who in turn provides her with a house and various comforts. Children are tools of a sort, in a barter which seems to create an equal division between men and women.

The mother seldom gives herself over to enjoying the newborn baby, but rather is engaged in other domestic chores while she breast-feeds the child. Children are often handled awkwardly, in ways bordering on brutality. They are placed outside in the sun with nothing to shade their eyes; they are bundled up to the point of immobility; or they are washed in water that is much too cold. Breast-feeding may suddenly be disrupted by the mother putting the child aside in irritation in order to do other chores.

It is as if the mother is testing the child's ability to survive, only allowing herself to form a attachment to the child if it survives the first year. This is probably a protective mechanism or a defense against too strong an attachment to a child, which the country's high infant mortality rates show can all too easily be torn away.

Many give birth by the "Indian method." In the mountains, Indian women give birth in a squatting position, with the man sitting behind her giving her support. He places his arms around her and follows her breathing, becoming a participant in the contractions. Physiologically speaking, it is a good position for giving birth, and psychologically, the husband's participation gives the birthing woman emotional support and a sense of security. A finely woven piece of material is placed on the ground under the woman. This cloth has belonged to the family for many generations and has always been the first piece of material that has received the newly born.

However, in Chemescua, this method of childbirth has been altered and coarsened. When the birth takes a long time, the Indian method is adopted. The husband uses all his might to try to press the child out, and to prevent the infant from getting hurt, some rags are spread out on the ground under the woman.

Man and Woman The symptoms of depression and the negative self-image in Chemescua resemble the conditions that Alicia and Gerardo Reichel-Dolmatoff have described in another Colombian village, Aritama (Reichel-Dolmatoff 1961). These conditions are expressed first and foremost in the paucity of interrelations: the individual has few close relations. The family is characterized by instability and an unmasked oppression of women.

Men and women rarely grow attached to each other, and most women are abandoned by their husbands.

Many men in Chemescua say, "Después de Dios, el hombre; después del hombre, el perro; después del perro, la mujer": "After God, man; after man, dog; after dog, woman." Men see themselves as superior to women in nearly all areas of life. Men can subject women to the most outrageous vileness, and still regard their own sexual promiscuity, laziness, and aggressiveness as a "human right."

This does not mean that male authority is a firmly established, incontestable force. A man is no more than a tolerated guest at home, where the woman plays the role that causes least friction, a *fait accompli* satisfying both parties.

The woman often says, "Yo no voy a comer besos," "I cannot live by your kisses." By this she means that if a man makes overtures, he must promise her something in return, for example, more money for food and clothes. A woman's first refusal of a man is not just a question of demonstrating her chastity, but an attempt as well at evaluating him and getting a cash return out of their relationship. Mothers raise their daughters to regard coitus as a means for achieving monetary rewards from a man, as *un favor,* a service she renders for which he must pay.

Marital quarrels are widespread in Chemescua and often develop according to a well-established pattern:

The wife accuses her husband of infidelity, and he accuses her of not serving meals on time, of not washing and ironing his shirts, and of not keeping the children and herself in a clean and presentable state. The wife replies that it is all his fault, because he is so lazy, which means she must slave even harder and cannot get everything done. These mutual accusations quickly lead to a regular fight. The man is dominant here as well. He often begins by smashing things in the home. With a sweep of his arm, he may send platters, dishes, flatware and glasses flying, and then go around the house systematically destroying everything within his reach. This takes place while both parties quarrel loudly. When he wants to direct the physical destruction toward has wife, he may gather her personal belongings—dresses, shoes, sewing gear—and throw them out of the house. There is a special expression for this moment in the quarrel: *sacar los chismes*—"throwing things out." The altercation is then replaced by yelling and screaming, and out of curiosity the neighbors begin to flock around the house. The man will then begin to beat his wife, either with his flat palm or with a stick. A popular moment is when the wife rips the straw hat off her husband's head and begins to trample on it.

Even though both parties declare loud and clear at this point that they will kill each other, they rarely suffer any physical injury. The dispute culminates with the man calling his wife and her mother whores. The woman will react by having an ataque, at which point the neighbors will intervene and attempt to smooth out the problems.

The man will then leave his home, go out and get drunk with his friends, or perhaps move in with his lover. If the wife nevertheless wants him back, she will send one of the children off to him after a few days with food and clean clothes. This is a symbol of peace and submission, and the man will then slowly return home.

The Psychological Point of View: Learned Helplessness In a psychological sense, the inhabitants of Chemescua can be said to be characterized by "learned helplessness," a concept stemming from laboratory experiments which showed that dogs had a poorer ability to learn when subjected to uncontrollable pain stimulus (Overmeir and Seligman 1967; Seligman 1974, 1975). The dogs were placed in learning boxes with two compartments and given electrical shocks through the floor. Those dogs that were not given the possibility of averting pain stimuli by jumping into the other compartment became apathetic and passive in subsequent learning situations, compared with the dogs who received warning signals and could learn to avert the pain. Thus, those animals that had earlier been conditioned for helplessness in their encounter with uncontrollable electric shocks, later showed tendencies to give up in any learning situation, becoming passive and apathetic instead.

Theories on learned helplessness have since been developed to describe behavior in patients who suffer from depression (Garber and Seligman 1980; Abrahamson, Seligman, and Teasdale 1978; *Journal of Abnormal Psychology,* vol. 87 no.1, 1978). The hypothesis is that the more often one experiences a lack of connection between one's actions and their results, the easier it is to develop a general belief in one's own helplessness and inability to master the world, thus establishing the grounds for depression.

In a way, it is this form of learned helplessness that characterized Chemescua's inhabitants. The trauma of colonization and the subsequent decolonization have placed the inhabitants in so many uncontrollable and negative situations that they have all gradually been thrown into a depressive state of learned helplessness. The outer factors have been transferred to inner personal relations, and singular, specific events have been internalized as generalized states of helplessness. The external traumas have thus contributed to a general depressive tone and a negative ego-perception. Since the inhabitants share the same external situation, the prerequisites for contagion are there, and depression has gradually become a common lot.

Theories on learned helplessness are nevertheless so seductively simple that one may easily be tempted to apply them uncritically to Chemescua. In a number of other cases, however, the theories do not stand up to empirical examination.

For example, there are no convincing cognitive-psychological tests in which the simple addition of a person's negative experiences proves that the more often he or she has experienced a lack of connection between behavior and result, the more easily the person experiences depression. Many people who have lived lives filled with negative experiences remain optimistic and involved, whereas others with positive life stories get depressed (Hammen, Krantz, and Cochran 1981; Hammen and deMayo 1982). Nonetheless, studies show that there is some small connection between having lived under objectively favorable living conditions and the experience of satisfaction (Costa and McCrae 1980). Symptoms of depression are thus a complicated interplay of many factors.

Similarly, epidemiological studies of the connection between life circumstances and mental illness have been criticized. Even though the first "life-event" studies could demonstrate a connection between a series of traumatizing and stressful life circumstances and the development of physical and psychological illness (Holmes and Rahe 1967; Holmes and Masuda 1974), later studies have shown that the connection was far from impressive, statistically speaking. The study could be criticized methodologically, in that the negative events in a person's life were not in themselves the stress factor that gave rise to the illness, but rather it was the meaning each individual ascribed to these events. The very reactions to life events was the point of departure. However, the reactions turned out to be so complex that they did not immediately lend themselves to measuring and statistical correlation with symptoms of disorder (Toits 1983; Lazarus and Folkman 1984).

The general critique of cognitive-psychological as well as social-epidemiological theories on the connection between living conditions and depression can be summed up as follows: an inflicted helpless passivity and depression is not necessarily a sign of poor adjustment. The kind of behavior associated with helplessness and depression is only inappropriate when the surroundings can be controlled or modified by the subject. If there is a high degree of uncontrollability and impassiveness, depressive behavior can turn out to be functional.

Studies show that the less control one has over a situation, the more easily there will arise a general feeling of insecurity, an undervaluing of one's own skills, and a loss of initiative (Tversky and Kahneman 1971, 1981). Depressive patients distinguish themselves from nondepressive by a lack of confidence in their own capabilities. Even though the two groups in reality often manage task situations equally well, depressed people will have a lower expectation of their experience of their capabilities and will be characterized in particular by their experience of their surroundings as being uncontrollable (Garber and Hollon, 1980; Tversky and Kahneman 1971, 1981).

If these psychological studies are to be applied to the inhabitants of Chemescua, one may pose the hypothesis that their depressive symptoms can be seen as a reaction to the experience of the uncontrollability of their surroundings.

Depression, like other feelings, can be a necessary forerunner of other emotional states. Like anger, guilt, and anxiety, depression often has a limited duration. Even the positive emotional states which come after one has achieved a long-desired goal will often be limited, because they are only one step on the path toward other goals. For example, a student may get a little depressed after an exam, because the completed exam has been overevaluated and is afterwards seen as only a small step toward a career (Lazarus, Kanner, and Folkman 1980).

Even if depressive symptoms may reflect poor adjustment and lack of control in an individual, the same symptoms in a larger context can be appropriate mechanisms of adaptation in a process leading to change and control. In the same way, depression among the people of Chemescua can be seen as a link in a process of development, an appropriate mechanism of adaptation to difficult living conditions, and not just a disturbed reaction to underdevelopment.

The Anthropological Point of View: "Illness" and "Disease" People in Chemescua suffer from the same symptoms described in other "cultures of poverty" that are in the process of dissolution and underdevelopment (Reichel-Dolmatoff and Reichel-Dolmatoff 1961; Lewis 1962). However, symptoms like dysphoria, sadness, hopelessness, unhappiness, and lack of delight in one's surroundings take on different meanings and forms in different societies (Kleinman and Good 1985). In a Western European society, one of the definitions of depression described in psychiatric textbooks is "a sense of hopelessness, accompanied by a gamut of feelings, ranging from distress, depression, and shame to anger. Feelings of hopelessness will not always be restricted to the provoking incident—large or small. It may lead to thoughts about the hopelessness of one's life in general. It is such generalization of hopelessness that forms the central core of depressive disorder" (Brown and Harris 1978, 235).

A more precise psychiatric description of the symptomatology of depression could have been selected, but the above description in fact fits the population of Chemescua. The villagers, however, do not regard the symptoms of depression to be a cause for treatment, but rather an inescapable part of human destiny. The inhabitants are tormented by depression, but they do not conceive of it as symptoms of a psychiatric disorder. The symptoms are inscribed in their own conception, woven into the local norms, meanings, and power relations.

The dilemma is that the symptoms which our culture sees as a disorder are regarded as signs of normalcy in other cultures, reflecting two different understandings of the concept of disorder. On the one hand, psychiatrists have a tendency to regard disorders as universal occurrences, while culture is just an external interpretation that is added on. On the other hand, anthropologists regard disorders as relative and mean that they cannot be identified independently of specific cultures (Marsella, Sartorius, Jablensky, and Fenton 1985, 300).

A distinction between "disease" and "illness" can perhaps lend some clarity to the discussion of culture-bound conceptions (Kleinman 1980). *Disease* is the professional definition in which symptoms are inscribed in the context of medical science and treated within the prevalent, well-established professional institution. *Illness* is the popular conception, to which is connected a treatment based on people's own experiences. Within biologically oriented medical science, disease can be distinguished from illness, whereas it is more difficult to maintain a distinction when there is talk of psychological disorders. Even in the case of a psychiatric disorder that has a fundamentally biological-genetic cause, social and psychological conditions can be superposed and the symptoms combined and given cultural and symbolic meaning. Taken to the extreme, it could be argued that a number of psychic ailments, for example, depression, exist as illness and not disease.

However, according to a traditional psychiatric frame of reference, it can be shown that some forms of depression have the same causes universally. Psychiatry has specific definitions for different types of depression (e.g., DSM III 1980). Thus with this diagnostic code as a point of departure, cross-cultural studies aiming at statistical epidemiological information can be carried out. Such studies show that depression in the Western form is found everywhere in the world, even if it is culturebound in its manifestation (Kleinman 1986).

On several occasions, it has been suggested that this conclusion is somewhat illogical and indeed even circular (Obeyesekere 1985, 136). It is highly doubtful whether one can consider symptoms like gloominess, lack of initiative, somatization, and hypochondriac, overdramatic complaining as symptoms of depression outside the Euro-American psychiatric tradition.

In only a few societies outside the Judeo-Christian belief system is depression associated with feelings of sin and guilt. The Buddhist would go a step further and say that generalizing hopelessness is one's personal fate, and salvation lies in understanding and living through this hopelessness (Kleinman and Good 1985, 134). Life consists of suffering and grief, and the cause of grief is connected with wants and demands. Similarly, grief is a religious experience for Shiite Muslims, for whom the ability to experience intense dysphoria, or anxiety, is a sign of deep understanding and maturity in an individual. In contrast, the people of Bali and in particular the Thai-Lao people regard the leveling off of emotional highs and lows as a virtue and the only way to maintain a stable and harmonious inner life.

In Western society, moreover, the depressive symptoms exist in a freer flowing form and are not in the same way bound to a cosmology (Obeyesekere 1985, 138). This is one of the reasons they are easier to identify and treat as a disorder.

It must be emphasized once more that the distinction between illness and disease does not exclude the possibility of isolating and identifying biogenetic and sociocultural conditions which are cross-culturally uniform and which constitute the operational core of what can be called depression. The cross-cultural point of view is not against the biologically based treatment of depression per se, nor is it opposed to the hospitalization of depressive patients.

The anthropological point of view supplements the psychiatric and the clinical psychological point of view. To the anthropologist, depression appears to be a state of grief which is to be translated and interpreted in order to identify a hidden meaning in a hidden system. To the psychiatrist, the same pattern of behavior takes the form of depressive symptoms, and against the background of, among other things, epidemiological studies, he will be able to decide if it can be treated. One point of view does not exclude the other.

The Inhabitants' Point of View: Sickness as Social Control On the basis of a "disease"-interpretation, the depressive diagnosis has many different variations. In a psychiatric and clinical psychological context, one distinguishes between endogenous and reactive depression or between different reactions to grief and crisis. However, regardless of the fact that some categories, such as reactive depression, contain culture-bound aspects to a large degree, they are insufficient to describe the depressive mode of reaction of the inhabitants of Chemescua.

Supplementing the professional disease model with the popular illness model gives an impression of how disorder can be used as a measure of social control.

The people of Chemescua have astonishingly little knowledge of physiology. For example, they consider the heart to be the organ with which one breathes and have a conception of it as a bird-like body with the lungs constituting the wings. These wings function as ventilators, bringing fresh air to the heart, and when someone dies, it is because the wings stop flapping and close in around the heart.

Sickness is a neutral part of nature and will always be present. But one only gets sick if two conditions are fulfilled: a lowered resistance to sickness and an aggressive act aimed at oneself by another person.

Lowered resistance is connected with explanations of the blood being "weak" or "strong," "thick" or "thin," "hot" or "cold." The composition of the blood varies according to sex and age, day and season, and is dependent moreover on the physical and mental activity the person carries out. A woman's blood is said to be hotter than a man's, making her more receptive to different sicknesses, like infections and indigestion. The blood, and thereby its natural resistance, changes all the time.

Sickness is an instrument used by others to harm or obliterate a chosen victim. Sickness and death can always be blamed on others thinking evil thoughts about one. In certain cases, a person can even bring on sickness in himself as a form of self-punishment and self-reproach. A glance, a gesticulation, and a prayer containing a hostile thought directed at another person can be the cause of his sickness.

Sickness functions thus as a mechanism of social control (Parsons 1958). Fear of having one's blood "weakened" can make someone follow local convention and rules for acceptable behavior. For example, it is not desirable in Chemescua for people to gather in groups to hear music or to dance and drink, not so much because of hygienic precautions, but simply to avoid situations of stress and potential conflict that arise when people in crowds begin to exhibit domineering behavior. Likewise, it is known that beauty, harmonious family life, and sound health are asocial and can give rise to jealousy and hostility from the neighbors, because they deviate from the norm. The people who possess these characteristics, and perhaps do many good deeds, are regarded as having weak blood, which means they easily can fall ill. Regardless of whatever qualities an act may have, acknowledgment and support will always be given to the situation that can be controlled.

Aggression creates an equilibrium and levels off individual differences. The infliction of sickness is the most efficient way of making people act in a manner which is neither dangerous nor threatening. The sick person cannot work, risks losing his physical attractiveness, incurs great expenses, and ends up reduced to a subordinate level. Therefore, anger, retribution, and jealousy are very important emotional states, a kind of social control which may well have arisen because Chemescua is placed in a no man's land, so far out that no other control systems have had any influence.

Sickness is a recurring theme in most conversations. By exaggerating one's pains and by dramatizing and drawing attention to oneself, one demonstrates one's helplessness and defeat. To be sick is to be harmless, that is, a "good" person. Such an individual is in a privileged position, which allows him to sidestep obligations and hide from enemies.

A sick person is in a sense holy, because his immediate social world

Chemescua, May 12, 1983

For a short period of time, I thought life in Chemescua was idyllic and romantic, simple and original. I decided then to live like the inhabitants. But I quickly discovered that daily life was so filled with cooking and providing the most essential necessities that there was no room for anything else.

For example, I tried to make the corn pancakes, called arepas, *that constitute a staple in most people's diet in Chemescua. The recipe was as follows:*

Corn cobs have to be harvested.

Corn cobs have to be dried.

The kernels on the cobs have to be removed.

The kernels are to be soaked in water in a big wooden mortar for a couple of hours, after which they are to be pounded until the shells fall off.

The corn has to be washed several times and strained over a finely meshed net in order to separate out the shells.

The corn is left overnight to soak.

Half of it is taken off and cooked.

The cooked and raw corn are mixed together.

The corn is ground to flour between two stones.

The flour is formed into pancakes and roasted over the fire.

It nearly took two days of uninterrupted work before the dry corn became pancakes, on top of which came all the difficulties of getting hold of firewood and petroleum and going around to the neighbors to borrow a strainer, a wooden mortar, and a stone grinder.

I had to try that only once to understand that life in Chemescua is arduous.

has demonstrated its powers in him. A healthy individual, in contrast, is asocial and dangerous. He is upwardly mobile and will perhaps move away from the village and into the big world. He may live in a better, more respectable way, which makes him disloyal to those left behind.

Sickness is then a social measure, which produces its own meaning in the individual's immediate social world and in an extreme sense creates equality.

Shamanism as Treatment and Survival To the inhabitants it makes no sense being labeled with a psychiatric diagnosis. They do not regard themselves as mentally ill and never refer to a doctor for psychiatric treatment. Nonetheless, this attitude does not exclude the fact that they perceive themselves as suffering and tormented and thus in need of help from their own people. Therefore, the inhabitants of Chemescua make extended use of the Indian shamans in the mountains. When they feel especially tormented, they return to their Indian roots, and the Indian, who otherwise is regarded as wild and primitive, becomes the embodiment of healing power.

The shamanistic rituals have a parallel with grief therapy and crisis intervention, in which one gets confronted with one's loss, and through a process of recognition, experiencing the pain, and reframing, one gradually matures and regains one's original ability to function. In the same way, one can say that the people of Chemescua can only get rid of their depression when they have recognized and lived through the dissolution and poverty that has afflicted them.

Even though Chemescua is marked by depression and learned helplessness, it is not only a broken-down, underdeveloped village. On the contrary, it has the possibility of becoming a town of survivors.

The survivors are those who have lived through the crisis of civilization and acknowledged the breakdown. In the same way, one can say that the people of Chemescua will have to have lived through grief and looked the colonial deathtrap in the eye in order to regain life. Precisely by way of their poverty and shabbiness, the hypochondriacal, depressed inhabitants of Chemescua have the possibility of looking their grief in the eye and again becoming heroes—not necessarily supermen, but disheveled heroes.

Many inhabitants in Chemescua believe that magic is their most important means of survival. The treatment of a disease will always have

the sense of a battle, a competition between the patient and his advisors, on the one hand, and enemies on the other. The battle is not primarily directed against the sickness, but against the evil spirits that produce it. If the patient dies, it is not because the treatment was poor, but rather because the enemy that produced the sickness was stronger and more knowledgeable.

The shamanistic rituals, which may involve the ingestion of hallucinogenic yage and peyote, take the form of epic theater. Under their influence one can directly address the evil force, enter into a dialogue with it, and look it in the eye. One can be nourished to the point where one can go back to society and demand that it fight off witchery and evil. This takes place in a poetic mixture of vomit and shit, which literally flows out of one's interior as a reaction against all the euphoriant drugs.

As a rule the patient lies still, while the healer talks and talks and fills up the room, in contrast with the psychoanalytic situation, in which the therapist listens attentively. The shaman sings, hums, or buzzes, and comes with small asides and stories, often in a language the patient does not understand. But the performance is more than a simple projection of the disorder into a magic ritual. It creates sympathy between the shaman and the patient, and the rituals become a part of an odd mosaic of thoughts that weave through the stories, jokes, interruptions, and humming. It is a performance that cannot be understood without participation in the pictures the patient creates in the process. Being brought together in this way gives rise to moments of understanding in which the process unites very diverse forces—movement and stagnation, humor and despair, insecurity and security—order and chaos.

The Journey Goes On Like a yage trip, the journey back from the last surviving Indians ends in Chemescua. Yage is a heavy liquid whose initial effect is to make the seeker throw up and lose control over his bladder. He thinks he is going to die, and images of wild animals and devils flood his mind. Only when the nausea and discomfort subside does he have visions, and then the treatment can begin.

Similarly, after the Indians have immersed themselves in Chemescua's misery they can begin to journey back to their own civilization. When they have lived through this necessary pain, the devils and demons of Western civilization can be exorcised. Images from the past can now be

projected into the future and be awakened, like a sleeping giant, to crush the mirror of history.

However, mysticism and magic are not the loci of liberation. Shamans are often charlatans who give false hopes and justify accidents.

Shamanism is the base from which the oppressed and the oppressor, the victim and the victimizer, the Indian and the white man, can see each other as images of order and disorder. But this does not mean that the recipient ends up getting healed and ridding himself of his opponent.

The journey goes on. However, when magic is the underlying principle one must be prepared to find liberation in other places than where one is searching.

4. *The Survival of the Indians*

One moral alone cannot be elicited from the journey to the last remaining Indians. Each new chapter, each stop on the journey into isolation adds new dimensions and new images: the lack of structure and the fluid boundaries of the Motilon; the rigidity and hierarchy of the Arhuacos; the depression and learned helplessness in Chemescua.

The psychology of survival develops and changes form at the different stages of the journey:

The missionaries went out into the jungle of the Motilon in order to fight back the wildness in themselves, and the Indians became a leaderless counterculture of anarchy. The result has been that the Indians are about to become culturally extinct, because they have only been able to preserve their traditional culture in isolated places. The Arhuacos were able to throw the missionaries out of their country, but the price they paid was to have to build up organizational structures that mirror our society. The inhabitants of Chemescua are in danger of wasting away in depressive and hypochondriacal states of mind, but they attempt to survive by seeking refuge in shamanism, which no one really understands.

In each place, survival is at the expense of something else. In each place, the price paid is different.

The Indians who have done best at keeping their autonomy intact, as the Arhuacos have, are those who have been able to separate themselves from the others, like "floating islands," which constantly keep themselves oriented in relation to their surroundings. The Motilon Indians, in contrast, have run into great difficulties, because they have attempted to survive by fleeing into remote corners of the jungle, where no one has been able to reach them. They have isolated themselves and attempted to maintain a status quo without putting up a battle against their opponents, without organizing themselves, and without bringing about any interplay.

The Murder of a Culture and a People There can be no doubt that the number of Indian groups has dwindled greatly (Dostal 1972), but in all fairness, it should be mentioned that no studies exist which clearly show that the number of Indians within the existing groups is declining. On the contrary, a study by Lizarralde and Beckerman (1982) shows that the number of Motilon Indians is probably slightly on the rise. Information about the Arhuacos, however, is so imprecise that it is difficult to conclude anything at all about their physical survival (Loaiza 1984, 8).

The great inaccuracy in documentation of the fluctuation of population is due to the fact that demographic studies of Indian peoples are very difficult to carry out and interpret. Methodologically, it is problematic to count a population that lives in isolation and is often out wandering. Moreover, there can be different political interests influencing the results of the studies. Some want to document that only a few Indians live in a particular area, in order to argue against the Indians' right to land. Others want to support the Indians and are interested in showing that they are many, in order to secure more money for aid.

In the cases where attempts have been made to bring together the most reliable demographic studies, it has been difficult to show anything unequivocal about which way the population is moving (Grey 1987). A few reports indicate that some Indian groups, like the Campa and Shipibo groups, have rapidly growing populations (Hvalkoff 1984, 197). There are many possible explanations for this. For instance, the vaccination campaigns of the missionaries have probably had a marked influence on the increase in population; the new land laws, which restrict the allotment of land to those who define themselves as Indians, may also have their effect, in the sense that people define themselves as Indians in order to get land.

Nevertheless, regardless of whether doubt can be cast on the question of the physical extinction of the Indians, cultural eradication is taking place. When traditional Indians disappear from the isolated areas, they may possibly turn up elsewhere, either as down-at-the-heel inhabitants of the ghetto in the provincial capital or as sanctimonious Christians at the mission station. The question is whether Indian culture as such can survive in the gutters of the larger society.

The question of Indian people's survival embraces a whole string of issues, for example, the issue of defining genocide and ethnocide, the issue of methodological requirements in demographic studies, and the issue of how political interests affect the results of studies. However, if we look at Indian survival from the Indian point of view, these definitions and limitations are irrelevant. The Indians believe unequivocably that survival is a problem for them, and some even believe they are approaching extinction. Certainly there are some few who claim that the Indian mode of thought will survive as transformations into other forms, no matter how much it is oppressed. This attitude, however, is mainly expressed by Indians who have moved into the larger society. The few Arhuaco and Motilon Indians who have been able to preserve parts of their traditional culture do not accept that a person defines himself as Indian, no matter what costume he appears in. In their view, Indian identity is contingent on a traditional mode of living that cannot be transferred to slum life in the big cities or to the villages around the mission stations. They distinguish between the "real" Indians and those who are culturally deprived of their Indian identity. Their attitude is that cultural survival is just as important as physical survival.

However, if one puts one's own definitions aside and follows Arhuaco and Motilon self-conceptions of being the last isolated bearers of Indian culture, a few comments are necessary:

First of all, there are no more Indians who are isolated in an absolute sense of the word: they all have contact with the society around them, and even if some of them live in isolation and may have far to go to their nearest neighbor, their seclusion is a reaction against being swallowed up by the surrounding society, as a means of protection from it. It is separation rather than isolation.

Secondly, the Indian societies that have been the most successful at surviving with their traditions intact are not just passive cultures preserving the past. Rather, they are countercultures that consciously or unconsciously accentuate and expose the parts of their traditional culture that constitute a contrast with the surrounding European culture.

The anarchistic structures of the Motilon have possibly always been present and have not arisen as a reaction to the larger society's hierarchical distribution of power. The way in which the Arhuacos use the loom is probably also more than just an attempt to avoid being defined as psychotic in our world. And shamanism in Chemescua is possibly more than just a way of opposing the mode of thought imposed on the Indians by colonial terror. However, in trying to understand Indian survival it is difficult to unveil the structures they have always possessed, one reason being that Indians do not present their past in such a way that it can be included in historical research with time as a linear measure. As Euro-Americans and representatives of the larger society, our point of departure is how we read Indian culture here and now. In this reading, some aspects of Indian culture appear in opposition to the larger society, elements that the Indians themselves see as representative of their traditions and essential to their identity. Whether these cultural traits have always been there is less important than understanding how the Indians emphasize and dramatize parts of their culture in contrast to our Euro-American culture.

A description of the survival of the Indians starts with the Indians' own self-conception of being the last ones left, even if they do survive physically and are succeeded by others. A sense of solidarity characterizes their view of culture, a view which is not necessarily pessimistic, in part because it does not exclude the belief that the last ones can become the first.

Shamanism In summary, one can say that the Indians seem to be metaphors of the crisis of our civilization, and that the long house of the Motilon, the loom of the Arhuacos, and the depression in Chemescua have become contrasting images to our culture.

The Indians do not doubt that the mystical and magical space they wrap around themselves is the most potent means they have against the terror of white society. Shamanism can be described as a force rising out of the history and conditions of their oppression (Taussig 1980, 39).

The era of conquest and colonization was a time full of paradoxes and contrasts. The New World was built upon the disproportionate terror and eradication of Indian culture, in which the church with its own use of magic represented both civilization and wildness. It was this confusion of contradictions and paradoxes that created the magic of the Indians. Its task was to oppose the order of colonization by setting up images that created disorder. This magical quality of reality and the role of myths in history was created by juxtaposing images from different periods of time in nonsynchronic contrasts.

More than any other group of peoples, the Indians have the horrors of colonization as a historical memory, and for that reason have good premises upon which to recreate images that conjure up disorder. Magic becomes a force coming from the Indians' history, connected with myths of conquest and wildness. The outcome of the treatment depends on how willing and ready one is to penetrate the sphere of death, lose one's soul, and allow the sickness-inducing trauma and the healer's manipulations to revive the creative forces inside oneself. It is a journey carried out by the healer as well as the patient in an underworld of sacred landscape. The decisive point is the journey to the kingdom of death or, rather, how one gets out of it. It can be an expansive land, flat and shadowless, or it can be a narrow tunnel with water running and animals swimming and flying. It can be a land full of colors, words, and music. The kingdom of death can be banal and quiet, a land one submits to, or it can be a demonic land where one fights heroically. The shaman offers the vision, but he needs the patient in order to return again to life.

The Indians still work with the magic that lies in their historical knowledge. After meeting a shaman and being present at his rituals, I was struck by his friendly and unthreatening manner, which instilled in me a sense of security. At the same time he has hauled me through the strangest stories, making no sense at all, and initiated me into rituals that had no continuity or logic. This experience may be attributed to my lack of knowledge of the language and its context. But I am convinced that his magic has also had the purpose of creating disorder. He has insisted on contesting and undermining my search for order. The magic of the Indians is in a broad sense an attempt at liberation from colonial terror. Like an allegory, it tries to create another order than that of Western civilization created by the Spanish, the whites, and intellectual travelers. The means is to create an unpredictable arrangement of images, in which the shaman himself becomes unmanageable and wild in his rituals, not for the purpose of eliminating wildness, but in order to reclaim it (Taussig 1987, 391).

Nonetheless, it is difficult to see the Indians' magical powers as a basis for their special ability to survive. On the contrary, magic is a means for furthering their oppression. It has some powers of attraction among the poorest of them, lending them characteristics that make it even easier for intellectuals to accept that they disappear. By assigning them some supernatural abilities and a little positive life wisdom, it is possible that both we and the Indians believe that they are in reality not oppressed.

Heightened respect for the primitive represents neocolonial reparation of guilty consciences.

Therefore, shamanism is only a starting point. Liberation lies elsewhere.

Indian Movements: Indianidad The historical and political consciousness of the Indians breaks with our traditional, historical train of thought, more closely resembling a secret agreement and concordance between earlier and present generations.

Some Indian organizations have termed the field of tension that is released between past and present *Indianidad* (Varese 1982). This movement stands for a collective consciousness that is based on common interpretations of historical events, interpretations which the Indians pass on to each other in the form of symbols in their own language.

This particular form of historical thinking and political action has made Indian movements the object of many of the white intellectuals' projections. The Indian liberation movement has become a romantic metaphor for hope in our own struggle for liberation. Indian populations are seen lumped together with the lower classes in the cities as the potential from which a new civilization will be able to be formed. From here arises the popular movement that can oppose exploitation, cultural oppression, and ideological uniformity. The Indians are said to have developed a culture that can form the basis for liberation, and the left-wing politicians in the cities have developed defense mechanisms which should be able to produce liberation. In certain cases, this romanticized interpretation of Indian culture has caused such big organizational problems that the Indians themselves end up in dissolution and suicide. The main reason is that there are no organizational models developed for Indian liberation movements which sufficiently take Indian culture or Indian formulations and metaphors into account.

From the start, the problems of the Indian movements have been structural. Colonialism is totalistic and one-dimensional in form, based on the view that there is only one way of administering the world. Reality becomes narrowed down and monopolized, containing only the visions of those who are colonizers. There is only room for one discourse, one consciousness, one ideology, and one science.

The dilemma for Indian people is that with regard to structure, breaking with colonialization necessitates a unified revolutionary movement, which can win only by being just as one-dimensional and monopolistic as the process of colonization. For the struggle to take place and for imperialism to be able to change thrones, the opponents would, structurally speaking, have to espouse the same uniformity and unity of ideology and organization.

Indian cultures cannot demonstrate this necessary unity, because they do not constitute a unified, distinct category. On the contrary, they are made up of hundreds of different populations, each with its own specific historical and ethnic origin. In practice, the Indian organizations have divided up into many factions, some of which fight for an ideological principle, while others are more concrete and put more emphasis on land rights and autonomy. Indian populations constitute completely different social groups that cannot be reduced to one downtrodden people. Their struggles are not the same as class struggle.

In many of the universities with a Marxist intellectual elite, the Indian people have proved to be a difficult academic subject, because they do not fulfill the traditional requirements for class struggle. In the social sciences one may well speak of Indians as having a revolutionary potential, but no content analyses of their speeches or writings have in fact ever been done. The Indian movements themselves have resulted in complaints about their being hedged in by a display of discretion that in the broadest sense can be attributed to the influence of colonial thinking on Latin American and left-wing social science (Varese 1982, 30).

This unspoken need for unity and one-dimensionality in the revolutionary struggle has led to accusations that the Indian movements are being split up into factions that wage war against each other. It has been said that the Indians formulate demands which are unrealistic and out of step with the present political situation, and they have had to defend themselves against charges that their ideologies were too romantic and impractical (Manuel and Posluns 1978, 216).

Anthropologists have also had trouble recognizing the multidimensionality that is an important characteristic of Indian mobilization. Even if they naturally have always stood on the side of the oppressed Indians, they have also tried to isolate them, structurally speaking. First, they studied the Indian people as such, describing their situation without taking into account their own points of departure in Western civilization. Then scientists documented the difficult survival conditions of various Indian groups, producing an impressive series of case studies,

Nabucimaque, August 11, 1982

The Arhuaco Indians told me later what happened on the day they took over the mission.

They had held a meeting for several days and then agreed to end it. Some of them were chatting, while others went to sleep. Late at night, a mamu came back from a nearby temple and said that he had seen something in a dream. They listened to him with interest. Suddenly, the mood changed to one of excited arousal, and in the course of a few minutes, everyone agreed that the time had come to take over the mission station. They ran around the houses waking people up, and after an hour, a resolution had been drawn up, which all the Indians present, about six hundred, signed. After that, they seized the mission.

Two white people were present during the meeting. They were friends of the Arhuacos and had fallen asleep, but were awakened to take pictures of what had happened. One of them told me later that the action apparently had not been planned ahead of time, and that she did not understand what had gotten the Indians to seize the mission exactly at that particular time. She had attempted to get an explanation, but was told that even though they were friends, it did not mean she was meant to understand everything.

from groups like the International Work Group for Indigenous Affairs and Survival International. However, only a few have tried to describe the destruction of a people in a broader perspective, putting it into a larger context and describing each separate Indian people, not only in relation to the state, but also to each other (Bodley 1982, 165; Veber 1984, 43).

Planned Collectivity or Collective Consciousness The larger society has tried in various ways to make Indians invisible by inscribing them within its own world.

One example is the idea of development which experts are ready to use in order to help Indians survive. Welfare experts and public authorities see them as a "resource problem," a "market problem," an "infrastructure problem," and a "technological development problem." They promise progress and talk about higher incomes and better nutrition, specific advancements that everyone agrees are desirable. However, the concept of development often disguises hidden intentions of getting the Indians to be more like their white neighbors. Development suggests "something carried out by foreigners who have more power than the local population itself" (Frank 1987, 41).

In contrast, left-wingers and intellectuals in the big cities want the Indians to go back to their original roots and search out the basic principles of Indian culture. In several Latin American countries, including Colombia, Peru, and Ecuador, the intellectuals maintain that their nations would be strengthened by acknowledging their Indian origins. Therefore, Indians must help the new nations to bring out the true national character, and the Indians themselves can only survive if they acknowledge their status as true Indians.

Nonetheless, no matter which concept of development the outsider utilizes, he or she still comes as an expert who tells the Indians that they are culturally deprived, that they do not have the right kind of culture, and that with a little help from the outside they could acquire what they lack at the moment. Whether or not the lack resides in the technological civilization of the larger society or in the original culture of the Indians, the structure is the same. The standard is set by the foreigners, just as it always has been (Friedlander 1975, 182).

In a traditional Marxist sense, the Indian movements belong to a residual category of "pre-capitalist remnants" waiting to be developed

(Tarp 1984, 97). Socialism is the means for achieving quick development and extensive modernization, whereas capitalism is often associated with slow, traditional growth. This is one reason why socialism became so popular in a Latin America that cried for revolution and rapid change. The socialist train of thought regarding development can be called "planned collectivity" in contrast to the Indian interpretation of the balance between history and nature, which can be called "collective consciousness" (Tarp 1984, 105).

However, no matter which theory of development has been used, or attitude taken, by experts and intellectuals, the reality is that the Indians simply disappear. It is as if words like acculturation, cultural contact, modernization, economic development, integration, and assimilation have been used to rationalize the cultural murder, or ethnocide, that takes place when a technologically powerful culture colonizes a less powerful one.

Traditional development researchers claim that ethnocide is unavoidable, as long as ethnic minorities cannot be kept in total isolation. For example, it has been said that "Men in every culture harbor unexpressed wishes to have more in order to be more. Once it becomes evident to them that it is possible to desire more, they will by and large want more. The structure of traditional village society becomes undermined because its traditional functions become displaced once superior economic and technological alternatives become available" (Dalton 1971, 29).

In a certain sense, this developmental train of thought was created simultaneously with the white class, the "colonial bourgeoisie's realization that it was impossible to maintain dominance over colonial countries. Therefore, they decided to stage rearguard attacks within the cultural sphere, and the natives were won over by other words and other, more insidious arguments" (Fanon 1967, 32).

Today, the idea of development is still going strong among many native people, and professionals still attempt to oversimplify the debate by claiming that the Indians cannot survive by being isolated on reservations and kept like animals in the zoo; they must be integrated into the larger society. Total isolation and no changes versus complete assimilation are two extreme poles by which integration comes to be seen as the only rational alternative. Integration is defined as taking the best part of native culture and putting it together with the best part of our culture, thus creating a new independent culture (for example, Foster

1969). Of course, it is emphasized that the process of integration has to be guided by the "free choice" of the native peoples, but at the same time development experts indicate that they will help the population to make the right free choices, or even to create situations in which the natives get forced into making certain choices in order to survive (for example, Goodenough 1963).

Through the years, as the various academic disciplines have developed, these formulations have become increasingly opaque. A new solution arose only when anthropologists began to reflect more consciously on the significance of their own effect on the research process. Once this influence was acknowledged they began to notice the bias of their Western origins on their view of ethnic minorities (Bodley 1977, 1982). Thereby the basis was formed for being able to respect the rights and autonomy of native peoples.

The Right to Self-Determination Cultural autonomy was formulated by organizations like the International Work Group for Indigenous Affairs, after testimony had been gathered about native people's own wishes (IWGIA 1971; Sanders 1977). The solution was a demand that tribal cultures should remain outside any government's political structure, thus rejecting any further talk of "development" and "integration."

Cultural autonomy was formulated as a series of demands:

1. National governments and international organizations must recognize and support tribal rights to traditional land, cultural autonomy, and full local sovereignty.
2. The responsibility for initiating outside contacts must rest with the tribal people themselves: outside influences may not have free access to tribal areas.
3. Industrial states may not compete with tribal societies for their resources (Bodley 1977, 43).

The demand for cultural autonomy has often been criticized for being a wish that came too late (Dalton 1971). It has been claimed that development is out of the hands of indigenous peoples, and that time cannot be turned back so they could withdraw again into isolation and rediscover their old way of life. Moreover, it is said, gone are the last of the untouched Indian tribes, living out of contact with white civilization, for whom it would make sense to maintain isolation.

However, the alternative to ethnocide is neither the zoo nor the museum. It is not a question of restoring a life of the past. On the contrary, the native peoples have shown in many cases that they themselves can return to traditional patterns after major changes have taken place. Pacific Ocean cultures, for example, managed to return to their original subsistence-level economies when they were thrown into isolation by the Great Depression of the 1930s. Similarly, in the Peruvian Amazonas, Campa Indians were able to return to autonomy and live isolated for more than a hundred years, after they had succeeded in revolting against the Spanish viceroy and a very dominating Franciscan mission. Likewise, the Arhuacos were able to return to their original cultural forms after they had thrown the missionaries out: they managed to establish their own education and began more than ever to make use of their traditional language and dress.

Native peoples are, then, capable of deciding when their original way of life is irrevocably lost. Cultural autonomy is neither impossible nor impracticable when native peoples themselves want it.

There are about four hundred Indian peoples in Latin America, each with their own ethnicity, some thirty million Indians in all (Varese 1982, 35). The most essential demand for each and every one of them is the right to self-determination. Self-determination is understood as the path to gaining the possibility of deciding oneself what substance to put into the rhetorical phrases on collective consciousness—that is, the right to be different. The demand for self-determination is a strategy of foreign-affairs politics, which can safeguard the security and continuity of the ethnic group in its foreign-policy relations.

None of the Indian peoples has succeeded in building up a new state that is independent of state society, which they fall under today. This can be attributed first and foremost to practical conditions, the fact that no native peoples in Latin America today have sufficient resources to be able to build up a government apparatus with all the institutions a modern state demands. However, nothing indicates that it is the small size of the Indian populations, nor the paucity of territorial possessions, that make it unrealistic for them to break away and live under their own flag (Veber 1984, 49). On the one hand, several of the Indian peoples have large populations: The Quechua of the Andes and the Maya Indians in Mexico each number in the millions. Furthermore, there are

Indian reservations in Latin America that are larger in area than the State of New Jersey. Thus it is the political conditions that prevent Indian groups from establishing themselves as independently governed units.

Indian survival often proves to be an unstructured process, in which the different Indian peoples mirror themselves in each other, and instead of finding a common goal, their object is to find a common footstep. Their meetings strengthen internal cohesion and reinforce external conflicts, but do not necessarily offer any precise strategies for action in their dealings with the state society that colonizes and terrorizes them.

The prerequisite for liberating the Indian peoples is the creation of an organization through which they can win respect for their diversity. This means, at the most profound level, respect for their wildness and for the shamanistic perspective of their culture, which was where we started.

PART TWO *Slaves*

1. *Maroons*

Survival is contingent on the way in which each single local community defines itself in relation to the larger society of which it is a part. When a people tries to survive with its own culture and identity intact, it is dependent on being able to achieve the subtle balance between not allowing itself to be swallowed up by and integrated into the larger society on the one hand and not letting itself be isolated from it on the other hand. In other words, a balance between integration and isolation.

The local peoples who have been able to survive the best are those with a historical consciousness that goes back to the time before colonization and conquest. Thus their identity is based on a culture made up of more than struggle and resistance.

The Domestic Cattle That Escaped In Surinam there are small societies of descendants of black slaves, called Maroons. They have survived as an ethnic minority, but their culture is one of more than just survival.

Long ago the ancestors of these people ran away from the whites and avoided becoming victims by settling in small villages in remote corners of the jungle, where the descendants have lived for 150 years in little or no contact with the outside world. They fled from oppressive conditions and have been able to maintain a self-image as descendants of slaves, without letting themselves be fenced in by white society. Through isolation, they have found a way of establishing themselves as one people and one culture. The reason for their escape has not only been to insure biological survival of their kind. The challenge has lain in having to preserve their dignity under conditions which tended to deny it.

The name Maroon stems from the Spanish *cimarrón* and is a designation for the domestic cattle that escaped, fled into the mountains, and formed wandering herds. Having slipped out of the stables, they reclaimed their resilience and mobility and became dangerous and aggressive.

Maroon cultures have existed since the first slaves came to Latin America in the early 1500s. They range from tiny bands that survived less than a year, to powerful states encompassing thousands of members and surviving for generations or even centuries.

Surinam, a former Dutch colony on the Latin American continent, has the largest population of Maroons. Today they live in independent enclaves, isolated in the inaccessible rain forests in the interior of the country. There are in all about twenty thousand Maroons distributed among six different tribal societies (Anderson 1980). They still constitute an antithesis to the slavery from which their ancestors fled. Their survival is based on individuality, expressiveness, and personal style; and a daily life that is pervaded by play, creativity, and improvisation. They have a strong historical consciousness, and many of them have remained faithful to cultural traditions that trace their roots back to Africa. The succeeding descriptions of the Maroons are heavily influenced by the work of Price and Price (1980) and Price (1983).

History Already among the first shipments of slaves to Latin America, there were some who escaped and formed their own "marronage." They became a threat and a heroic challenge to the white masters, standing as proof of the existence of a consciousness among the slaves that could not be encompassed and enclosed by white manipulations.

During the first decades of the colonies, brutal punishments were carried out against the slaves who attempted to flee. Herlein, a Dutch tradesman, wrote in 1718:

> One recaptured town slave whose punishment shall serve as an example to others was laid on the ground, his head on a long beam. The first blow he was given, on the abdomen, burst his bladder open, yet he uttered not the least sound; the second blow with the axe he tried to deflect with his hand, but it gashed the hand and upper belly, again without his uttering a sound. The slave men and women laughed at this, saying to one another, "That is a man!" Finally, the third blow, on the chest, killed him. His hand was cut off and the body cut in four pieces and dumped in the river. (Herlein 1718 in Price 1983, 6)

Around 1670 the first troops were organized to fight the Maroons, and in the next century several military expeditions went out into the jungle. But even if great efforts were made, the results were small. The

Maroons quickly became experts in just about all aspects of guerilla activities and managed to protect their villages with considerable engineering skills.

In 1730, a small unit of troops, consisting of forty white plantation owners and two hundred slaves, was sent out. At the end of three months, sixteen Maroons had been killed and four men, six women, and ten children captured. In addition, twelve slaves from the ranks of the expedition succeeded in disappearing during that period (Price and Price 1980, 16). Most of the other expeditions at this time were just as fruitless, and the plantation owners realized that stepping up the number of expeditions only led to more of the slaves catching a glimpse of the free life and the possibility of deserting.

Stewart, an English historian, tells about an encounter between Maroons and whites in inner Surinam, in 1823:

> The troops marched in their proper regimentals, as if they were going to fight a regular and civilized enemy, and sometimes had even the absurdity to traverse the mountainous roads with drums beating. . . . The customary accoutrements were too clumsy and burdensome for traversing the woods and clambering over the rocks, and the red coats were too conspicuous an object to the Maroon marksmen, who seldom missed their aim. . . . The regular soldiers . . . disdained for a time to have recourse to rocks and trees as a shield against their enemies' fire, accounting it base and unmanly in a soldier thus to shrink from danger. (Stewart 1823 in Patterson 1973, 8)

The Maroons quickly learned to turn inaccessible and hostile nature to their own advantage, as a hiding place and a defense against the troops that pursued them. Paths leading to their village were meticulously hidden and instead false tracks leading to perilous pitfalls and traps were laid. The villages were often regular fortresses, with palisades, trenches, and shooting holes. The Spanish-speaking Europeans called the Maroon societies *palenques,* the spanish word for palisades.

The Maroons were dependent on being able to secure new supplies from the plantations. Therefore, they returned to the coast to commit small robberies and at times regular raids. They also had contact with some of the remaining slaves who now and then provided them with tools. Thus, some of the Maroon societies were supplied with consumer goods of the times and were able to get guns and ammunition.

One example of a Maroon survival strategy is their alliance with pirates. From the early 1500s there are descriptions of pirates fighting side by side with escaped slaves during sea battles, and of Maroons acting as guides on the pirates' plundering raids inland.

On one of Sir Francis Drake's pillages in Panama, forty-eight Maroons joined him and helped him as hunters and guides. It was primarily because of their assistance that he succeeded in recapturing three tons of silver from the Spanish. When Drake left the country, he gave the Maroon chief a coronation sword that had once belonged to the French King Henry II (Price 1973, 14).

In 1760, after nearly a hundred years of waging war, a peace settlement came about. The Maroons had grown to such large numbers that from the points of view of both military strategy and economy they represented a threat to the plantations. They were given their freedom in return for promising to stop their attacks on the plantations. This peace treaty was soon broken and new wars broke out.

With the end of slavery in Surinam in 1863, the Maroons achieved a new status, and in the subsequent century a gradual assimilation took place.

Around 1960, the use of airplanes and canoes rigged with outboard motors led to increasing traffic between the coastal population and the Maroons in the interior of the country. In 1978 the Maroons formed their own political party and gained representation in parliament.

A Village Today there are about fifty Maroon villages isolated in the jungle. A typical village consists of an irregular cluster of small houses, open areas and squares, big shade trees, an occasional hen coop, various shrines, and scattered groupings of brush and wild vegetation.

The settlers live in a close-knit, complex kinship system. The families are matrilineal, that is, people live in families descending along the female line, and everything in the village, from place of habitation and marriage to access to political and social power, is decided on the basis of who one's mother is. Most men have more than one wife, though seldom more than three at once. Children spend the first four to six years with the mother, but after that responsibility is taken over by their father or another relative.

Rituals occupy a large part of the Maroons' daily life. Activities like weeding a vegetable plot, building a house, taking a trip up the river to the nearest village, punishing a thief, or bringing up one's child all take place after consultations with the village ancestral shrine, one's ancestors, the spirits in the woods, the snake and monkey gods, and other similar powers.

Daily life is characterized by great personal independence. Every adult has his or her own canoe and goes off alone to do such things as engage in horticulture, visit friends and family, go to the doctor at the nearby mission, or participate in a funeral in the neighboring village. Each individual's network of kinship relations extends to many different villages, often a few day's journey away, resulting in a free coming and going in many houses over a large area, invitations to dinner, overnight stays, and other forms of participation in the social obligations of the place. Due to a high rate of divorce and the practice of letting children be raised for long periods by different people, each child has a very individualized social network, resulting in varied visiting patterns.

Furthermore, the pattern of settlement is influenced by the fact that normally each adult has more than one house, and that each house is owned by individual adults rather than families. For example, most women have a house in their own village, a house near their garden, and a house built by their husband in his village. When the men are in their own village, they often divide their time among three or four houses built at different points in time for themselves and for their present and former wives (Price and Price 1980, 18).

Daily life is structured according to very personal, individual patterns, which are nearly impossible for outsiders to decipher. Characteristically, Maroons often try to get away from the complexities of social life. In accordance with their great need for individuality, they may seek solitude on long hunting trips or sojourns at their isolated garden plots. Even though the days spent on these plots are characterized by hard physical labor, in contrast to the most easygoing work tempo in the villages, the atmosphere is considerably more relaxed. The women in particular enjoy working in their gardens, as we in the Western world might enjoy life in a summerhouse in the country. In their gardens they can wear their old, worn-out clothes, which would not be acceptable in the village. Here they can take meals less seriously, and men and women can eat together and talk more or less about whatever they please. For the men, the woods are a romantic and adventurous place. They can spend hours telling about solitary hunting trips and being left for weeks on end at the mercy of the woods, their gun, and the hunting dogs. The Maroons consider this solitary individuality so important that several of the old people say that the hardest thing about old age and decrepitude is that they get tied down to village life and can no longer withdraw to their gardens and the woods.

In the villages, much time is spent on social and ritual obligations. Acquaintances pass through, needing to be fed and sheltered, which has to be done without arousing any conflicts and quarrels, and preferably without the guests feeling they are causing an inconvenience. At the same time, there is always a lot of work to be done; houses need maintenance and repairs, gardens have to be weeded, and food prepared. Thus, life in the village is strenuous and can lead to much social tension.

Many Maroons spend hours by the river. They sit in their canoes and look out over the water; they bathe, fish, wash clothes, scrub pots and pans, clean fish, build canoes, gather in small groups, gossip, and laugh. The river functions as a cool place where one can relax and get away from the social life of the village.

Individuality, Expressiveness, and Personal Style To understand the social psychology of the Maroons, one has to start with their early history as slaves, when loss of personal identity, the eradication of social and cultural affiliations, and their treatment as nameless, working bodies were as great a threat as the fear of physical violence and annihilation.

Paradoxically, the humiliating aspects of slave existence engendered the development of a high degree of personalized traits, by which each slave could differentiate him- or herself from the others; these were exactly the traits no slave owner could eliminate. In this way slaves developed an individualistic pattern of behavior, involving a particular sense of humor, a particular type of knowledge, a certain way of walking and talking, or some little detail of apparel such as the manner of wearing one's hat.

As early as 1796, Stedman wrote of a journey on a slave ship crossing the Atlantic:

"All the slaves are led upon the deck . . . their hair shaved in different figures of stars, half-moons etc., which they generally do the one to the other, (having no razors) by the help of a broken bottle and without soap" (Stedman 1966, 205).

In their villages today one sees how slave descendants have maintained this individuality by expressing themselves artistically, each with his or her own personal style. Every object gets reworked so that it becomes aesthetic and artistic in its visual appearance. A fragment of glass is used to etch various patterns into calabashes, which serve as utensils for eating, drinking, or food storage; the pattern reveals who owns them and for what they may be used. Order is maintained in this way. However, many of the other decorative forms have no functional value, but exist only to express graphic design and aesthetics. Manioc cakes are baked with patterns on them, and material for loincloths is cut into small pieces and sewn together again as patchwork. A scarf gets embroidered. The torso and face get tattoed in different patterns, and hair is cut in various shapes. Imported metal spoons are decorated with a design made with the help of a nail, pots are imprinted with a design, handles are painted in strong colors, different colored ribbons are tied around one's upper arm and calf. The house and canoes are decorated with woodcuttings and painted in different patterns. The rifle butt, the paddle, the wooden bowl, the grain mill, the stool—all get carved, decorated, displayed, ordered, and exhibited in their little houses. Nothing is left to functional form; objects must be reworked to express a personal style. Many of the Maroons' possessions are felt to be a part of their personalities. Thus a person who becomes separated from a valued object experiences the separation as a loss of a part of himself.

On the road to the international airport outside the capital of Paramaribo, some Maroons have opened a shop in which they sell different kinds of wood carvings to tourists. They bought anthropologist Muntslag's book *The Symbolic Meaning of Maroon Motifs* (Muntslag 1979; Price and Price 1980, 188) and work on copying patterns that are depicted in the book. When a tourist asks about the significance of a graphic pattern, they refer to the book. However, if one is visiting an isolated village, it is very difficult to buy their things or to get explanations of signs and symbols. Their artistic lives are no one else's business and not available for translation. They keep it to themselves as a way of protecting their individuality.

One of the first anthropologists to do field studies among the Maroons was M. J. Herskovits, who wrote:

> When I made my suggestion that I might care to acquire the board, the woman became apprehensive. She took up the board, and excusing herself, disappeared with it inside her hut.
>
> "No, no," she called from the house, when her brother went to tell her of the offer we had made for it. "I don't want money for it. I like it. I will not sell it."

Dangogo, October 10, 1985

The two Maroon women asked me only two questions: Where do you come from? And, What do you have for us?

I answered the first question by saying I was a European and tried to tell where Denmark was. However, no matter how much I explained, I could not shake their belief that I was from Surinam. For them everyone outside of their own tribe had to be from Surinam, no matter what they said. They expressed their self-sufficiency in this way, showing that they did not need further elaboration on the question of who I was.

I answered the second question by giving them several kilos of rice. They thanked me in a friendly way, but remained silent from then on.

Later, it occurred to me that one of them was responsible for all of Dangogo's business transactions with the surroundings. She was also the one who received my payment for boat transportation, room and board. She was always friendly, but after getting an answer to the two questions of who I was and what I had brought her, her lips were sealed.

The sum we offered was modest enough, but not inconsiderable for this deep interior. We increased it, then doubled our original offer. There was still no wavering on the woman's part, but the offer began to interest her family. Such wealth should not be refused. Her brother began to urge her in our behalf.

"With this money you can buy from the white man's city a hammock, and several fine cloths. You should not refuse this."

The old woman took up the discussion, then another sister, and a brother. At last the Headman took us aside, and asked us to leave his sister alone with them.

"We will have a meeting, and tomorrow you will hear. She is foolish not to sell. But she cares for the board. It is good, too, when a woman loves what her man has carved for her. We will meet about it, and you shall hear."

Three days passed before the woman's permission was given to dispose of the piece.

"When they see this, your people will know our men can carve!" she claimed in a voice which held as much regret as pride. (Herskovits 1934, 281; Price and Price 1980, 45)

Play, Creativity, and Improvisation An ordinary conversation among the Maroons takes the form of a lively exchange of utterances that repeat themselves and develop. New figures of speech are invented. There is improvisation, the fluctuation of pitch in different keys, and much fooling around and grinning. Standard expressions are substituted by new phrases. A watch becomes a "back-of-the-wrist motor," food, "under-the-nose material," a stool "the rump's rejoicing," and a piano, "a black box upon whose teeth one strikes to make people cry" (Price and Price 1980, 167).

Mannerisms and personal style are greatly appreciated, and people imitate each other's figures of speech and gestures. "Good morning," for example, can be said in innumerable ways, describing whether one woke up that morning quickly or slowly, what mood one was in, what dreams one had. Two people meet, and they exchange vociferous outbursts of expression. One of them may begin to do humorous imitations of the way a neighbor of the other dances. The other one, who has no trouble recognizing the resemblance, then begins to imitate the way his companion's wife dances.

These expressive and theatrical social conventions go on throughout the day. An elderly woman, who has patiently been fishing down by the river without catching anything, finally catches a modest little fish. She squats in the water, cools herself off, and breaks out in song and dance, while she twists the upper part of her body back and forth, praising her good fortune. Another woman may see her neighbor with a bouquet of flowers go by her door and greets her with a little song: "The red bouquet of flowers suits my sister-in-law. See how well the red bouquet befits my sister-in-law" (Price and Price 1980, 167).

These spontaneous outbursts can slide into more formal, delimited forms of music, dance, and word-art. For instance, a woman sings a melodic stanza to break the monotony of grinding rice. The song will perhaps be repeated during the next village festival, with the woman leading the singing to which a chorus responds. A spontaneous song develops into a stylized dance. A man's entertaining description of having once seen one of the sacred gods of the village develops into a stylized dance, carried out to the accompaniment of drum beating and hand clapping. Another person reproduces the sound of a machine bottling Coca-Cola, which he saw once on the coast. This sound-picture becomes a popular number among the local people, which they incorporate into their drum playing.

During such performances one cannot distinguish sharply between audience and actor. People getting together for an evening of storytelling do not tell their stories one after another. On the contrary, each story gets interrupted at different points and various short stories are told by others, so that a story ends up consisting of a complex interweaving of side stories. The pattern is the same with song, dance, and drum performances, during which performer and audience are constantly interchanged. Maroon performances more closely resemble a jazz jam session than a classical piano concert. Counterpoint arises all the time, and roles are exchanged. Even when the relatives who live in the cities along the coast send letters home in the form of recorded tapes, they leave spaces where the listener can come in with applause and commentary (Price and Price 1980, 168). In that way a structure is maintained in which shared participation and individual virtuosity complement each other.

Consciousness of History One of our civilization's greatest threats to survival is the increasing loss of a sense of history. Identity is no longer something taken over from one's family that predetermines one's life.

The Maroons are, in contrast, very conscious of history and tradition. The past for them determines their identity, and one of their most important survival mechanisms involves preserving accounts of the first days of slavery as as reminder of times that must never return.

The Maroons often speak of "that time" and can give many accounts of how oppressive and degrading slave existence was. These stories have been passed down orally from generation to generation, and several of them can be affirmed by Western historians (Price 1983).

The Maroons believe that every act is a consequence of deeds done in the past, and that they themselves are able to affect the future by their present behavior. Not only can every mishap, illness, or death be blamed on a specific misdeed in the past, but any insult or crime will at some time in the future bear its bitter fruit. Every act constitutes the material from which history is made.

Illness or accidents lead to an invocation of the gods, who use different signs to reveal which specific action was the cause. With the help of rituals, order is then restored: the ancestors speak, the gods dance, the past comes alive, and becomes visible and tangible. This perception of time passing requires a periodic retrospection into symbols of older periods, at the same time the society continues to move into the present.

For the Maroons there is a special period, "First-Time," which possesses particularly strong forces. It ranges from the arrival of the first slaves in Surinam in 1520 to around 1800.

Anthropologist Richard Price has gotten the Maroons to tell about this First-Time (Price, 1983). However, they have shown a great deal of caution and reserve, for as one Maroon said to him: "First-Time kills people. That's why it should never be taught to youths. . . . That's why when you pour a libation at the ancestor shrine, you must be careful about speaking in proverbs because you may not be aware of all their hidden implications. There are certain people's names that if you call them you're dead right on the spot! There are names that can't be uttered twice in the course of a whole year! It is with such things that we are raised."

Another person said, "I don't tell children and foreigners about this. My mother's brother used to say 'Talk with them [the foreigners] but don't *tell* them. Because if you tell them, those things will rise up and come listen' " (Price 1983, 7).

It is said that a persecuted people will always be preoccupied with the past in their efforts to make themselves free. Knowledge of one's origins is a source of personal security, because, in a sense, with this knowledge one is no longer alone. The people from the First-Time with their enormous powers are there as support. Many persecuted minorities have been scrupulous about their family history. The Jews, for example, wrote their genealogy in two ecclesiastical books, which were kept in two different places for reasons of security. If one of the books disappeared, there was always a copy somewhere else.

Among the Maroons, knowledge is power, and the more one shares knowledge, the easier it is to lose one's power. Therefore, when they are asked what they know about First-Time they feel that answering such questions will make them lose some of their power. They advise one instead to be present when the old people begin to tell stories and to sit quietly, making neither sounds nor movements, and listen.

It is assumed that a person's knowledge increases slowly and only a little bit at a time. For this reason, different parts of the story are told in small portions and adapted in such a way that the listener only gets to know a little bit more than he knew before. In order to disguise the importance and strength behind these narratives, they usually come up as digressions, interruptions, short side-stories, or as footnote material.

One of the storytellers said to Price that "First-Time things don't have only one head. . . . Your ears must truly grow tired of the thing before you will really know it" (Price 1983, 9).

This protection of the prehistory of the Maroons is a double-edged sword. The belief, as some people say, that you should "never tell another more than half of what you know," can simply lead to a loss of the First-Time narratives. The Maroons say, "There are certain papá songs of which it is said, 'If you sing this you will die,' yet people still must sing them." Thus, people of knowledge are denounced and ridiculed if they are too indiscreet (Price 1983, 12).

There is gratification in knowledge and pleasure in learning, but there is a risk involved in telling it to others. Knowledge is power, and if one shares knowledge too generously, the clan and the society can lose power. On the other hand, possessors of knowledge get denounced and ridiculed if they do not tell some of what they know, for they risk losing the narratives for all eternity.

Or, as the Maroons say, "If you don't stir up a hole, you won't find out what's inside" (Price 1983, 14).

Thus, they have their strategies for avoiding time running out.

The Maroons as a Counterculture Some characteristics of the Maroons, as we have seen, are: an emphasis on personal style, a dramatic

Dangogo, September 29, 1985

Granman Loanzo and his brother came one day to Dangogo by boat and stayed for a couple days. Loanzo had been in contact with a few missionaries many years ago, but the only thing that came out of it was that he learned to speak a little English.

My mood was elevated at the thought of being able to talk to someone and get answers to my questions. This made me bold, and after a while I began to ask about anything under the sun. Suddenly Loanzo fell silent, and when I asked why he wouldn't talk anymore, he replied, "One ought to be careful about shaking an old tree, as one can risk being hit on the head by a falling branch."

and theatrical self-conception, a decidedly expressive way of living, and a strong appreciation of individuality; a firm historical consciousness; a preference for new aspects, new discoveries, creative games, improvisations, and an expectation of constant changes and developments in artistic forms of expression; an aesthetic view of the human body and a widely structured conception of rhythms and tones; and a knowledge and categorization of color contrasts, and ways of expressing the importance of balance and symmetry.

In order to survive and put up a resistance, the Maroons first had to assimilate and adapt. In more concrete terms: the house slave who poisoned her owner's family by putting glass splinters in the food, first had to become the family cook; the slave who organized an armed protest at the market place first had to be able to produce for the market and obtain permission to sell his products there.

Maroon societies are not a primary African culture, based on a collective memory of traditions, norms, and values from their homeland. They are rather a counterculture, developed in a struggle to survive in a world that neither culturally nor geographically resembles Africa.

The people who formed Maroon societies were possessors of a very complex mixture of African language and cultures, stemming mainly from West and Central Africa. Some of the inhabitants were Africans who had just arrived on the slave ships, and others were slaves who had worked for generations on plantations. Thus, the group of people who established themselves in the rain forest was varied and complex.

Even though the Africans in the New World often had very little in common when it came to origins, slave existence gave them a shared Afro-American way of approaching life. Shortly after the founding of the colony of Surinam, a common language, *Sranan*, developed among slaves, a language which has become the unofficial main language of the country today. Afro-American cultures that still exist today arose on many of the plantations. For example, groups of Maroons travel every year from the interior of the country out to the places on the coast where the old plantations used to lie, celebrating and exchanging rituals and ceremonies.

However, Maroon culture is more than just an escaped slave culture. The Maroons of today produce art and religion having an aesthetic and expressiveness that was not found in slave camps and has no resemblance to its African roots. Their woodcutting art, their use of colors, their religious myths, and the names of their gods are entirely their own invention (Price and Price 1980).

Nonetheless, the Maroons feel strongly tied to Africa and have always had an ideology of Africa as their true homeland. In reality, however, this has mostly been an expression of nostalgia directed toward an Africa they have constructed. Anthropologists have not been able to find direct carry-overs from African systems to Surinam (Anderson 1980).

The Maroon culture is not small pieces of Africa transplanted to the interior of Surinam. To say that the Maroons represent Africa in Surinam is a view of culture based on the principle of fossilization. On the contrary, they are constantly changing and adapting, tenaciously staying alive. The Maroons' ability to survive rests on the freedom to extrapolate from African ideas and adapt them to their ever-changing situation. Their origins are more connected with an underlying principle of mutability and functional adaptation, than any direct African inheritance.

The Maroons as the Theater of Survivors I lived for a while in the isolated village of Dangogo. I did not know their language, and a sixteen-year old boy functioned as my interpreter. However, his English was so hopeless that I often had to make do with seeing the Maroons as theater without text, an incomprehensible performance about survival. I had chosen to put my books away, and my pencil served to let my thoughts flow when they became too restless. I took on an attitude of restive awareness, watching the Maroons carry out their daily doings over and over again, until all logic was extracted from them.

After a few days, Maroon time began to penetrate. Everyday life did not move systematically forward here. Inhabitants did not work toward a higher goal. Time as a concept was unthinkable separated from its content. Daily life went on, governed by supernatural forces that humans could not transcend. Tasks were carried out without their taking place in time, being of time itself. The time it took to go down to the river, to boil water, to eat, to sleep was what structured day and night. Consciousness was tied to concrete sense experiences, to nature and its rhythms. Time was cyclical, and past and future were one, as in the Maroon rituals in which the dead are rediscovered in new forms.

In my own culture, time has been hammered into our bodies in a different way. Descriptions of the rise of the factory system in eighteenth- and nineteenth-century England tell how people found it hard to understand and accept the new concept of time (Foucault 1980; Olsen 1978). They had sold their working power for a miserable salary and had to be at work precisely on time regardless of their own needs, the weather, and the season. Their own leisure time was reduced to rest periods, when work was done. Time became an abstract, disciplinary concept.

My time was distinct from the Maroons', as the linear is from the cyclical. Maroon culture as a performance is based on simultaneity, on contradictions and paradoxes, on improvisations that give rise to breaks and turning points. Development is non-continuous and yet always circular. Time repeats itself and revokes causality.

Moreover, time is accompanied by a particular spatial experience. Mine was a three-dimensional space seen in perspective, as opposed to the Maroons' two-dimensional, simultaneous space.

In my civilization, perspective was developed according to a set of rules and codes in the art of the fifteenth century. By assuming a specific, fixed position as observer, one looked into three-dimensional space, in which size and proportions were determined with the aid of straight lines seen from a particular point in space. The meaning of space required that one accept the existence of one and only one point of view. With the development of perspective drawing, we began to master the motif, but became enslaved by the chosen spectator stance (Christoffersen 1986, 15). One could see infinitely far into space, even if in reality it was two-dimensional and time was a linear movement, which followed physical movement. One could move as far in or out as time permitted.

The Maroons do not use perspective in their drawings. Among them one rediscovers our medieval, cyclical concept of time and its corresponding two-dimensional concept of space. Even though they decorate things as much as possible, they use patterns which are repeated and transformed into a whole that is more than the sum of its parts. Similarly, their stories are filled with subsidiary plots, expansions, unfixed ordering of elements, and rapidly changing scenes, which are not necessarily a part of the whole, but appear simultaneously and complement each other in one uniform expression.

Among the Maroons, action is carried out on a stage of simultaneity that reminds one of the medieval compositional mode. Time is limitless and events do not have a subordinate relation to causal thinking, in which one action triggers the next.

In contrast, history in our world-view submits to a law dictating that time, place, and action constitute a unity and that causality and continuity are the basis of narrative development.

The current stage of our culture is directed toward naturalism and psychic realism in contrast with the Maroons' stage, which leads one into the sphere of medieval carnivalism, with its physicality, fertility, and bantering.

Being among the Maroons is like walking in the dark. The darker and more incomprehensible it gets, the more all of one's senses become sharpened.

Left to my own devices and theatrical thoughts, I stayed in Dangogo while the local inhabitants teased me, told stories, hung around, and laughed.

The Floating Islands and the Third Theater Within the world of group theater, the term "third theater" is used for the floating island on which actors live in awareness of the necessity of keeping a distance from established society. The third theater is a community of asocial actors, in which asociality is a concrete way of living together (Barba 1986, 193). The Maroons resemble this Third Theater, which emphasizes an awareness of individual differences, and harbors no dedication to formless emotionality or vague sentimentality about all of us being brothers and sisters.

It is living far apart from the surrounding world, from time and from a larger society, that allows the Maroons to achieve the necessary distance needed to create. It is the life that recluses have chosen through the ages (Gad and Gad 1982; Storr 1988). Distance and separation also characterize the anthropologist, for whom the core of fieldwork rests on a "balance between emphatic involvement and disciplined distance" (Mead 1972, 248).

Within the sphere of avant-garde theater, this conscious distancing has been developed into a weapon against traditional dramaturgy. The concept *Verfremdung* expresses this interplay between empathy and distance. The actors do not identify themselves entirely with the role, but every now and then inject commentary into the play. The characters on the stage are a kind of metaphor for the part they are playing. Or as theater people put it: "Characters in a play are only seemingly people;

in reality they are simply symbols, reflections in a mirror, dreams in a dream" (Esslin 1968, 56).

Similarly, the Maroons can be experienced as a metaphor for survival, as a picture of our civilization's Middle Ages. However, as psychoanalysts we must examine them thoroughly in order to understand our own present.

No Survival without Communication For Maroons to be included among the ranks of the survivors, they must have a meaning.

The moment Maroons are regarded as theater, their language becomes a codification of secret messages, making room for all the spectator's projections of inner dreams and images. Subtle interchanges, movements, expressions, outbursts, pauses, and gesticulations create a kind of physical language based on signs and not words, like the theater of cruelty, the theater of alchemy, and the theater of metaphor.

But when all is said and done, it cannot be denied that it is a theater with a very small audience; thus, the seed of doubt as to their survival is sown. Theater is communication; without an audience it dies.

One of the Maroons' most important rules of survival is the moral that knowledge is power and that one must never reveal everything one knows. However, the more they hold back their power, the more easily they lose their possibilities for dialogue.

The Maroons have never reduced themselves to a passive culture, a receptacle of traditions and past events. On the contrary, they have been able to go the path of rediscovery and development. Nonetheless, this large capacity for mutability has not led them to break with their past. Their strength can be attributed precisely to this combination of being able to reorient themselves, to deconstruct and reconstruct, and at the same time maintain a knowledge of their prehistory.

However, if all these ingredients, all this life, does not gain meaning, the Maroons will die, just as a theater dies when it cannot be instilled with meaning in relationship to an audience. Most anything can be dispensed with—scenery, costumes, lights, spectator space, stage, makeup, and even text. But without actors there is no theater, and no theater without spectators (Grotowski 1975, 56). If communication is not important in itself, then "I am like a partner in dialogue left to my own devices, as when a beautiful landscape speaks to me and I invest it with anima in order to keep the conversation going. This is what people have done all through the ages without achieving anything but their own reinforcement" (Bredsdorff 1986, 168).

Survival is contingent on a balance between integration and absorption on the one hand, and separation and isolation on the other. Many Maroons have simply chosen to be themselves and make a virtue of rejecting all visitors. Many of their villages have been placed on the official maps with false names, in the wrong places, and many of the stories anthropologists have been told, like those about the period of slavery, are pure fiction created for the entertainment of the white man.

The Maroons have shrouded themselves in darkness, but if their survival is to have meaning, it must give off some light. Otherwise, others will only experience them as a theater of the absurd, and power will remain where it always has.

In 1970, three village chiefs went on a three-week tour to West Africa, invited by the governments of Gambia and Ghana. The anthropologist Silva de Groot wrote a diary of this trip (De Groot 1973). The diary tells that even though Africa made a great impression on the chiefs, they never expressed their delight or astonishment.

They traveled around and met official ministers, generals, and presidents. The chiefs were clothed in old, discarded police uniforms, which they refused to put on once they discovered that these outfits showed a remarkable resemblance to the uniforms worn by the hotel porters who were constantly running around and opening doors for them.

Many places they went, the three Maroons showed their surprise at how well Africa had developed into a modern state, at the same time as it was able to keep its original traditions intact. The Minister of Education in Ghana offered the explanation that since earliest times, Africa has always been able to mix different cultures, owning and absorbing the best aspects of them all. To this the granman Gazon replied, "The same wind that long ago took us away from Mother Africa against our will has now helped us to find our way back again."

However, a few days later, the same granman gave a blessing to a few people in *Kromanti,* the original and secret language of the Maroons. Meanwhile, not one of the surrounding Africans understood a word of what he said. He was furious, and scolded them for having spoken so much English that they had forgotten their own language.

In another context, one could say that when the Maroons performed their own theater, no one understood the meaning of it, and the actors lost their minds.

2. *Jonestown*

To place oneself in a closed system without self-criticism and without interaction with one's opponents is to risk self-dissolution.

One of the keys to understanding dissolution is to be found in the kind of leadership and concentration of power that develops the moment people isolate themselves and deny their history. A lack of history leads to a loss of identity and paves the way for the acceptance of a Messiah who can offer a new millennium and a new timeless paradise. The leaders will often be self-appointed prophets, generals, or dictators. They present themselves as God's elect or as the best interpreters of a political ideology. They end up becoming the total center of power in the society, and members are only admitted to the cult, sect, or political movement by undergoing conversion in the presence of the leader. The conditions for incest and loss of culture are thereby fulfilled.

Internal Relations

About a thousand emigrants from the United States had settled in the jungle in Guyana to build up an alternative, collective society. They had chosen a totally isolated place in the dense rain forest, cut off from the surrounding world.

Eighty percent of the jungle commune consisted of black people from slums in midwestern and West Coast cities. They were descendants of slaves and came from the culture of the black ghetto. The movement was called the People's Temple and the colony, Jonestown, got its name from its leader, Jim Jones.

In November 1978 they wiped themselves out. Nine hundred fourteen people were found dead.

A large part of the population could neither read nor write. They were a symptom of miserable living conditions in the United States. However, they never managed to become a reactive force that could formulate a precise ideology and lay a strategy for change directly affecting the system that had created their misery. Their extermination was only an inarticulate, desperate scream.

The scream of the inarticulate evades our intellects and speaks directly to our feelings. We do not understand. We cannot argue with it; it puts us off balance.

The Anamnesis: The Story of Jim Jones The first seeds of the People's Temple were sown in Jim Jones's childhood and early youth. The following anamnesis is made on the basis of interviews with Jim Jones's friends, family, religious followers, and people among whom he grew up (Kilduff and Javers 1979; Reiterman 1982).

Jim Jones was born in a little provincial town in the Midwest in 1931. He was the only child of a mother who worked outside the home, and an invalid father who spent most of his time in the Ku Klux Klan. The boy had a dark, Asiatic appearance that made him an outsider in the little town.

At the age of 10, he already used religion as a means of dominating others. A childhood friend recalls an altar the boy built out of a few boxes in the attic of his childhood home. He would light some candles and sit on a chair with a white sheet around him as a cape, while his playmates sat around him on the floor. On one of these occasions, one of his friends refused to obey his orders, whereupon Jim ran down to the living room, stole his father's 22-caliber rifle and shot it at the friend. Although the child was not hit, the shooting episode gave rise to a great commotion. Jim was expelled from school and forbidden for a long time to play with others.

At fourteen, Jim Jones delivered his first sermon in a church of the charismatic sect, the Pentecostal Holy Rollers, and at sixteen he began delivering sermons on street corners. At eighteen, he finished high school, got married, and entered a university in Indianapolis, but he had trouble completing his education. As a student he started an animal protection group promoting the cause of kindness to animals, at the same time he was earning extra money by selling monkeys imported from South America door to door.

In 1953 he founded his own church, the Community Unity Church, financed in part by the sale of monkeys. Three years later he formed what he called his "rainbow family" by adopting children of different races.

In 1964, Jim Jones had a vision of an atomic cataclysm. Believing the world would soon be destroyed during an atomic attack, he traveled around barren stretches of the United States with a large group of his followers, looking for safe havens where they could survive.

In 1963, Jones had thirteen hundred followers and he was given official permission to form his own religious movement: the People's Temple. In this period he came out with statements claiming that someone was trying to eradicate the People's Temple. He believed that his telephone was being tapped and feared that his food was being poisoned. A lawyer was hired to investigate who was conspiring against the movement. While speaking in his church Jones would sometimes go into a sudden fit of cramps and lose consciousness. Some of his followers recount how he would sometimes throw the Bible on the floor right before these attacks and say "too many people follow this instead of following me."

In an interview, Jones once revealed that in reality he had always been an atheist, but regarded the People's Temple as a "means for getting people to stop using religion as a narcotic." He said that people needed a leader who could find the true socialist goal for them.

Several members of a small group of whites who always surrounded Jim Jones at this time told later how they participated in the staging of various healing tricks. They filled small plastic bags with blood, which they passed to the leader during the service. Jones would tear the bag with his nail, allowing the blood to spread over his palms, which he would display as a manifestation of the stigmata.

By 1972, Jim Jones was using armed body guards. He had become a public person, usually managing to get favorable press coverage. According to the *Washington Post,* in August 1973, "The 660 wonderful people from People's Temple win the honor of being named 'Best Tourists of the Year.' This group of church followers has traveled around large parts of the U.S. in 13 buses, spending an hour every day removing garbage from our public parks and recreation grounds."

In 1974, the *Herald-Examiner* in Los Angeles named Jim Jones "Humanist of the Year." The Governor of California and the Mayor of San Francisco were present at the ceremony. The following month, Jones was appointed chief of the re-housing board, a leading position within the public city planning administration.

However, in 1977, the first articles criticizing and casting doubt on Jim Jones and his movement appeared in the newspaper *New West.* Some of his earlier followers started turning their backs on him, revealing what was going on in the movement. On the basis of these disclosures, Jim Jones seriously began to feel that he was the butt of a conspiracy, and in the summer of 1977, the exodus to Jonestown began. A few years before, the People's Temple had begun negotiations with the Guyanese authorities to establish a farming project in the dense jungle. At the beginning of 1977, sixty people lived in Jonestown, and in the course of the summer, Jones and around eight hundred others moved into the camp.

The Clinical Impression: An Encounter with Jim Jones I visited the colony eleven days before the collective suicide took place. By a series of coincidences I was the only foreigner who came into the camp and met Jim Jones without having had any earlier connections with the People's Temple (Elsass 1980, 197). Our first conversation took place over the telephone, in the radio room of the camp. I was told that for security reasons he could not meet strangers face to face. Nevertheless we did meet and he appeared to be under the influence of medicine and said that he had fever due to a stomach infection. He was worn down and tired, speaking in a slow, forced manner, as some people do when trying to overcome fatigue.

In my diary of that November 1978 I wrote:

> Jim Jones tells how difficult it is to establish a socialist movement. Even though they have chosen to give it the religious cover name, the People's Temple, and have moved to one of the most remote and isolated places in Latin America, they are constantly threatened by conspiracies that try to annihilate them. In particular, in April and May of this year, they have been under CIA attack. Jim Jones says that I would not believe my ears if I heard what experiences of persecution they have had in the jungle. For several weeks, the CIA has had a force of twenty-five to thirty men in the jungle, shooting after them and attempting to poison their food. Jim Jones tells in great detail about the methods used by capitalist conspiracy to get rid of them. I don't know what to believe.

When Jones spoke to me, for one and one-half hours, I attempted to write down as much as possible. He spoke in an endless stream, and in an attempt to make some sense out of his words, I resorted to my trade, clinical psychology. The conversation was recorded on tape, and I asked to hear it again, winding forward to two passages, which I then wrote down word for word:

> CIA is using every trick to gain control of me. At times they even control and influence my thoughts, so I cannot think clearly. They have their means, so they poison my food, and that poison also affects my brain activity.
>
> In periods I am so absorbed by the idea of socialism that I really am Lenin and speak with his voice.

Within traditional psychiatry one would designate such statements as symptoms of paranoid delusions. But I did not pay much attention to them. What could one say in a personal conversation, out there in the isolated jungle? I let myself be seduced and did not see the impending catastrophe.

Selection of Members and Isolation Other specialists have attempted to avoid letting themselves be seduced. Sociologists, psychologists, and psychiatrists have examined all aspects of the case and completed scientific reports.

For example, the American Psychological Association dissected the case of Jonestown at its annual meeting in 1979. Various work groups and commissions were set up and given access to all related material the U.S. State Department possessed. The work of these commissions has resulted in a series of analyses of the logic of suicide.

Jonestown was an isolated society with minimal contact to its surroundings. The members were not allowed to leave the camp. They had no place to go to test their sense of reality, no place to vent their feelings, and no place where they could get support, apart from Jim Jones.

The background for establishing Jonestown was a meticulous selection of followers. In some instances, members dressed up as garbage collectors in order to examine an applicant's garbage before he was admitted to the movement. They formed an impression of his eating habits and looked through the mail he had thrown away. Other members might visit the applicant in his home. While one of them started a conversation, the other would ask to use the toilet. This allowed him to get into the person's medicine chest and write down the names of pills and the doctor who had prescribed them.

All this information was then handed over to Jim Jones, who used it to demonstrate that he had magical abilities and could see through people. New members would be impressed by the leader's divine powers, and the first condition for submission and control would be established.

One of the criteria for the location of Jonestown was its isolation. The campsite was so remote that no one had the physical possibility of escaping. Only a very select few were given permission to go to the Guyanese capital Georgetown, on short excursions.

I wrote in my diary:

> I took a little Cessna plane from the capital, Georgetown, to Matthew's Ridge. A flight of one and a half hours over the densest, most uninhabited jungle I have ever seen. No roads. The trees were so close together that you couldn't see the ground. Now and then some small flat stretches with dark red mud. From Matthew's Ridge a two-hour drive in a Land Rover on a miserable dirt path to the entrance to Jonestown.

In Jonestown, Jim Jones was always the one to read the news out loud over the camp's loudspeaker system. He often demanded that the members not discuss the items among themselves, but instead write down their reactions and send them directly to "Dad."

Surrounded by dense jungle, without newspapers and with only sporadic news interpreted by the leader, it was impossible for the members to have their distorted sense of reality corrected by outside influences.

The stay in the jungle was shrouded in secrecy. Before the departure for Guyana, the members were forbidden to say good-bye to their friends and relatives. Most of them were first told they would be leaving twenty-four hours before departure and at times just a couple hours before. Families usually received no answer when they inquired at the temple in San Francisco about the whereabouts of members.

Thus, by cutting off connections with the environment, members became dependent on staying in the camp. They turned their thoughts and feelings more and more inwards, with the result that the outside world slowly lost its reality. This emotional truncation is of the same nature as that described in other totalitarian institutions, like concentration camps, prisons, and traditional psychiatric asylums (Goffman 1968).

Members of the Temple surrendered all their valuables in the form of property, cars, and securities to the People's Temple. When they arrived at Jonestown all their money and valuables were confiscated and hidden away with their personal identification papers. Not only did the movement thus secure what it needed to run its daily economy, but confiscation became a means of establishing control. Over time the valuables accumulated, and survivors say that "Jones gave out money to philanthropic causes in Guyana and in San Francisco, just to get rid of it" (Kilduff and Javers 1979, 85).

The members had no other choice but to stay in the camp. As one of the temple members said, "the Temple eventually got everything I owned. That was what made it so difficult to leave the place. We had no place to go and we had nothing to return to" (Reiterman 1982, 420).

Just as a hypnotist tries to influence his subject to close out all influences and receive only those he is sending, all channels of communication in the camp that could refute the leader's statements were cut off. The leader became a substitute for reality.

Public Confessions and Punishment At large gatherings, members of the People's Temple were forced to step forth and make public confessions. These confession meetings were held in an atmosphere of emotional catharsis. The behavior of the members, their personal attitudes and moral values were on exhibit and scrutinized by all those present. People were subjected to physical and psychological humiliation. Survivors of Jonestown tell how men and women would be forced to take off all their clothes and confess in a naked state that they were lesbian or homosexual. There was an isolation cell in which those who had committed crimes against the ideas of the People's Temple were kept locked up and anesthetized with psychopharmacological drugs. This cell was often referred to as the "extended care unit" and consisted of a narrow box placed directly in the sun.

During the gatherings, Jim Jones said over and over again that the camp was being spied on by the CIA. He gave accounts of how the members who left the movement would be caught by CIA agents and killed or exposed to torture and lengthy prison sentences. Therefore, everyone was encouraged to watch out for spies among themselves.

The gatherings were nightly events, and the members had to listen for hours to Jim Jones's long speeches, which were often interrupted by acknowledging responses from the listeners. His speeches were taped and played throughout the camp during the day via a well-functioning loudspeaker system.

Public punishment, torture, mutual confessions, and accusations among the members created a psychosociological atmosphere which resembles Bruno Bettelheim's descriptions of concentration camps during World War II (Bettelheim 1986). Those members who did not develop a child-like dependency on the leader were accused of threatening the group's security. It was inevitable that they would regress to an earlier psychological stage of development in which one lived like a child, in the moment, and after a while lost all sense of time. "The prisoners were incapable of laying plans for the future and of establishing lasting friendships and emotional bonds. Friendships developed as quickly as they were dissolved" (Bettelheim 1979, 79).

The Break with the Past and the Denial of Feelings In order for the new life to become acceptable, everything connected with the members' earlier existence—friends, relatives, social and personal values—had to be eradicated. People were even forced to deny their own names. One of the survivors recollected that when his name was called out, those sitting next to him would shout, "Sit down. That's not you anymore." (Feinsod 1981, 14). Or a person might be put on exhibit at a public meeting, after which all his friends would come up, one after the other, and swear off or deny their friendship. Any loyalty, any solidarity and any connection that existed among the members had to be eradicated. They were not allowed to believe they could depend on anyone, at the same time they were forced to lose their belief in their own individuality.

One of the members wrote in a letter to Jim Jones: "Now I know that I have become a vegetable, a banana that can be eaten like any of the others in the bunch, I have really developed" (*New York Times*, November 29, 1978).

One of Jim Jones's most efficient ways of exercising power over the members was by controlling their sexual and emotional connections. From time to time, they might have marathon gatherings where they talked for hours and hours about how important it was to abstain from sex. He asked members to spy on each other and tell him if anyone was holding hands, or showing feelings for someone else. Many marriages were split up. Marital partners had to live separately and were forbidden to have sexual relations. The children were reared in the children's houses separate from the parents.

However, as in other so-called greedy institutions, it was not far from sexual abstinence to sexual promiscuity. The two opposing forces kept each other in reciprocal balance, because Jim Jones himself was not sexually inactive. He had sexual relations with his adopted children, and with women as well as men. Jim Jones told the camp's lawyer that he had had intercourse with fourteen women and two men in the space of one day. His explanation was that it was to insure their loyalty to him (Lane 1980). Jones was not abstinent in other areas, either. During the last years of his life, he was described as an amphetamine addict, and large quantities of narcotics were found in his house in Jonestown after the massacre (Reiterman 1982).

The opposing sexual forces served the same purpose. Both promiscuity and celibacy break down a stable relationship between couples, after which the emotional connection can be made to society and its leaders instead. Sociologically speaking, it is irrelevant whether the members abstain from all sexual relations, as in the case of the Shakers, or indulge in a controlled form of promiscuity, as in the case of the Oneida movement. In most totalitarian societies the emergence of personal relations has always been undesirable, because relationships between couples and close friendships absorb emotional energies, which can no longer be controlled by the leaders (Coser 1974).

Self-Hatred That Led to Suicide Life in the camp became permeated with self-hatred. One of the followers wrote to Jim Jones: "Dear Dad and Savior. I have often felt disgusted with myself. I despise being old, I hate it. I know you are truth and salvation. I hope I die before I betray you and let you down" (Reiterman 1982, 345).

Whatever feelings people had before coming to Jonestown, the life in the camp was to a large degree a reflection of Jones's own self-hatred. Their pain and anxiety became an expression of self-sacrifice to Jones. His constant need for omnipotence, and for being everyone's first lover, covered over his own self-hatred and inferiority complex.

He himself did not practice many of the things he preached to his followers. For example, he was bisexual, but hated homosexuals and let them be publicly punished. Such contradictions between the obedience he demanded of others and his own actions created the same dissonance among his followers. They confessed publicly to things that deep down inside they did not believe in.

Psychological studies show that in the face of such cognitive dissonance, or contradictions between thought and action, one often reacts by becoming apathetic and unenterprising (Festinger 1957). During the mass suicide, when the many hundreds of adults stood in rows waiting to receive the lethal poison, barely any tried to escape. Only some very few managed to get away. One who succeeded in escaping, Odell Rhodes, tells that it was impossible to make eye contact with any of the other inhabitants, while he stood in line. They stood listlessly, waiting for it to be their turn. Only through great efforts did he succeed in pulling himself together and coming up with an excuse about having forgotten something that he had to go back and get. Then he ran away and hid in the jungle. Later he wrote, "We were like dead people inside" (Feinsod 1981, 14).

Trial runs on the suicide were held on a few of the previous nights. During these "white nights" everyone was awakened by sirens and led by armed guards to stand in front of a big tub with red liquid in it. They were given small plastic cups to drink from, and then sat down in one of the big pavilions to wait for the poison to work. A couple of hours later Jim Jones would then declare over the loudspeaker that the whole thing had been staged in order to test their loyalty, after which the members would mechanically and passively return to sleep.

All the testimonies that have come forth after the massacre indicate that the great majority of Jonestown inhabitants participated in the suicide of their own free will, and without resistance. The People's Temple was dissolved a year and a half after the massacre. However, several of the old members have since publicly stated that if they had been in Jonestown that November 18, 1978, they would have been the first to stand in line to receive poison, and they would have done it with gratitude (Naipaul 1981; *San Francisco Examiner,* November 18, 1988).

Jonestown greedily swallowed its followers in total isolation and secrecy. By eradicating all the alliances between single members and by erasing borders between what was public and private, a collective consciousness of mutual control was recreated in the camp. All feelings of mutuality were controlled by the leader and directed toward the common external enemy, which he had erected.

One of the letters to Jim Jones said, "Must only be read by Dad: If you should die a natural death tonight, I would make my life available too. I would continue on my own fighting against as many enemies as possible—and if it were necessary take my own life too."

Nine hundred fourteen people died; the suicide took four hours, in all. Only three members succeeded in running away and hiding in the jungle, once the death ritual began and people waited on line to be given the poison. Miraculously, a fourth person survived. She had lain down in order to take a nap and slept through it all.

The suicide was recorded on tape, as was the custom with all activities within the People's Temple. At one point, scattered shooting can be heard, but testimonies and investigations indicate that most everyone went to their deaths without resistance.

Finally, it should be mentioned that Jim Jones did not commit suicide. He was shot by one of his followers.

Apocalypse and Incest When the balance between integration and separation tips to one side and separation turns into isolation, the community begins to engage in apocalyptic interpretations of history. Large groups change into utopian communes and begin to erect an everyday life based on romantic and over-idealized experiences of self. People begin to see the world of today as permeated with so much evil that it will soon perish, after which the right ones, the chosen few, who live in accordance with God's will and the true ideology, will take over.

Self-sufficiency alone does not determine dissolution. On the contrary, some of the Indian peoples over-idealize themselves a great deal. The Arhuacos, for example, believe that their culture is the center of the world. In a certain sense, this grandiose self-conception gives the Indians the pride and self-esteem that allows them to survive.

However, dissolution begins when single individuals deny their history and break with their past. As soon as they abandon their prior understanding of the meaning of life and subjugate themselves to a whole new world system, undergoing conversion and entering a sectarian or cultic movement, the prerequisites for dissolution are present.

Thus, the themes of dissolution and self-destruction are as follows: separation leading to isolation and withdrawal; an apocalyptic, over-idealized self-conception; setting aside democratic principles for the benefit of the sectarian movement; concentration of power; initiation by way of conversion, which requires that initiates deny their earlier history; a loss of history which creates a loss of identity and makes space for self-appointed prophets or Messiahs—the community's true and total center of power.

The People's Temple placed both a vertical and horizontal frame of fundamentalist conceptions around its members, conceptions that were full of sin and apocalyptic destruction, authoritarian to the very core. With the aid of concepts like "the saved" and "the damned," the Temple terrorized its members into submission instead of liberation. The result was neither racial justice nor socialism, but a messianic parody of both.

The mass suicide was Jim Jones's last total exercise of power. Social researchers have described Jonestown as an example showing that utopian societies, which seemingly build upon rationalist ideas of world improvement, usually contain so many irrational motives that the group members end up regressing and subjugating themselves to an authoritarian leader (Coser and Coser 1979). The socially engaged and the morally courageous, who have been physically and psychologically oppressed, will at times show a tendency to subjugate themselves to a utopian community. However, behind many of the rational fantasies of world improvement lies a web of what later can be recognized as totalitarianism (Coser 1974). What begins as an experiment in liberation may end as an experiment in submission and total absorption of the personality. Communal utopian movements often have the tendency to transform themselves into what social researchers call "greedy institutions" (Coser 1974).

They may not always end in the destruction of their members, but may dissolve instead into contending factions and intrigues among rival leaders.

Social researchers claim that for a society to survive, it must be able to channel feelings and friendships, or libidinal energies, to people on the outside (Slater 1963). The society will dissolve if emotional connections can only be made through the members, and if the members are always placed in a position of tightly controlled dependency on society's authority figures. These kinds of conditions are the real basis for the incest taboo.

Not only in a literal sense was Jonestown an incestuous society. As mentioned, the leader was called "Dad," and he had sexual relations with many of the Temple's followers, including his adopted children and both men and women.

Structurally, it was the evasion of the incest taboo that brought about the dissolution of Jonestown. The incest taboo is a defining characteristic of human society. The anthropologist Lévi-Strauss has emphasized the introduction of the incest taboo as the step through which human beings tore themselves loose from nature and entered into the sphere of culture (Lévi-Strauss 1969). It functions as a symbolic marking of the culturally possible and impossible, the permitted and the forbidden (Héretier 1982). The taboo does not necessarily have anything to do with the preservation of biological kinship. It is a symbolic boundary marker of universal significance. The incest taboo is the most basic and decisive rule for the social administration of sexuality, and in a greater sense, between separation and integration (Hastrup and Elsass 1988).

Separation and the establishment of identity boundaries are necessary, but if interaction with others is neglected, the identity loses its sense of reality. Incest is, then, an expression of interaction with others coming to a standstill. This does not only mean interaction among daughters and sisters within a family, but also symbolic interaction, which is a prerequisite for being able to maintain an independent identity.

In incest families, sexuality is administered according to the rules of the father, the self-appointed center of power. However, even though the boundaries fluctuate inwardly, there is often a sharp drawing of boundaries outwardly (Herman 1985; Goodwin 1982).

Just like Jim Jones's subjects, the victims of incest keep the secret because "they feel dead inside." They have lost their self-esteem by submitting to power. Mothers, who often know about their husbands' incestuous relations with their daughters, repress the knowledge in order to keep the family together. Only by staying together can they keep the secret and defend themselves against transgressions by the world outside.

Incest is also an expression of the fact that outside the family, there no longer exists an authority in the form of an indisputable social morality or a shared historical consciousness. Jim Jones may well have been father to his members, but his psychotic defense mechanisms made it impossible for him to construct an unequivocal morality. Furthermore, from an ideological point of view, he did away with the connection between sexuality and reproduction, so there no longer was any link between the individual sexual act and the group as a whole. Jonestown was left to its own improvisations over the authority theme and its own history. The abolition of the incest taboo became a sign of loss of culture.

The Psychology of Large Groups I visited the colony eleven days before the collective suicide. The background for my visit was that I had made a film on Latin America with photographer Morten Bruus. He had met some of the Jonestown people in New York. They had contacted him to hear if he could make a film for them on the People's Temple. Morten Bruus passed the invitation on to me, and when I happened to be in Venezuela, I made a side trip to neighboring Guyana. By a series of coincidences, I was the only foreigner with no prior knowledge of the People's Temple to enter the camp.

During the two days and nights I spent in Jonestown, I was seduced by this incestuous society into seeing it from its positive side. I was constantly watched over by a guide who followed me around in the camp and never left me alone. Only once, by mistake, did I get to see inside a house, where people were crowded together under very unfavorable conditions. But I did not make special note of the scene, because my thought was that all beginnings are difficult when an alternative society is being built up.

The day after I left Jonestown, I visited a lawyer, Robbin Stoby, in Georgetown. He was pursuing a case against the People's Temple for one of its former members, Deborah Layton Blakey, who had succeeded in getting out. The testimony she gave on June 15, 1978, contained the following passage:

> All members of the jungle commune were expected to behave in a specially friendly and happy way, when the rare guest came to visit. Before the guests arrived, Jim Jones instructed us on which facade we should show. The work day was shortened. Food improved. Sometimes there was music and dance in the evening. Apart from such days as these there was almost no hope or joy in our daily lives.

Such was the manner in which I was seduced by the People's Temple. I was the next-to-last guest (Elsass 1980, 219). The last was Congressman Leo Ryan. Some former members of the People's Temple had complained to the U.S. Congress about conditions in the camp, and an investigation commission was set up with Leo Ryan as the chairman. Prepared not to let himself be seduced, he was accompanied by journalists, who wanted to get a close-up on Jim Jones and Jonestown, and a group of avowed critics of the People's Temple. As a result he was shot as he was leaving the camp, and his murder became the concrete event that triggered the collective suicide.

In my own defense, it should be said that it takes certain qualifications to be able to resist seduction by a large group of people isolated from their surroundings. Psychosociological experiences with groups of people between twenty and several hundred, so-called large groups, show that regressive and destructive behavior can develop more quickly and uncontrollably than is the case with small groups.

The Tavistock Institute in London is one of the few places in which academic research on behavior in large groups has been done. Through the years, the Institute has gathered researchers together at Tavistock Conferences, and has experimentally formed large groups in order to study such phenomena as authority and leadership. In one instance, a group consisting of around eighty people, was gathered together in a room, in which everyone was able to see and hear everyone else several times a day for periods of two hours over a lengthy stretch of time.

Evidence shows that members of a large group have experiences which are of enormous significance for the group's explicit political life, formulated as morals and attitudes. First and foremost, the large group has a strong potential for developing feelings which very easily become unmanageable or overflow and become irrelevant, imprecise, and inappropriate in an extreme panic situation. In the best cases, the group as a whole can develop into "a very sensitive" thought apparatus, "but only on the condition that it has the necessary time and place to develop its organization and content" (de Maré 1975, 147).

The ancient Greeks already understood what forces reigned in large groups. They held large group meetings, called *poleis,* at which several thousand people sat face-to-face in a large circular amphitheater, where each member could be seen and heard by everyone. A chorus placed at the center of the stage, called the *koinonia,* used a kind of "spiritual humming" to express the "koinonia principle"—the ethical and aesthetic dimension of the meeting. The power and significance of the group for the individual was expressed by expulsion and ostracism. The most serious punishment was exile, which in the case of Socrates drove him to choose death. The fear of being expelled and isolated from the large group or punished in everyone's presence was an instrument of power. The same power play was used at Jonestown, and can be seen in our own society as well. For example, Laing (1970) and Cooper (1980) have described how neuroses and psychoses are developed as a reaction against expulsion and social alienation. Against this background, they have worked with the "therapeutic society," in which the effect of the large group on the individual is the object of treatment.

Experiences from large groups show that anxiety and psychotic mechanisms easily erupt and become the focus of the group's attention. Freud has discussed the effect of large groups on releasing psychoses (Freud 1959). In psychoses the ego-structure is underdeveloped and prefers carrying out actions with the help of processes like splitting, rather than repression. The psychotic patient has difficulty learning from large group experiences; in addition, large groups can release a latent psychosis. One of the pioneers of research on large groups, Patrick de Maré, says that "every new large group shows similarities at the early stage of development with schizophrenic thinking disorders. Schizophrenia resembles a suspended large group process in which the individual psyche corresponds to splinters of the mirror in Hans Christian Andersen's story about the Snow Queen" (de Maré 1975, 151).

In comparison with the behavior of small groups, which lend themselves more readily to a psychodynamic, commonly psychoanalytic, point of view, large groups let their behavior take place in a totally different group-dynamic space, which still cannot be adequately described. It can generally be said that while the problem for members of small groups is how they can feel and experience in the situation, the large group's problem is, rather, how members can think. In the small group, unconscious factors penetrate its members, whereas in the large group, consciousness itself is in danger. The feelings that large groups can arouse are so powerful, unpredictable, and chaotic that anxiety takes on a psychotic aspect. However, when this anxiety is contained and organized, it can become a very powerful political expression.

The therapeutic significance of the large group is of a different nature from the small group's psychoanalytic situation behind closed doors. The therapeutic communities that work with large groups can develop very powerful forces and have always gained public attention, at times being threatened or even destroyed by political and administrative forces.

External Relations

The History of the Slaves It would be a dangerous illusion to place all the blame on internal conditions in the camp, large group psychology, and incestuous relations.

A few months after the massacre, the Guyanese Ministry of Information lost patience with the enormous energy being invested in the work

Jonestown, November 6, 1978

I wrote in my diary:

The sunlight is bothering me and I want to fetch my sunglasses in my room. But the guide calls someone standing nearby and asks him to go get them. I insist on doing it myself. I also have to go to the bathroom, and with a "be back in a minute," I am finally on my own in Jonestown.

I take the liberty of going the wrong way and ending in a part of the colony I haven't seen before. There are four large barracks here, and through the windows I see people packed together as tightly as in the slave ships—eighty to a hundred people in bunk beds with less than a meter's space in between, mostly old people.

I don't take special note of that sight. These living conditions are probably not worse than in the black ghettos in the U.S.A. Beginnings are always difficult, when you are building an alternative society.

This is how I was seduced by the people of Jonestown into not seeing the impending catastrophe.

of explaining mental illness, agents, and conspiracies. An inquiry was sent to the American government:

> Why has no one been occupied with figuring out the background for all these people leaving the wealthiest and most highly developed nation in the world to start a new life in a wild, impassable jungle in an underdeveloped country?

The majority of the inhabitants of Jonestown were black and in many cases descendants of slaves. The establishment of the People's Temple can thus be seen against the background of the historical development Afro-Americans have gone through since the abolition of slavery (Huggins 1981).

Even though slaves in the United States formally got their freedom at the end of the Civil War in 1865, tyrannical conditions continued. Moreover, emancipation resulted at times in even worse conditions for blacks than they had had before. The presence of free blacks caused the whites to fear social disorder. In light of their history of oppression, blacks were potential revolutionaries. Class differences were formerly determined by race differences, but now one could fear that a free black might acquire a social status which allowed him to exercise authority over whites.

Society was supposed to be "civilized," and when the colonists looked at themselves, they wanted to see Europeans and not an uncontrolled mixture of strange people of different colors. As a civilized white man, one was not supposed to give the impression of having been let loose in a foreign, uncultivated country of wild men.

Free blacks began to gather in movements and organizations. They established their own churches, partly because their religion differed in temperament and style from white religion, and partly because they wanted a sanctuary in which they could protect themselves against derision. Some of their gatherings had to take place in secrecy and under the names of funeral parlors, song clubs, or jazz orchestras, in order to hide the political activities that actually went on behind the scenes (Frazier 1974).

However, many of the black organizations were full of inner divisions, a mirror image of the contradictory white society surrounding them.

These divisions derive from slavery, under which blacks were tied to white power and materially speaking totally dependent on the slave owner's mood and whims. Thus, the black man was a part of the white man's game, but as his opposite and opponent. After blacks were emancipated, many tried to identify with whites and become part of their class in order to gain influence. The result was that class differences developed among free blacks. The acquisition of a little piece of property could give a person status and thereby the right to distance him- or herself from other blacks. The poor whites and the native Americans of the United States, who lived in desperate competition with the blacks, often were their worst enemies.

However, regardless of what strategies were chosen, the freedom of the blacks continued to build on an illusion, even over a hundred years after the abolition of slavery.

The people of Jonestown were such a group in conflict with itself, attempting to find a way out by establishing themselves as one people and one culture outside of all others. Nonetheless, they became the victims of a white leader and a white system.

The People's Temple as a Substitute for a Left-Wing Movement Before the exodus to Guyana, the People's Temple had its headquarters in San Francisco, where there was a strong tradition for left-wing politics among the population of well-educated academics.

Many explanations have been offered for why people let themselves be seduced into the People's Temple. One was that Jim Jones had a "program" for them to live by. In the 1960s, the United States was an angry, but in a sense, apolitical nation, without political organizations. There was a strong attraction to any group that could present a plan of action, show that it had attained concrete goals, and give an explanation for most personal frustrations in simple words and phrases borrowed from the left wing.

The People's Temple was an offspring of the many left-wing movements that arose in the 1960s. At first, Jones recruited members by stereotypically hitting on motives like "alienation from and disgust with the inhumane, American capitalist system" and "racism, which poisons human interrelation." Jim Jones became a well-known person with his left-wing rhetoric, and the movement attracted attention, because it was always capable of getting several thousand poor people and blacks to participate in demonstrations and election campaigns. In left-wing circles, there was considerable fascination with Jones and his Temple, because he could do what few other groups managed: get things done, reach out to people, mobilize, and act. When some group contacted the Temple and convinced them to support an issue, their discipline could always be relied on. They kept their promises and with very short notice could mobilize a large group of members to come to demonstrations or compaigns.

Jones knew that his visions of a utopian society had to be followed up by concrete tangible results. Jones was a good organizer, and when the People's Temple moved to San Francisco, he initiated a long series of relatively unpretentious activities for the black people living in the neighborhood. They started a public kitchen at which around two hundred people a day could buy a cheap meal. Inside the temple building a medical clinic was set up, where people could have free consultations. Members of the People's Temple ran activity centers for the elderly, and a printing press and photography lab for the young. Many of the elderly living in the neighborhood received home visits by members who offered to help them by contacting public authorities regarding social and medical problems.

With decided political charisma, Jones appealed mostly to blacks, who constituted 80 percent of the members. He condemned racism and accused the American government of being behind the murder of Martin Luther King. He had close connections with some of the most influential black politicians in California, often speaking to their cause and proclaiming that he would personally carry on King's work.

The Fillmore district, in which the temple was situated, was a desperate area in the 1970s. During the Second World War it had been a dynamic part of the city for more well-to-do blacks. Twenty-five years later it was run down, the houses were dilapidated, and unemployment, welfare, alcohol, and drug abuse were as widespread as in the black ghettos of New York and Chicago.

This was the area from which Jones got most of his followers. There was another small but important group, recruited among whites who had formerly belonged to the cultural and social protest movements of the sixties and seventies. Some of them were hippies.

The People's Temple may be seen, then, as a substitute for the left-wing movement that had dwindled in large parts of the United States. Since the turn of the century, there had not been any strong political organizations in California. Politicians often had to face arbitrary voter organizations, which were disinterested and apathetic. Immediately prior to the suicide, the People's Temple had around eight thousand members in San Francisco alone, potentially one of the largest groups of politically active people in the area.

Two Kinds of Political Consciousness: Elitist and Popular The People's Temple contained two kinds of political consciousness.

One was formulated by Jim Jones himself and the little group surrounding him, composed primarily of whites. This was the ideology that outwardly characterized the People's Temple and appeared in the media. At first, it was characterized by progressive left-wing thought, but around 1977, a paranoid element entered into it. The movement declared publicly that the FBI conspired against the whole left wing and in particular against the People's Temple. In October 1977 their newsletter *People's Forum* carried the following headline: "Conspiracy, Blackmail, Bribery, Perjury, Anonymous Accusations, and Media Manipulation Characterize Plot to Destroy People's Temple."

In 1978 Jim Jones spoke to his members in San Francisco over the camp radio in Guyana:

> I know that some of you want to fight, but that is exactly what the system wants you to do. It wants to use us as sacred sacrificial animals, as scapegoats. Don't fall in the trap of resorting to violence, no matter what lies are told about us.
>
> The People's Temple has so to say helped all political prisoners in the U.S. Our message has reached all oppressed people, and that's what is worrying the system. We have organized poor people and given them a voice, a possibility of expressing themselves. The system has nothing against giving power to the ruling class, but for the first time we have given a little support to the little man, and that is an unforgivable sin. That's the whole problem in a nutshell. (Reiterman 1982, 372)

When Jim Jones spoke these words, the People's Temple had twenty thousand active members. Its newsletter was distributed to around one hundred thousand people. A thousand had moved to Jonestown in Guyana, and about $20 million had been deposited in foreign banks. At this time it was revealed in the People's Temple newsletter that the group was not a religious sect, but a human rights movement, which had socialism as its goal. The People's Temple was a cover name.

The other kind of political consciousness was made up of the large body of members, who were more attracted to the sense of community they could find in the People's Temple than to the leader's ideology. Of the thousand members who emigrated to Guyana, only a few went along because they shared Jim Jones's paranoid ideas about conspiracy. Most of them followed because they wanted to show that they could establish a life liberated from the material and psychological oppression they experienced in American cities.

One of the few who managed to evade the suicide, Odell Rhodes, declared afterwards that it was not encountering Jim Jones that originally brought him into the movement. It was the people in the People's Temple who made the greatest impression on him. They were so different from the self-centered and lonely people he knew from city streets. He explained, "They made me feel like a fool for not having been with them my whole life. I saw it at once. It was just what I was looking for, and it was what I had been looking for my whole life" (Feinsod 1981, 15).

Rhodes, by the way, did not find the conditions in Jonestown unacceptably oppressive. He had been in the military for eight years in Vietnam, and by comparison Jonestown was a positive experience. Rhodes considered the discipline in the camp the necessary price one had to pay to obtain that kind of community.

According to Rhodes, working in the manioc fields was "the hardest work I had ever had. But it wasn't as though you just waited for the day to be over. You were at work with all your friends, and you knew that the work you did would bring food to the people you liked. I didn't mind. I was happy with that work" (Feinsod 1981, 15).

These two kinds of consciousness, the elitist and the popular, supplemented each other and were the reason the People's Temple became a well-disciplined political machine that was difficult to see through and contest.

Left-wing circles in particular voiced words of praise. Black political activist Angela Davis said in a speech to the People's Temple in 1977: "I know that you are in a very difficult situation right now, and that there is a conspiracy against you. . . . When you are attacked, it is because of your progressive viewpoints. We feel it just as much as a direct attack on us as on you. Therefore, we will do everything in our power to strengthen your security and your possibilities of continuing the struggle" (Reiterman 1982, 369).

For several reasons, left-wing circles were willing to overlook what they knew about the inner workings of the Temple. First and foremost, there was an unwillingness to oppose an organization with so many members, most of whom were black. Furthermore, critics feared that the People's Temple would turn its political power against them in the form of smear campaigns, rivalry, or direct threats. Also, many people on the Left were of the opinion that it was wrong to criticize each other publicly. Finally, some of the socialist movements had their own problems with authoritarian leaders and oppressive party discipline—and of course those who live in glass houses should not throw stones.

Intelligence Activities: CIA One of the ways of avoiding dealing with the People's Temple after the suicide was simply to claim that Jonestown had been annihilated by an enemy from the outside. The Black Panther Party, for example, claimed that the massacre could be blamed on the CIA neutron bomb tests. Others demanded an investigation of the intelligence activities which the U.S. State Department had carried out in the camp.

Guyana is the only socialist country in Latin America and the only English-speaking one as well. So when a thousand American citizens emigrated there to build up a socialist society, the CIA had to be interested in making the experiment fail. A large quantity of psychopharmaceuticals, which were claimed to have been developed by the CIA for brainwashing and behavior control, was found in the camp. The Alliance for the Preservation of Religious Liberty accused the CIA of using the so-called mind control drug, MK-ULTRA, to control the camp. Journalists identified a People's Temple member, by the name of Philip Blakey, as a former CIA agent. Among other things, Blakey had led a UNITA action in Angola, in 1975. His name was not among the 914 dead; he escaped and has not been seen since.

The United States has always had great interest in the Caribbean. Earlier it was claimed that Guyana's President, Forbes Burnham, was installed with the aid of the CIA and an official of the American Embassy in Georgetown was identified as the mediator (Naipaul 1981). The latter was, in fact, the government's contact to Jonestown.

Leo Holsinger, who was Congressman Leo Ryan's right-hand man, and a part of the group whose visit to Jonestown triggered the suicide, claimed later that Jones's intention was to avoid the suicide and make a getaway to Grenada with a few select members. A sum of $100,000 dollars had been deposited there in a bank ahead of time. After the massacre a few members of the People's Temple arrived in Grenada to claim the money, but the President, Maurice Bishop, said that the money belonged to Grenada. A year later he was deposed with the aid of the CIA.

It is impossible to find out how big a role the CIA played in Jonestown. Tim Reiterman is one of the journalists who has examined the Jonestown material most thoroughly and written a report that is both the most extensive and the most praised by the press (Reiterman 1982). According to him, neither the FBI nor the CIA had any significant information in its possession. The CIA, it seems, did not even know how badly off the inhabitants of Jonestown were. Consequently, Reiterman and some other journalists have accused the CIA and the American Embassy in Georgetown of irresponsible ignorance.

In a way, Jim Jones's paranoid ideas coincided with many of the romantic, revolutionary dreams of the sixties, in which some people saw their socialist utopias enveloped in CIA conspiracies. There may well be a certain measure of truth in paranoid illusions, but in this case, staring narrowly at intelligence activities in the camp would leave other important questions unanswered.

Reaching an Understanding of the Jonestown Trauma Jonestown presented a problem for many of the black organizations.

If they dissociated themselves from the People's Temple, it meant that they wrote off an organization based on a black constituency and supported by liberals and left wingers. If they defended the People's Temple, it meant that they condoned and concealed the death of 914 people. Hence, many blacks in the United States reacted to the suicide with grief, but evaded the question of responsibility. Many of them neglected the key questions or avoided them by pointing once again to the danger of blacks following a white leader.

Another reaction on the Left was to condemn Jones and his little inner circle of whites. Some views compared Jones with Stalin and sought to explain how a leadership of this sort could be allowed to develop unchecked. The point of view was person-oriented, focusing on an analysis of the leader's demonic powers, instead of being system-oriented and analyzing the People's Temple as an organization that created an impenetrable, authoritative structure.

Different testimonies showed that in reality Jones's power built upon a group of members, each of whom had his or her sphere of power. As it happened, most of this inner circle eluded the suicide, having attended a baseball game in Georgetown while it took place.

One of those who escaped was Jim Jones's son, Stephan Jones. He has later said about his father, "Jonestown was not Jim Jones's, even though he believed it himself. Jim Jones will be used to discredit socialism. People will use him to give a bad name to everything we have built up" (Yee and Layton 1982, 51).

Dick Tropp, one of the whites in the inner circle around Jim Jones, said to me during my stay in the camp:

> Jim Jones is the instrument that created our movement. He is not the movement. In the U.S.A. you can't just start any old movement without there being a strong leader. Most Americans lack a father figure. The People's Temple has made use of this psychology. But when people come to Jonestown, they are told that they have to take responsibility for their own lives. They can't blame Jim Jones for whether things go well or not. . . .
>
> But here in the camp, Jim Jones doesn't mean much. Besides, he's a sick man and we hardly ever see him.

Many people saw Jonestown as proof of the dangers of accepting an authoritarian leadership. They spoke of the danger of channeling the needs of an oppressed people into one single organization with only one leader. Instead, they emphasized the need for a democratic left wing, which wrote off any kind of authority, thereby dismissing the power and strength that had nonetheless resided in the People's Temple before its excursion to Guyana.

One of the most formidable aspects of Jonestown was that the members expressed dissatisfaction and passivity at the same time. They were dissatisfied with the society they came from, but submitted passively to Jim Jones's authority and let themselves be led into suicide. For many people, pervasive desperation and unformulated dissatisfaction was part of their daily lives. In the United States of the seventies, these were the people who primarily formed the basis of the movement. The People's Temple proclaimed that it could give them social security, existential

Jonestown, November 11, 1978

I eat breakfast with the camp's leaders. The atmosphere is relaxed and we talk about unimportant matters, the jungle, the heat, and Guyana. While the others are talking, the man sitting next to me introduces himself: Mike Prokes, former filmmaker. He is very interested in talking to me and pulls me aside, asking me about anything and everything. Suddenly, he winks in a knowing way and pinches me on the arm, as if we share a secret. It makes me wonder, and I make a note of the incident in my diary.

This afternoon I want to take a picture of him. But he is reluctant and says that it must not be a closeup. He goes back a way and poses with two others in front of the leader's house.

Later I find out that Mike Prokes evaded the suicide and was arrested in Georgetown with a suitcase containing $50,000. He then came to the United States and filed a testimony in which he described how he had been contacted by an official of the American government in 1976 and offered a good salary if he would go into the People's Temple and report back to the authorities. He had accepted the offer.

Prokes published his testimony a month after the suicide. He signed it at a press conference, after which he went into the bathroom and shot himself.

meaning, and political courage. However, it made its promises without demanding that its members had to participate actively in the democratic process.

Revolutionary involvement was measured by the extent of the members' willingness to sacrifice themselves, rather than by their regular work effort and the influence of their contribution to the Temple. Jonestown became a textbook example of a movement wishing to use people's desperation in order to manipulate.

In many right-wing circles, the Jonestown massacre was a reinforcement of their belief in traditional American individualism. Jonestown awakened a fear of collective actions and a mistrust for going into movements and political parties. The People's Temple offered stimulation to the prohibitive aspects of collective experiments. It became a nightmarish vision of the impossibility of socialism, with passivity and escapism taken to their utmost extreme.

In several left-wing groups, Jonestown was the point of departure for analyzing their own nightmare and acknowledging the difficulty of building up a democratic, popular, left-wing movement.

Analyzing Jonestown was so frightening to many people that they often had to protect themselves behind political rhetoric, which only served to make the discussions even more impalpable. Thus they ended up resembling Jonestown itself, where platitudes and rhetoric were a contorted expression of anger and desperation. An uncontrolled outburst of anger was legitimized by being termed a "socialist act." Passivity was called an expression of "political discipline," and desire for defense was transformed into self-hatred by being termed a "revolutionary suicide."

Words like "equality," "freedom," "community," "justice," and "solidarity" move and inspire most people, even if the words are spoken by murderers.

No one understood this better than Jim Jones.

The Anthropology of Violence Who was responsible for violence arising? Was it the members in the camp or Jim Jones? Was it the right or left wing in the United States. Was it the American government or the CIA? The easiest answer would be to make a sweeping claim and squarely place the blame on Jim Jones, as most have done. However, the more deeply one digs into the material, the more one is forced to accept that the cause of violence can be located at many different points in the internal relations of the various parties involved.

The word "violence" may be used either by those who witness it or by those who are its victim. The practitioners of violence, on the other hand, will use other terms and regard it as a necessary and just act. The terrorist, for example, would argue that his actions are legitimate, while the victim of course would claim the opposite. Both parties appeal to social norms and values, and each one claims justice to be on his side. Therefore, the word only has value when one knows who is using it and how the perpetrator fits into the political scene (Riches 1986, 5).

The massacre in Jonestown shows the relativity of violence. The People's Temple did not term the internal relations in the camp leading to the suicide as terror, but rather as a legitimate political strategy, which was necessary for stopping the violence and oppression perpetrated by the American government. The right wing in the United States claimed the opposite view: the People's Temple was a terrorist organization against whom they had to defend themselves. Both parties regarded the other as the violent intruder, competing for power on the public scene.

Violence has three parties: a perpetrator, a victim, and a witness. At times, however, the boundaries between them can become imprecise, and the nature of violence unclear. In Jonestown, the consequences of violence were visible, and no one was in doubt as to who the enemy was. In Chemescua, on the other hand, the population was split into different attitudes, for and against modern development, and even though the inhabitants were plagued by depression and internal conflicts, they had trouble diagnosing the symptoms and agreeing on who the enemy was. Only in shamanic rituals did violence become visible and terror get named.

Violence, then, does indeed assume many different forms, and is not a homogeneous constant. It can be physical or psychological, visible or invisible, instrumental or metaphorical.

Physical violence aims at destroying objects and people; mental violence aims at destroying identities. These two modes cannot always be juxtaposed, just as the inner world of the mind and the outer world of physical surroundings do not always go hand in hand.

The Jonestown suicide was an example of the opposition between the physical and psychological world. Violence did not simply arise along with the members' increasing difficulties in making their mental ideas on socialism fit in with their outer reality. On the contrary, it exploded at a time no one had been able to predict.

The structure of the physical world is continuous, while mental landscapes are discontinuous. In outer reality there is movement, and in the inner ideal world, displacement. Efforts will always be made to bring harmony and continuity between these two spheres, while "the essential characteristic of violence will be to attempt to bring imbalance and disorder between the two worlds" (Corbin 1986, 29). Thus it is extremely difficult to understand the Jonestown massacre, because its essential effect has been to elude our intellect.

Violence originates in our efforts to create predictability and continuity. However, if conditions become too unpredictable and chaotic, violence erupts as a defense mechanism against anxiety. The incomprehensible part of the world is labeled enemy and eradicated. Paradoxically, the very unpredictability one fights in the enemy becomes an essential characteristic in oneself. The structures reproduce themselves. The oppositions filter into each other, negations are abolished, and equity between friend and enemy emerges—all for the purpose of creating order.

Violence is, then, the only means at hand for dealing with the intolerable situation that has been created. Democratic solutions, discussions, and a gradual solution of conflicts are no longer realistic possibilities.

The Jungle in Guyana Is Not So Far Away Characteristically, few scholarly contributions of substance have aided our understanding of the Jonestown massacre. When great tragedies and accidents take place, sociologists, anthropologists, and psychologists have little to contribute. Certainly, the catastrophes, massacres, concentration camps, terror, and annihilation get placed in a polemical context in which moral and ideological conclusions are drawn. But not many conclusions can be drawn, nor strategies for prevention be adapted, on the basis of professional contexts and studies alone.

Since the Jonestown massacre, only one or two scholarly conferences have been held on the subject, and the results have been made public in some sparse work papers published by the University of California, Santa Cruz, in May 1981 (Woods 1981).

Jonestown has been mentioned in more general psychiatric contexts as a cult (Galanter 1989, 156, 324; Shupe and Bromley 1982). The distinguishing characteristics of cults include authoritarian leadership, suppression of rational thought, deceptive recruitment techniques, coercive mind control, a totalistic group structure, isolation from conventional society and former relationships, and exploitation of group members by leaders (Bromley and Shupe 1989, 310). Jim Jones has been described as psychotic, with signs of megalomania and paranoia (Weightman 1983). His need for total control and domination over his subjects, and his paranoid fears of betrayal, have been explained as a result of the narcissistic nature of his relationships. Due to the permeability of his ego boundaries, he experienced and dealt with external objects through projective identifications as a part of the self.

These objects may represent or contain representations of unacceptable parts of the self; controlling them can be equated with controlling the self, and changing them, with changing the self. The ability to externalize in this way had the purpose of saving the narcissistic patient from intolerable internal conflict and warding off a psychotic break. The admiration or tribute from external objects mitigated a dangerous lowering of the disturbed individual's self-esteem (Deutsch 1989, 157). The followers of cults are generally young persons whose self-esteem needs the mirroring entailed in receiving recognition or approbation from the grandiose leader, or more regularly through a "merger" with the idealized person. But both old and young may be involved in cults, as demonstrated in the demography of the dead at Jonestown (Zimbardo and Hartley 1987).

But beside these general conclusions, no scientific report based on concrete empirical material specific to the Jonestown case has been published. The same forbearance can be found in the publicizing of investigative reports on concentration camps during World War II. It took twenty-nine years before the psychological studies of war criminals at the Nuremberg Trials were published (Borofsky and Brand 1980). One of the reasons it took such a long time was that the conclusions touched on our last defense mechanism against our own destructiveness. Admitting our own part in the world in which such crimes were committed was so emotionally provocative that even psychological experts tried to stay silent as long as possible.

History repeats itself, and we are still waiting for the final report about Jonestown.

I will never be able to shake off the experience of staying in Jonestown. I have read all the many articles and books collected on the subject. I gaze at the pictures of the victims. I can recognize some of them I had been with for those two days at the beginning of November 1978. I talked and laughed with several of them about something, the subject of which I no longer remember.

The massacre took four hours. While the inhabitants waited to receive the poison, some of them took the time to write letters to their families:

> They will never be able to destroy what we have built up, because we decided a long time ago that if they come after us, they will have to take all of us together. Martin Luther King said it like this: "A person who has not found something to die for will not feel he is alive."
>
> We have found something to die for. It is called social justice. Then it doesn't matter how they choose to do away with us at the moment or how we will be described later on. At least we have had the satisfaction of living in justice here. It's not because they have promised us success or reward, but simply because it was the most right thing to do—the best way we knew of living our lives.

Some of these statements could have come from the mouths of other oppressed people as well. In a sense, the jungle in Guyana is not so far away. The eradication and destruction of a people could happen again.

3. *The Survival of the Slaves*

In protection against its eternal opponents, violence and destruction, survival takes different forms at different stages.

Among the Maroons violence was invisibly present in the form of memories and metaphors for the past. In Jonestown, in contrast, it was openly identifiable in the form of murder and physical destruction. However, even if violence may assume many different forms, either physical or mental, visible or invisible, the kind of violence slaves have been exposed to is generally different from that of the Indians.

When the Africans in the New World were originally subjugated in master-slave relations, they were separated and sold away from everyone they had known soon after their arrival. The Indians, in contrast, were exposed to the terror of the colonizers as a united people. Thus it was easier for them to base their survival on political and organizational contexts and on historical tradition and shared memory. For the slaves, on the other hand, terror was individualized, and their survival needs are more psychological in nature.

The following is a survey of the history of the slaves to demonstrate the development of certain psychological mechanisms, based in particular on Huggins (1981) and on Frazier (1974), Galeano (1977) and Kovel (1970).

The Past as Weapon The slaves came from West Africa, from an area which spread like a fan from the delta of the Senegal River, down along the Bay of Benin and inland to the south, corresponding to what we today call Angola. Slaves were taken from just about every single village in this vast area stretching three to four hundred kilometers inland and brought to both North and South America.

At the high point of the slave trade, healthy young African men could be bought for ten dollars in Africa and sold for up to six hundred dollars in the New World (Huggins 1981, 49). Even sick or dying slaves could be expected to bring in a price, like other damaged goods.

The transport of slaves was not only a nightmare of physical pain. Mentally and spiritually, the slaves had to travel from one world to another.

Loss of freedom was not *the* most essential characteristic of slavery. The African had always been tied to one place and one people, with a daily life consisting of innumerable obligations. The idea of freedom, if understood to mean unfettered by connections and able to act without regard for others' decisions, attitudes, and prejudices, would have been frightening for him.

The radical change in slave existence was, in fact, in the very conception of what it meant to be a human being. In the New World economic value was the measure of a slave. During the subsequent 250 years, the basic substance of slave existence consisted of being pawed over and examined, discussed as an object, moved from one place to another, bought and sold. Each sex, each age, each appearance, each state of health had its own price.

However, even if the slave were regarded as cattle, there was the decisive difference that he was a thinking being, who was assumed to know the difference between right and wrong, and in contrast to a horse or cow, could take responsibility for his actions. A horse that trampled his master to death was not a murderer, but a slave who defended himself against brutality was.

The slave could plan and organize and thus become a threat to his master. When the slave began to understand how little stood between him and his master, his imagination could begin to work on finding an escape, defying his position, and rebelling.

There were many contradictions involved in the fact that salable goods were also human and that a human who was not his own master could be responsible for his own actions. Moreover, this dilemma was difficult to solve in a society of whites, who in fact claimed to follow the Bible and place a high value on human rights. The solution to the dilemma was sought by assuming the inferiority of the black race, and thus racial prejudice began to develop.

As time passed, racial differences were no longer the real problem. At first, it was not difficult to justify differential treatment of people, whose appearance and language were exotic and strange. Later on, the similarities between the races became the problem. The longer blacks and whites lived together in the same culture, spoke the same language, and were tied to the same habitation and work, the more difficult it was to justify that one party was to be denied what the other regarded as a birthright.

Similarly, just as lack of freedom was not the central disgrace of slavery, neither was inequality its most disturbing aspect. Both Europeans and Africans were accustomed to living in societies in which some people were higher-ranking than others. Neither masters nor slaves had ever experienced the realization of the concept of equality among all people.

What made the whites masters over the blacks was their possession of social and collective power. In the first stage of the slave trade, power resided in a superior weapon and navigation technology. Later on, the master had the force of government behind him, and he could always gain help from the army, the authorities, and the police in order to crush slave rebellions. This power was concrete and visible. Slaves were undressed, tied to trees, pinned down by others, whipped, branded, mutilated, or killed in front of other slaves. Such scenes served as preventive measures, reminders of who really had the power.

There were all types of slave owners, ranging from the perverse and brutal to the gentle and intelligent, and in all cases, being white was sufficient grounds for having power. If a particular slave was lucky enough to have a master who was against the use of violence, he could observe the widespread use of it at neighboring plantations.

The adaptations of slaves ranged from defiance and resistance to extreme subservience. To protect themselves from oppression, they attempted to retain some elements of their life in Africa, often intangible aspects of culture that could not be thrown away or used up and that served as a means of survival. For example, slaves retained African music, a particular way of singing a song, and of moving their bodies in dance.

Music was in a sense the African's soul. It survived the passage over the ocean and the changing generations. Just about every event in Africa had been accompanied by some particular music. However, when the African came to the New World, he came to a world lacking in familiar sounds. He managed to provide himself with instruments, and in situations where drums were prohibited, he used his own body to produce music. There was hand clapping, thigh slapping, foot stomping, and the jangle of jewelry as the body moved. Music was used as invisible baggage from Africa, as one rowed down the river, cleared the earth, sowed, weeded, or harvested. Each kind of work had its own particular rhythm and created its own worksong; "as it was back home, it should be in this alien world" (Huggins 1981, 86).

To Africans there was no sharp division between the sacred and the secular. While white Christians drew a sharp dividing line between the physical and spiritual, Africans were accustomed to dancing and singing during funerals and sacred rituals. The New World was divided into good and evil and, literally speaking, into black and white. Blacks who became Christians transgressed these divisions. Even if they cultivated God, their bodies continued to move to psalms and liturgical music as their ancestors had done. Their call-and-response songs and rhythms made their way into black church services, becoming gospels and spirituals. In the secular world, marches, waltzes, and ballads were transformed by their influence into a new kind of music. Thus the slaves became a creative element in the New World and were able to retain something from their homeland.

Slaves Who Became Masters In some instances, whites and blacks shared a common understanding of the nature of external relations. They were friends, and their relationships were based on mutual respect and love. The realities of power and violence could at times be concealed behind personal, everyday interactions between master and slave. They adjusted to each other in the course of time. Some slave owners regarded their slaves as a part of their family, and their slaves reciprocated in kind. However, in most cases, these feelings were based on unstable sentimentality. The master could run into economic troubles and find it necessary to rent or sell even his favorite slave. Even if the owner had written in his will that his slaves were to be given their freedom after his death, the outcome was dependent on acknowledgment by the court. In far too many cases, the white inheritors succeeded in overturning the dictates of a testament. Even the most genuine family sentiments toward the slave were dependent on the outer world, which could suddenly lead a trusted slave to become ungrateful and run away.

There is no hiding the fact that the aim of the slave system was to give the slave owner economic advantages. The whites selected different strategies for getting slaves to work as efficiently as possible. Some attempted to clear their consciences by appealing to the slave's credulity with displays of friendliness and loving care. Others chose a firmer, more forceful strategy. The former was guided by family sentiments; the latter, by incitement to brutality. Each saw its advantage in getting slaves to yield the greatest work effort.

Even though power was naked and direct, slaves understood how to place themselves in situations which, paradoxically, enabled them from time to time to get their needs and wishes fulfilled. For example, at an early age, slave children began to fawn over the master and family. The whites might be surrounded by little black children who shouted with joy at the sight of them, told them everything they had learned, begged for sugar and candy, and ran in front of them with their continual chatter. Most whites, finding them cute, were reinforced in their familial sentiments. However, for the slave child it was in reality an education in manipulation, a way of learning where the limits of the master's tolerance were. How long should he keep on begging before something came his way? When did the master become impatient enough to give something away and when did he get angry instead? This knowledge was the ballast with which the slave could gain control over the white man.

Slave-white relations contained many contradictions. On the one hand, slaves had to give the master the impression that he was incontestably the wiser, the more powerful, and the superior of the two; on the other hand, whites acted like children, helplessly appealing to the slave in many small ways in daily life. The white mistress managed to get into such a state of dependency on her slave that she was unable to get dressed, make the simplest morning toilet, or make decisions about what she should eat without the slave helping her and supporting her. By infantilizing whites, by keeping their clothes clean, by keeping order in their things, and reminding them of their duties, the slave could cultivate dependency, which led to increased influence. The master's weaknesses, like whiskey, women, and gambling, were not hidden knowledge to the slave, because he was often the one who drove the master home from sprees at which he had either gotten drunk or was otherwise in trouble. In such situations, the slave could press various promises out of the master or even lay the foundation for more of the same kind of situations.

Having well-reared slaves and a well-kept plantation was a matter of honor for most masters; being a good master was something to be proud of. However, it was precisely this vanity which opened up possibilities for blacks to manipulate whites.

Blacks and whites often lived their whole lives in the same household, generation after generation. Young and old, black and white gave each other a feeling of intimacy and continuity. Black and white women helped each other give birth, the white infant fed at black breasts and was rocked to sleep in black arms. Blacks nursed whites through their illnesses, and black hands washed dead white bodies, preparing them for eternity. Many white men, wanting to sow their wild oats before they got married, had their first sexual experience with a black woman.

Against the background of this intimacy, slaves were at times able to create a situation of transference and become masters.

The Psychology of the Slave The survival mechanisms of the slaves had the aim of avoiding three major dangers: becoming a victim of fear, making compromises and being hypocritical, or giving in to hate.

The fear of being exposed to physical torture and punishment was always present. This fear could seduce the slave to believe that it was better for him to withdraw and be self-sufficient, avoiding marriage and a love relationship with another person. The less one gave of oneself, the better one could protect oneself against injury and violation. However, giving in to this attitude led to a loss of self-esteem. A slave might cower every time the master went by, or smile, become an affectionate lapdog or a groveling bootlicker to avoid being hit or humiliated.

The danger of assuming hypocritical behavior was a loss of personal identity. The master was often a vain narcissist who could easily be manipulated, and the slave who wore a mask that pleased him could get things. However, if he played his role too well, compromising himself too much, the mask could become a permanent fixture. For example, whites loved to believe that blacks were always like children, and some blacks pretended to wear this naive "Sambo mask" in order to make life a little easier. However, if they did so too often, the lie might become reality.

The danger of surrendering to hate was that the continual debasement and potential for physical violence could fill the slave with hatred that could lead to desperate self-destruction. Hate combined with powerlessness could become self-hate and fatalism.

In the face of these three dangers, slaves managed nonetheless to maintain a spiritual strength that could recreate a separate culture. The most important means was their well-hidden communication system of codes, which were inaccessible to their oppressors. Religion and music, for example, were an important shield in which they could create an expressive mode that was characteristic of slave culture, with traits that the whites could not control. It was precisely the slaves' ability to develop a distinctive individualism and creativity under conditions which denied them this possibility that made whites notice the blacks' strength and worthiness. Moreover, it was also these characteristics that made many blacks not want to gain the advantages of the whites and become like them. They did not want to be integrated, even though they had been promised freedom and economic security after the abolition of slavery. If they could choose between conquering the whites, rebelling and gaining a share of the power, or escaping and establishing their own separate communities, they chose the last. Some of them fled into ghettos and few remained behind to try and gain a place in white society.

Ghettos At the same time society was becoming more "democratic," black ghettos were being formed. Even though slavery ended, the status of blacks worsened. A black man had trouble entering into any business relations, because there was no security for the validity of his signature. If he was exposed to continued persecution or harassment, no court would uphold his contention. Limits were placed on the free black worker, so that he could not debase competition in the white labor market.

Because he provoked the whites' fears of disorder in society, there was no place where a black could feel safe. Racial prejudice blossomed, and blacks became the opposite of what whites considered civilized. They became identified with stupidity, greed, laziness, and childishness.

Blacks attempted to organize in various ways, such as creating their own school systems. Although blacks were usually excluded from white schools, independent black education was nevertheless disparaged by whites. The whites would gather in protest and close the schools or burn them down. To protect themselves, blacks set up political organizations

Dangogo, August 20, 1985

When I entered the Maroon village, most of the children were terrified. This may be the reason why the inhabitants staged an act of retaliation, which consisted of my having to go hunting with Kanzi.

It turned out to be a terrible trip. He walked so fast that I quickly got exhausted. Every time he caught sight of some prey, he raced off, forgetting me entirely, and I might have to wait for hours until he returned. Sometimes I thought he could not find me, and I would start bellowing with all my might until he showed up.

It was very unpleasant after dark. He ran off several times with his battery-driven headlamp and left me sitting alone in the dark, at the mercy of all the sounds and at the discretion of the wild animals.

After a while, he began to enjoy the situation. He would disappear suddenly and when I'd been shouting a while for him to come back, he would jump out and frighten me with a loud "boo." In the end, I regarded his teasing as pure and simple malice, revenge for the day my sudden appearance as a white man in the village had frightened the children.

under false names, such as lodges, organizations, jazz clubs, and religious movements (Frazier 1974).

However, black organizations all too often imitated white ones in order to gain power and influence in society, basing their premises on the notion that one had to appear hard-working, conservative, and docile to be accepted as a free man and rise in society. To gain access to white society, one had to be careful about what one said and fully accept white reality as it was. It was necessary for blacks to show that they had more common interests with whites than with their own race. Denial of one's own background was a prerequisite for being born again. These contradictory survival strategies penetrated into several of the black movements, making them ambiguous and weak (Fanon 1970, 37).

Blacks brought this slave psychology with them when they settled in the People's Temple in Guyana, or as Maroons in Surinam. In both cases, they saw the necessity of staying clear of established society. They lived in ghettos, as floating islands, in which they were aware of their distance and separation from the larger society.

Of course, the Maroons and the People's Temple were formed in entirely different periods. The Maroons fled from a slave existence and were in clear opposition to white domination. In contrast, the People's Temple was formed long after the demise of slavery, with the result that oppression and contradictions were more insidious and opaque. The boundaries were so unclear that it was possible for this black movement to have a white leader.

Among the Maroons, individual differences were fully accepted, and there was little devotion to formless emotionality or vague feelings of everyone being brothers and sisters.

The People's Temple, in contrast, was based on the sentimental idea of community. The movement was born in the 1970s, at a time when grass-roots movements appeared in reaction to big institutions and political parties. According to the psychoanalytic philosophy of the times, repressed eros was regarded as the basis for social institutions (Marcuse 1955; Brown 1968). Linear thinking and rational goal-orientation was to be replaced by expanded consciousness—"Make love, not war." Politics was supposed to be grounded in feelings, and the personal was to be seen as political.

This sentimental vagueness was what destroyed the slave psychology in Jonestown. Slaves have always drawn clear boundaries around each person's individuality. But in Jonestown, everyone had to be a part of the community, and the boundaries between what was person-oriented and society-oriented became unclear. This made room for the self-hatred and destruction that has always been present in the ghettos, and which, in the end, took the lives of its inhabitants.

The survival of slaves is always dependent on their being able to nourish themselves on their slave history without feelings of inferiority. Characteristically, however, in contrast with the Indians, slaves must submit to a greater demand for personal and psychological variability. Without being able to refer to the kind of fixed, shared cultural tradition the Indians have, slaves would have to adjust constantly to different masters merely in order to stay alive. The survival of the slaves descendants has rested more on the freedom to extrapolate from their past and from African cultural traditions. Slave psychology contains a radical principle of variability and adaptation, more than of direct African carry-overs.

However, behind all this variability, there was a stable core in the psychological mechanisms that allowed slave descendants to retain individual expressiveness and creativity. As shown in the case of the Maroons, a presupposition for being able to respect the inner life of each individual is the clear demarcation of boundaries between master and slave, or between the community and the larger society, a boundary that is placed between isolation, on the one hand, and total integration and absorption, on the other.

PART THREE *Analysis and Conclusion*

1. *The Psychology of Survival*

The journey to the last remaining Indians and descendants of slaves is over, and we are left with some fragments of a psychology of survival.

What are the conditions that allow some communities to survive, while others perish? Survival is dependent on external relations, such as the Indians' geographical location, colonization of the area, and illnesses that intrude as a result of contact with foreigners. However, it is the interaction between these external factors and certain internal relations in the community that constitutes a psychology of survival.

Among Indian groups the prerequisite for survival was the formation of an organization that respected their many-sidedness and was able to accommodate mutual differences in cultural forms. The countercultures developed by the Indians often contained hidden recesses and traditions that were in counterplay to the larger society. One important aspect of Indian survival can be seen, for example, in shamanism, an alternative healing process, by which some Indians were able to produce a mode of thought that created disorder and wildness in our own civilization.

Among the descendants of slaves, the form of survival that developed was more individualized and psychological. In this case it was dependent on the community achieving a subtle balance between resistance to integration and absorption on the one hand, and not letting itself be isolated from the larger society on the other; or a balance, that is, between isolation and integration. In order to live in seclusion, these people had to fill their lives with themes that were life-giving. They had to be sustained by their own slave history, and had to develop the capacity for expressing a many-sidedness to their identity in order to avoid being overpowered by self-hatred and destruction.

These experiences from journeys into cultures on the periphery of our society do not immediately allow themselves to cohere into a simple study of survival. Nevertheless, some of the fragments do come together to form a message about what we need to watch out for in our dealings with other cultures and marginal groups, as well as what we need to hold onto if we ourselves wish to endure as a civilization.

The Indians and slaves give us no answers if we ask too directly. We have to stand at a distance from the details and see if, by assuming a stance of ignorance, we nonetheless can assemble the disconnected pieces.

Instead of going out into the world, we could return home and start by using our scholarly disciplines—psychology and anthropology—as points of departure, investigating where they lead. As the Maroons say, you cannot find out what is inside a mudhole without using a stick to stir it up. The stick could be psychological and anthropological science.

The Matrix of Culture Analytic group psychology maintains that a culture's ability to survive is contingent on being able to develop a shared body of knowledge, a matrix, or web of individual relations, in which the whole is greater than the sum of its parts (Bion 1961). A matrix is a fund of knowledge characterizing an organization; it is a structure that can be talked about and that has not only an emotional content, but cultural and ideological content as well.

The basis for a matrix of survival is the shared development of a body of knowledge, which gives a form of solidarity and inertia to the group. This shared knowledge binds the strong forces which exist in large groups into a shared concept.

Among the Arhuaco Indians, for example, the matrix finds expression in their loom. Using it as a shared concept, they managed to build up modes of thought that kept chaos at bay and provided security and continuity instead. The loom was the point of departure for part of their counterculture. Although it was used in ways we would call psychotic in our culture, in the Arhuaco context it was part and parcel of their worldview, creating order in society and nature.

Among the Motilon, the long house was their matrix. It could accommodate their apparent anarchy and lack of structure, imparting order and security. The long house was a kind of cultural center, containing in its mode of construction such information as kinship patterns, functional leadership, and the organization of equality. In a manner of speaking, the long house was woven into nature and became the point of departure for several of their concepts on horizontality and verticality. When the mission destroyed the Indians' long houses, their matrix disappeared and the group dissolved. Fleeing into isolation was the only way they could get sufficient space to build their long houses unperturbed, thus preserving their cultural matrix.

Each community has its focal points which express the core of the culture. In Chemescua it was depression and learned helplessness that became the inhabitants' matrix, which they attempted to correct and treat with shamanism. Among the Maroons it was the medieval stage, with all its improvisations and individualized creativity.

However, even if it is possible to distill the core of each culture through its matrix, one is not automatically provided with an explanation for why some cultures survive and others perish. The survival of the Indians is also dependent on external conditions. The concept of matrix may well contain the various ways in which the culture can defend itself against the larger society, but it is not the matrix as such that insures survival. Rather it is the way in which the cultures create an interplay between the matrix and the surrounding society.

There are very strong forces in a large group, and if the group articulates an inexpedient matrix, it will dissolve. Intelligence gets transformed into power and coercion, and leadership becomes hierarchy and the worship of authority. As in Jonestown, the group fell into dependency on the leader and on coercive organizational forms. Here, the matrix was Jim Jones, who with his paranoid and divisive defense mechanisms got the group to close in on itself, so that in the end it ate itself up.

If a community is to survive, the most important goal for its matrix is to keep the chaos of the larger society outside. According to Patrick de Maré, whose field of study is large groups: "Where there is chaos, there shall be matrix" (de Maré 1975, 155).

In a group-analytic sense, there are several ways of describing how chaos can be kept away. For example, one could say that a group's ability to solve a problem is influenced by the various basic assumptions it forms regarding the way it works, and thus the extent of its possibilities for existence and survival. For example, a group may be characterized by the following traits: conflict avoidance, or fighting among its members; pairing off, or rivalization; and submission to, or rejection of, the leader. Bion says that these basic assumptions "develop immediately, unavoidably and instinctively" (Bion 1961, 153). Each group is characterized, then, by some of these basic assumptions. However, if the group hangs onto them too long, its work and survival possibilities get inhibited. The mature group, in contrast, is capable of maintaining order in its own chaos by attempting to get acquainted with some of the basic assumptions it has made about itself, which thus enables it to stand apart from these assumptions.

The most diminished groups of the Indians and slaves can also be described on the basis of these group-analytical concepts. Those societies that have had the greatest difficulties surviving are the ones that have not been able to free themselves from their basic assumptions. Chemescua is an example of a society that was inhibited by its dominating pairing and rivalization. Among other things it had a concept of illness that might lead a man to accuse his neighbor of casting the evil eye on him, or to form an alliance for gossip and drinking with the man across the street, in order to build up his self-confidence. After the Motilon had come into contact with the missionaries, they were characterized by dependency and rejection of a leader. They had become all too dependent on the self-appointed leader, the missionary, and could not shield themselves from him by fleeing.

In a group-analytic sense, one can make the hypothesis that the group best at surviving is the mature group which has acquired the greatest knowledge of its unconscious formations, such as its matrixes and basic assumptions. The Arhuacos and the Maroons could then be seen as mature groups, because they had a thoroughly clarified relationship to their matrix and knew precisely what to say and what not to say, when asked about their loom or their history. Their matrix had taken centuries to develop, and it slowly became conscious for them through confrontations with the white colonizers and slave owners. In contrast, the People's Temple never built up a matrix, but rather lived on an ideology that was emotionally based, vaguely formulated, and dependent on the moment. Jonestown had precisely the criteria of an immature group: escapism, dependency on a leader, and hostility toward its surroundings.

The Ecological Psyche: "The Earth Is Our Mother" If we are bold and transfer the psychological experiences from large groups to communities, we can say that survival is contingent on the ability of communities to develop a matrix and gain consciousness of its basic assumptions. However, these group-analytical concepts do not afford the entire explanation. On another psychodynamic level, one can say that this matrix is necessary as well to prevent members of the society from experiencing anxiety that is overwhelming.

Challenging existential anxiety is, in another sense, the challenge of separation and individuation. In the ultimate psychological sense, it is about how the child separates from the mother. In large groups this anxiety is transformed on the one hand into a fear of not belonging to the group, and on the other hand into a fear of being swallowed up by it.

In Jonestown this anxiety about separation and engulfment was used as an instrument of power. While punishing a member at a public meeting, Jim Jones once said, "You are being expelled from the masses, but by the masses you will again be restored" (Reiterman 1982, 342). Among the Maroons, in contrast, cultural obstacles were used to keep individual members from being absorbed by society. The defense strategy they chose was to place top priority on individual expressiveness.

The individual's way of resolving the problem of individuation and separation from the large group determines the form of his anxiety. Each and every individual is singular and unique, right down to his or her fingerprints. Thus, a societal form that is valid for many people will inevitably contain aspects which are foreign to the individual. It is the experience, interpretation, and resolution of this foreignness that determines the individual's survival. The weighing and balancing of the significance of the individual against that of the group recurs on a larger scale in the relationship between the significance of the community as opposed to that of the larger society. Just as an individual appears to the group, the community is also unique and foreign to the larger society. It is the balance between this separation and integration that determines the community's survival.

It should be emphasized that psychological experience shows that only the anxiety that gets expressed can be combated. This means that when a unique individual, either a person or a community, is confronted with others, the interchange—the speaking, the action, and reaction—is important as an outlet for anxiety. It is the information about the differences between the parties that permits survival; this applies to individuals in relation to large groups, just as it applies to ghettos in relation to the larger society.

From an anthropological point of view, it can be said that truth lies in the act of communication. Or as Lévi-Strauss has put it, "We cannot avoid the act of exchange, because it is through exchange that culture as a system is built" (Lévi-Strauss 1969, 145).

However, even though anthropology claims that we must exchange our differences in order to survive, it is not thereby the case that the matrix of survival always takes the shape of an exchange or communication between two dialectical poles, as for example, unique individual/general civilization, or instinct/culture. On the contrary, survival is dependent on the group being able to form new dimensions that substitute and transcend the old oppositions.

Arhuaco Indians have managed this transcendence, as seen in their expression, "the earth is our mother" (Elsass 1987). They define themselves in a larger context than that of individual and the larger group, which gives them good possibilities for survival. Similarly, the Maroons define themselves in relation to slave history when they use the expression "First-Time" or say "Once when we were born of Mother Africa" (Price 1983).

Thus Indians and slaves can choose to solve the psychological question of how the child liberates herself from the mother by defining human beings as being just as dependent on nature as a newborn baby is on its mother. Survival for them is a new kind of consciousness, in which separation anxiety gets substituted by a universal symbiosis with the earth, history, and offspring; an ecological psyche in which personal identity enters into relationships in ecological as well as historical contexts. Unlike our way of erecting boundaries in relation to our surroundings, the large group, and nature, the Indians see themselves as part of a much larger context. They consider the self to be a false delimitation, only a verification of an all-embracing and coherent process.

Indian and European Ego Perception We are about to arrive at a matrix for survival which the Indians themselves might formulate as "the earth is our mother." However, when we use an expression that belongs to the Indians, there is the latent danger of reading it incorrectly, putting our own projections into it about what the Indians are like. To the Indians "the earth is our mother" is an expression of their ecological psyche, which bespeaks a world-view and an outlook on life, whereas in our context, ecology is rather the backdrop for romantic dreams that in practice rarely extend beyond our own vegetable gardens.

There is indeed a difference between the way in which Indians and Europeans delimit themselves in relation to their surroundings, a delimitation that stems fundamentally from differences in their experiences of identity. Among us, the self has been separated and individualized, in contrast to the conception of self among many Third and Fourth World cultures, in which the self does not exist as an isolated entity (Marsella 1985). In our civilization, the self is first and foremost an entity that relates to the individual, connected to a lesser and lesser degree with his or her family, the surrounding culture, and nature. People have become so individualized that responsibility for one's life has to a large degree been left to the individual alone. To us identity is something the individual tests, changes, discards, and retrieves. It has become more fashionable than ever to go into therapy, and there is a constant supply of new living patterns in which individuals have certain possibilities of creating their own lives through the process of "finding themselves" and transcending their framework as well as familial prerequisites for change.

In contrast, identity among the Indians is a common assumption, immediate and continuous, not only a concern of the individual, but owned, in a sense, by his family and close community as well. Life in the isolated villages is to such a large degree tied to tradition that identity is often something one "inherits" from earlier generations. Similarly, it was not the loss of individual freedom that constituted the greatest threat for the slaves. Earlier they had lived very restricted lives in Africa, tied to one place and one people, and with a daily life consisting of a long list of obligations. The idea of freedom, understood to mean lack of ties and dependency on others, would have been frightening to them.

In our civilization, in contrast, subjectivity has become so fashionable that life, so to speak, is no longer transmitted in a directly dominant hereditary succession. The traditional reproduction of psychic identity has broken down, and a veritable explosion of pictures, dreams, and fantasies have been created in our heads, to an extent unknown to any of our ancestors (Brückner 1974; Bauer and Lunn 1984).

Jonestown was an extreme illustration of this psychic lack of history. Its inhabitants broke with their past and left at short notice for a new world and a new life.

The downside of this "liberation" is increased psychic stress. The less tradition spares us from responsibility, perspectives, and decision-making, the more our own identity conflicts and feelings of insufficiency impose themselves.

It is precisely this insecurity and narcissism that can lead us to an incorrect reading of "the earth is our mother" matrix of the Indians. Our separation conflicts, our individualism, and our much-too-punctuated experience of self make us long for the opposite; unity with the whole world, including the Indians and slaves. We believe as well that their earth is our mother. The result has become that slaves and Indians can only protect themselves against our narcissistic omnipotence by establishing an even greater separation from us.

The New Type of Human Being: The Survival Artist The attempt to articulate a psychology of survival presents some cognitive problems that stem from our own unclarified relationship to the very same concepts we are attempting to describe in the context of Indians and slaves, notably separation and individuation.

It is precisely when working with the idea of matrix—an analogue rather than a digital concept—that dynamically unconscious processes can penetrate into our comprehension. In order not to be trapped by our own defense mechanisms, we must attempt to become acquainted with as many aspects of the psychology of survival as possible, and look, for example, at the meaning of the concept of "survival" in our own context.

Critical theory claims that our narcissistic culture has become a culture of survival. This critique of modern civilization accuses us of self-pity and hypocrisy, and of defining ourselves as being among the last survivors—as victims, that is, who are still alive in spite of our civilization's dissolution. The background for this critique is our weakened ego-structures, which no longer can resist and contain the plurality, disunity, and in the ultimate sense, unintelligibilty, of our surroundings. In order to manage everyday life, we protect ourselves with survival strategies that create control and order. According to scholars of the culture of narcissism, such as Hans Kohut and Christopher Lasch, we often act out of selective apathy, emotional distancing, disregard for the past and future, and on the basis of a decision to live one day at time, here and now (Kohut 1977; Lasch 1979, 1984).

Our civilization has developed a new type of human being: the survival artist. He fixates on any and all bad news and takes it for granted, thus warding off his own personal despair. His ideology is that crisis lurks everywhere, and one has to be prepared for the worst. He is uncritical and lets himself get agitated about any bad news. He refuses to distinguish between the information that truly threatens the future of humankind and the news that simply threatens his peace of mind. Survival becomes over-dimensioned. Extreme situations are transformed into everyday stress, and in a dramatic way, he sees small, everyday transgressions as signs that crisis, catastrophe, and doom are close by.

There are several reasons why our civilization has developed this new human type. From the point of view of a psychology of personality, the survival artist's strategies are a defense for protecting his narcissistic personality.

However, all the talk of the culture of narcissism has by now made the concept of narcissism into our own hypochondria, in which just about every crisis can be seen in light of our increasing ego-weakness. There may then be other reasons for the increase in the number of survival artists, reasons that can be found in structural relations and in the uses of language by which terror and catastrophe are communicated to us.

In the very formulation and description of terror there are some characteristics that rapidly exhaust our ability to react intellectually as well as emotionally. Bruno Bettelheim, one of the few psychiatrists who survived a stay in a concentration camp, and who has since written several books on the psychology of survival, describes how defense mechanisms against information on terror and mass murder quickly set in. His experience from the camps was that "a few screams filled us with extreme horror and a desire to help. Endless hours of screaming only led us to the one wish that the screamers would be quiet" (Bettelheim 1979, 260).

One of the reasons for this repression is that the destruction and eradication itself are carried out in an extreme language, which can only be used in the very same extreme situations. The language of terror loses its force when repeated. It is as if the moment of annihilation can only be remembered in a way that deprives the victims of their significance and meaning.

Thus, there are characteristics in the way extreme situations are communicated to us that put our intellects out of function. When we hear

Campigne, August 6, 1973

I had a polaroid camera with me when I went out to the Motilon. An anthropologist had told me that the best thing you could do was give the Indians photographs of themselves. In a visual sense it affirmed their identity without giving rise to false dreams of big-city temptations. One day I gathered the Indians together and said that I would take a picture of them—on a little piece of paper I would recreate them in their own reality. Unfortunately, however, I had gotten the wrong film, and every picture I pulled out of the machine was black with a few stripes of light.

The Indians giggled and looked at the pictures with surprise. Thus I came to understand that the way a photograph captures reality does not necessarily lead to permanence, but on the contrary, to irretrievable loss.

about terror, we may lose our grounding. Our mode of thought may become much too abstract and global. If we think too much in terms of larger systems, we lose the ability to think in a politically strategic way, staying in touch with the concrete transgressions that take place. We may, for example, degenerate into romantic ecological notions, taking the statement, "The earth is our mother" at face value, both as an expression of the disappearance of the rain forest and of our nation's pollution. But we have few ideas of what we can do concretely and politically.

On the other hand, terror can make us so emotionally upset that we completely lose perspective, and can no longer think globally or focus on the future. Our orientation is rather toward the immediate here and now, and we turn to our vegetable gardens, living by the precepts of "the earth is our mother," which we cultivate according to non-toxic ecological principles.

Information about destruction and apocalypse can agitate us, but it can also seduce and pacify us into avoiding taking a stand and acting concretely. In our descriptions of the last remaining Indians and slaves, it is easy to fall into the trap of appearing as survival artists ourselves. The Indians are defined as the last survivors, and our rhetorical key words are expressions like "annihilation," "colonization," "extermination," "catastrophe," "crisis," and "ruination."

We ought, then, to be on guard against a survival psychology in which Indians and slaves are only a study for ourselves, and in which our pervasive ethnocentrism cannot leave them in peace. In our intellectual games we may exploit their death, popularizing and interpreting it, and present their extermination merely for our own scholarly or polemical purposes.

The Heroes of Survival To avoid being seduced by the rhetorical expressions of the survival artist, it can be useful to turn toward our own civilization and examine the concrete data that lie at the base of our psychology of survival.

Research in this area has primarily taken as its point of departure the extermination of the Jews in Nazi concentration camps during World War II. While it would be a banalization of the Jewish experience to apply it directly to that of Indians and slaves, descriptions from the Holocaust can nevertheless add several dimensions to an understanding of how people survive under extreme terror. In particular, the descriptions show various aspects of our need to give the victims the status of heroes, in the case of Jews, as well as Indians and slaves.

Early accounts of survivors from concentration camps were remarkably matter-of-fact and factual. Not before the 1950s and early 1960s, with the Holocaust at some distance, did survivors begin to build up theories and speculations about what they had seen. One theory focused on Jewish passivity. Why did millions of Jews go calmly to their deaths without putting up a resistance? Prejudices and projections were the basis of seeing Jews as meek and nerveless people who let themselves be led to the gas chambers without a murmur, descriptions that were close to the Aryan ones, in which the Jew was seen as a slight, cringing man of feeble build, a moneylender with his nose in a book.

To get behind the prejudices against the weakling Jew, psychiatrist Victor Frankl, a survivor himself, formed his theory of logotherapy (Frankl 1966, 1970). He had observed that prisoners died at the point at which they gave up finding a meaning in life. Some were capable of living a long time, and perhaps surviving, even though their physical condition was miserable, precisely because they felt life had meaning. The goal of the concentration camp was to deprive the prisoner of a sense of life's meaningfulness, allowing terror to become a threat to his will to live. To survive the prisoner had to give suffering a meaning and find significance in a meaningless world. This was Frankl's way of turning the prejudices against the weak Jew into an existential problem. Later he extended his experiences from Auschwitz to the psychiatrist's consultation room. Psychiatry became a survival mission of sorts, with carefully planned therapeutic sessions that brought the patients to discover their own personal values, enabling them to repossess the meaning in their lives (Frankl 1970).

Bruno Bettelheim, who, as mentioned, had also survived a stay in a concentration camp, took personal integrity as his point of departure in pursuit of a prerequisite for survival. His survival psychology attempts to describe what types of personalities survive. His assumption was that apart from hoping for the Allies' victory over Hitler, there was very little concentration-camp prisoners could do to secure their survival. The prisoners' only possibility was to cling to their individuality and, like the slaves, strengthen their expressive and creative selves in the small details of everyday life—details that could not be controlled or detected by the prison guards. By keeping individual and spiritual morality high, they could combat personality dissolution and hope that a little something would be left if the improbable should happen and they should come out alive (Bettelheim 1979, 1986).

However, Frankl's and Bettelheim's theories of survival being contingent on a meaning in life, or on a highly individual and spiritual morality, are not completely congruent with the descriptions of experiences that later came out of the camps. On the contrary, it turns out that many survived by cooperating with the executioners, by informing on each other, and by stealing from the ill and dying. Those who survived were often the ones who were best at procuring food and eluding the toughest work. Thus it was not always the heroes who survived. Physical survival would often exceed concern for spiritual morality; in an almost animalistic sense, the life force was stronger than ideas and ideals. Bruno Bettelheim wrote that under extreme conditions prisoners regressed, living in the moment without hope or solidarity with others. Friendships were formed and dissolved from one moment to the next (Bettelheim 1979, 79). The biosociologist Terrence de Pres says that the people who survived were often emphatically dogmatic fundamentalists, such as Jehovahs' Witness, or—at the other extreme—petty criminals who cooperated with the guards, sacrificed their friends, and knew how to build up a relationship with the executioners involving sexual dependency (de Pres 1980).

Old-fashioned hero morality failed as a model for survival. Morality based on personal responsibility became an antiquated notion. Instead of elevating spirit over body, the experiences from the death camps were a resurrection of the body's unheroic and unglorified grief. Many of the survivors had discarded hope, and thereby also despair, surrendering instead to a biological will to live. In order to survive, the individual had to surrender to his or her biological and animalistic drives and to suppress the spiritual values of morality and ethics. The camps eliminated the possibility of there being a higher meaning of life. The survivor became, in a sense, the person who had lived through the crisis of civilization and suffered its breakdown.

Applying this psychology of survival to Latin America, it can be said that for the Indians to survive and bring themselves back to life, they would have to live through grief and face the colonial death room. Like the Indians in Chemescua, survivors do not necessarily become supermen and worthy Indians—but often minimal heroes, disheveled people who all too easily fall prey to alcohol and suicide's easy way out.

Many Indians and descendants of slaves end by taking their own lives. In a parallel sense, many of the survivors of Nazi camps feel guilty for living (Bettelheim 1979). They get weighed down by feelings of guilt for having stayed alive while someone close, or even someone they did not know, died instead. Many former concentration camp prisoners end, like the Indians, in suicide, because they feel morally unworthy and powerless (Eitinger 1964).

The Hardy Personality In recent years one has begun to generalize and extract psychosociological patterns of survival from death-camp experiences. Some representatives of modern stress research regard accounts from concentration camps as survival manuals (Lazarus and Folkman 1984, 203). One of the central focuses is on the fact that many prisoners survived by using defense mechanisms like denial and selective apathy. Some developed totally conscious adaptive mechanisms, concentrating on narrow and limited goals. Today the same adaptive mechanisms have been redefined by our stress researchers as "coping behavior," which they claim characterizes people who face stress and burdens in their everyday life. Certain personal traits, it has been found, allow some people to manage the daily struggle for survival better then others. For example, those identified as "hardy personalities" live longer and have fewer stress symptoms than others (Kobasa 1979; Kobasa, Maddi, and Kahn 1982). According to Hinkle (1984), they are characterized by a marked ability to concentrate on the segment of reality they can deal with, and at the same time to achieve a state of psychic numbness and resignation toward the inevitable. Personalities of this kind are said to utilize more effective coping behavior, because they experience fewer situations as threatening and are quicker at mastering them.

Thus, part of modern stress research has redefined the old hero as a hardy personality. However, it is difficult to determine how much reliable research supports this new type of survivor, and how much is prejudice and ideology. From a scientific point of view, the delimitation of the hardy personality from other personality types has been criticized for not taking its point of departure in prevalent methodological principles within psychology (Lazarus and Folkman 1984, 212). The hardy personality comes close to living up to the demands made on a survival artist to be able to manage a separation between the *observing* I and the *participating* I, to be able to decide to forget the past and live exclusively in the present, to cut off emotional ties periodically to family and friends, and to cultivate indifference to the pleas of others for help.

Thus parts of modern stress research reinforce the crisis of our civilization, by putting priority on ahistoricity and individualism as important character traits among survivors.

This focus stands in glaring contrast to the Indians and slaves, who were able to survive because they placed their highest priorities on collectivity and historicity. Parts of stress research have thus been allowed to be infected by the dramatic and catastrophic nature of the extermination camps, which document a loss of faith in the future.

Normal People Commit Violence The very process of articulating a psychology of survival seems to contain some obstacles which make us look time and again at our own denial and repression. The researcher who sets out to describe the characteristics of survival discovers that he is part of the violence which combats this very survival. Our problems with understanding this are in the deepest sense connected with our being a part of the society that practices terror against the Indians.

A look at psychological research on the ability of the ordinary person to use violence and terror may help us shake off the survival artist's rhetorical statements.

The psychologist Stanley Milgram carried out some experiments in which he examined the ability of ordinary people to terrorize someone they did not know, if they were ordered to do so. The leader of the experiment ordered each participant to give electric shocks of gradually increasing painfulness to another person, in order to investigate the relationship between punishment and learning.

The subjects used in the experiment were told to press a button which transmitted an electric shock to someone restricted to a chair in another room. Although no such person actually existed, screams were audible over the loudspeaker. The first time the subject pressed the button, no sound was emitted, but after a while the screams got louder and louder, and the voice finally shouted for help and asked for the experiment to cease. If the subject refused to continue at this time, the leader of the experiment insisted that they go on. If he refused again, the experiment was discontinued.

Among the participants in the experiment, 65 percent continued with the torture and obeyed the leader at all stages of the experiment.

Milgram reported, "I once saw a mature and dignified business man come into the laboratory smiling and self-assured. In the course of twenty minutes he was reduced to a cowering, stuttering wreck on the verge of a nervous breakdown. He kept tugging on his earlobe all the time and wringing his hands. At one point he hit himself on the forehead with his fist and muttered, 'Oh God, let's stop this,' but he continued and responded to every word the leader said, until the experiment was over" (Milgram 1974, 377).

Other examples can be mentioned of normal persons committing violence. For example, the war criminals who were placed on trial at Nuremberg were subjected to psychological examinations. Harrower (1976) let the tests be evaluated blindly, setting up a comparative control group in order to investigate whether an unbiased psychologist could arrive at the existence of a particular "Nazi personality." He concluded, "These personalities are not generally a particular type or character and are neither mentally ill nor in other ways deviant, but can be found in any country in the world today" (Harrower 1976, 362).

Indeed, psychological research shows that normalcy can be the basic substance of anyone who commits violence (Jensen 1978). This knowledge is relevant to an understanding of the Indians' situation: it is a point of departure for acknowledging similarities between ourselves and the intrusive missionaries, oil hunters, and landowners.

Victim and Victimizer In "The Survival of the Slaves" we have described the character of violence as illegitimate and unacceptable behavior, both irrational and bestial. These emotionally loaded words, however, are only used by those who become witnesses to, or victims of, violence. Its practitioners, in contrast, justify it as a rational and legitimate necessity. When violence becomes most uncontrollable and destructive, the tendency is for both perpetrators and victims to start accusing each other of being violent. Both parties fight to get power in the public sphere; each regards himself as hero and the other as a representative of barbarism. In structural terms the contrasts merge, and equality between friend and enemy arises.

In other words, it is not always obvious who is guilty of violence, who is the victim, and who is the victimizer. It has been mentioned several times in the preceding sections that whites and Indians relate to each other as victimizer and victim, or that the slaves have often placed themselves in a relationship to the master in which a mutual dependency arises. All are components of the same system, to which each contributes through stabilization and consolidation.

This interpretation of role switching between victim and victimizer is not to be taken so literally that one might judge Indians and slaves guilty of their own suppression and destruction.

In order to gain a better understanding of the role of victim we assign to Indians and slaves, we can start by looking at the victim-victimizer relationship as it is played out in a torture scene. The structure contains an asymmetrical relation, similar to that of other unequal relations, like teacher-student, doctor-patient, coach-athlete, or judge-defendant. In order to play the second part, of the victim, one has to exercise self-control and allow oneself to be subjected to suffering. The victimizer, on the other hand, has to communicate a method, or ideology, that under the heading "I'll teach you," contains various forms of pleasure for him. The relationship is like a game between opponents, in which one symbolizes powerlessness, and the other possession of power. In this asymmetrical relationship, however, the center of gravity can suddenly change, and just as Jesus received a crown of thorns at the Crucifixion, the powerless victim can be elevated to the point of achieving perfection in death. Thus, in the relationship between victim and victimizer, there is an image of a theatrical stage with onlookers who are ready to recognize the sublime and elevated status of the victim (Brandt 1980, 141).

On the stage of the unconscious, the victim-victimizer relation passes through various phases. After the victimizer's initial indication of who has the power, a phase ensues in which the torture victim reports that there is a change of mood. He now can experience moments of feeling an unexpected and paradoxical affection for his torturer, a feeling of sympathy which can unite the two of them (Brandt 1980, 141). The torturer inflicts wounds, pain, and mutilation on the victim in order to make him break down and confess. However, not only must he confess what he knows, he also is supposed to do more than that: to break down and give what he does not have. This attempt to give something one does not have is, in a psychoanalytic sense, the same structural relation that characterizes desire (Lacan 1981). The victim "desires" the victimizer in order to make him stop. He beseeches the divine powers for help, or invokes a political cause, to get strength to withstand the suffering and humiliation.

Torture and terror rarely create any change in the victim's connection with his ideology or political conviction. It is very possible that the victim breaks down and confesses under torture, but when he comes back to his cell the pain and suffering will often make the victim feel more strongly bound to his convictions, which are the locus of the meaning of his suffering.

The meaning of torture is that suffering leads to truth. "One must endure much suffering" before arriving at the truth. Per Åge Brandt says that this truth "is acquired through bestiality, which transforms it into a purifying pleasure, a pleasure which in principle is received by the torture victim in the throes of his fear of dying" (Brandt 1980, 142). With this assertion we have penetrated into the logic of the unconscious, where negations and contradictions are mediated, where desire is displaced by suffering and vice versa. In a figurative sense, the victim has become more closely linked to the victimizer.

Perhaps Freud can bring us back to the Indians. He offered an explanation of how desire and suffering could displace each other. He distinguished between desire and violation, claiming that due to the offensive constraints on the fulfillment of needs early in the development of so many people, desire will often be connected with violation at a later point in life (Blond 1977). These connections between violation and desire, suffering and pleasure, victim and victimizer, often arose in societies which no longer had an ideological base and a common spiritual morality and ethics (Freud 1961).

Put another way: When it is no longer possible to maintain a supporting matrix for survival, new cultural forms develop, with demonstrative and dramaticized mechanisms of suppression, and with the public as participating audience. Like the victim, Indians and descendants of slaves have to endure much suffering, because they disturb the new and all-too frail ideological base and matrix that the New World is trying to build up. In a reformulation of Freud's words, it can be said that by taking the Indians' suffering upon us, there is an unconscious hope that they will show us the way to a new truth.

The background for our assigning the Indians and slaves this role is that our civilization, despite all its material and cultural goods, has nonetheless not been able to satisfy us and supply norms and control. We have revoked the incest taboo and lost our culture, as discussed in the chapter on Jonestown. Here incest was an expression of there no longer being an authority outside the family in the form of an unambiguous social morality or a common historicity.

Every time there has been an ideological breakdown in the course of history, and the matrix of a culture has suffered destruction, new forms of bestiality have arisen. The regulating mechanisms have turned into prejudices, and become the rhetoric and stereotypes of an enemy image, like that of the white man and the Indian. When the rhetoric no longer sufficed, violence broke out in its direct, naked, and repressive form—and murder of a culture became murder of a people; ethnocide became genocide.

The Mimesis Myth If we push even further into the arena of the unconscious, we can supplement this Freudian rhetoric with some considerations made by the French historian of religion, René Girard. On the basis of an analysis of Western myths, he claims that aggression and terror have always been present, but in order to find a cause, and place the blame for it, the group invents a victim that incarnates violence. Harmony can only be reestablished when this victim has been lynched and done away with. As long as the victim is alive, he is pointed to as a disturbing element, and only by his death is peace and order restored to society. With the aid of this victim, society gets split into two parts, a winner and a loser of the desired object. To achieve peace and prevent the two parts from destroying each other in battle, the object is regarded as taboo, off-limits, and non-acquirable for either of the contending parties. The victim, who formerly bore the guilt, now becomes sacred, and in order to eliminate evil violence, one resorts to good violence, the sacrificial offer that creates order and harmony.

As the real object never does get conquered, our culture has to continue repeating the sacrificial ritual. Thus Girard describes our society as having entered a "mimesis crisis," in which we keep on seeking revenge in one long chain reaction, which cannot be stopped and which disguises and circumscribes violence (Girard 1982).

Using this mimesis crisis as a point of departure, the Indians can be said to have become scapegoats for the inner conflicts that plagued

Europe at the time of Columbus, and with a sure sense for repeating rituals, we have continued to sacrifice the Indians to our own inner conflict. Our half-hidden violent character has made us all complicit, so that no one really knows how he or she contributes to the terror.

What were the Indian societies like before Columbus's arrival? Girard claims that violence and aggression have always been present in society, that is, that the pre-colonialized Indians were also characterized by disturbances and disharmony, structurally speaking, of the same inner conflicts as today. Many people prefer to imagine the Indian societies as fundamentally harmonious and peaceful, and that our presence changed them into belligerent and self-destructive peoples.

History does not help us here. It has a peculiar way of closing around groups like the Mayas and Incas, societies which it describes as having suddenly disappeared, as if they expressed a communal hocus pocus, went into the jungle and were never seen again. This description has made room for many of our romantic projections about the peaceful Indians that had to perish at the expense of our aggressive culture.

If we turn to the biosociologists for an explanation of the Indians' administration of aggression, we do not get much help either. They offer some vague statements about aggression being the species' preservation instinct, essential for its survival (Lorenz 1966; Marvin 1979). We are driven by the same instincts as our ancestors, but we differ from the animals in that our aggressive drives can be self-destructive and lead to our extermination. Freud, too, regarded the human being as fundamentally destructive and healthy only when eros won over the death instinct. Biosociologists would probably join Freud in saying that with Columbus's arrival, aggression in Indian societies turned into destruction.

Some of these statements may repeat the same relations over and over again, each time clothed in new rhetorical phrases. However, when they are included here, the intention is for them to supplement each other. The psychology of survival neither can nor ought to be conjoined into one coherent body of theory. Concepts like matrix, victim-victimizer and mimesis crisis do not in themselves contain sufficient explanatory value. However, when they are juxtaposed, they can become concepts of the relation between relations. The psychology of survival does not make this relatively intelligible by using a single, one-dimensional, analytical-logical language. Its concepts are analogous, rather than digital. It is not concerned with "either-or," but rather with "both-and" and "more-or-less" thinking. Thus it is possible to involve many more sciences and carry out systematic examinations, including, for example, the dynamic unconscious as well.

Silence as a Presupposition of Terror The study of the unconscious processes in the psychology of survival points toward a theoretical and cognitive change in paradigm. However, other more concrete and cognitive aspects of a psychology of survival also make it imperative to find new descriptive modes, erase old modes of speech, and defy the immediately seeable. In a larger sense, the change is needed because survival relates to terror as an opponent, and it is in the very nature of terror that opposing it necessitates a change in the mode of speech.

The most important characteristic of terror is that no one is allowed to know anything, and yet everyone has to be responsible. Terror demands silence and unambiguity. Protest, survival, and resistance must then institute the rule that it is under all circumstances more important to talk than to be silent.

Terror during the persecution of the Jews presupposed the cutting off of all information from those who knew to those who did not. The extermination could only be carried out as long as it was not discussed. Words like "murder" and "extermination" did not appear in any of the highest-ranking secret documents. Instead the words were camouflaged as *Endlösung der Judenfrage, Sonderbehandlung,* and *Evakuierung:* "final solution of the Jewish question," "special treatment," and "evacuation" (Hilberg 1980, 23). These repressive mechanisms not only had the purpose of getting terror to function efficiently, but as Reich said, they were psychological protective mechanisms for the executioners, "a way of making violence fall into place according to the unconscious needs of the masses" (Reich 1972, 75).

Terror against the Indian peoples has also been shrouded in silence. It is perhaps not as apparent in European and North American contexts, where a good deal of informative material and scientific reports on their situation have been produced, especially among radical intellectuals, anthropologists, and sociologists. However, the closer one comes to the Indians in a physical and geographical sense, the less information there is available. The Latin American governments who are responsible for the Indians, and who often declare themselves protectors of the Indian cause do not publish any reports. Furthermore, very little is heard from the missionaries, who have followed the Indians more closely and longer than anyone else. Unfortunately, there are only a few Latin American anthropologists who have produced scientific reports which measure up, both in scope and scientific standard, to what is published in the United States and Europe. Informative material on the Indian peoples, then, is largely produced outside of Latin America and is directed at the young intellectuals at universities in Europe and the United States.

To break this wall of silence regarding the extermination of the Indian people, it is important to find new modes of speech which transcend customary Western university traditions. A new formulative mode may well not create a dialogue with Latin Americans, but it is the first necessary step in the direction of producing a clearer understanding.

Thus, a ground rule in the psychology of survival is that it is under all circumstances more important to talk than to be silent. Struggle and resistance in the face of terror entails the necessity of speaking, describing, communicating, naming, discussing, taking risks even in wrong contexts, mentioning relations that may not be important, and even lending significance to trivialities.

A New Understanding A new mode of speech and a new understanding are needed, but not at any price. The demand for a change in paradigm must not lead to value being placed on any and all new articulations. It is still necessary to demand a scientific standard, so that we do not end in uncritical verbosity.

A prerequisite for finding out where our new mode leads us is that we start by examining our own point of departure, and the cognitive difficulties we are immersed in.

One of the general interpretive problems in describing an Indian society is that we are seduced by our own culture to believe that every Indian expression is authentic, inherent in nature, and physically present. From a linguistic and structural point of view, when a capitalistic culture encounters a non-capitalistic community, it embraces it with its own concepts and a cocksure belief that it is observing and interpreting comprehensive, objective truths (Taussig 1980). The essence of the suppression of Indians and slaves can be said to reside in the way our concepts attempt to make non-capitalistic thought modes redundant.

Resistance essentially consists of reestablishing this lopsidedness by using other thought modes. In the 1970s, we thought Marxism bore new hope for survival, but the linearity of the logic informing the Marxist concepts became so predictable that it lost its powers of renewal. Today we are forced to find other associations that can disturb the metaphors of suppression.

However, in the search for new forms of understanding, it is all too easy to get seduced into a new kind of idealism, an uncritical nostalgia. If we avoid sharpening our demand for methodology and just say that the Indians have their own logic, which each of us must attempt to capture through impressions and intuitions, we will very likely project our wishes for another and better life onto them. Traditional native societies become burdened with our dreams and wishes to return to a mythical Golden age. We use them as a projection screen for our own longings.

I became aware of this power of projection when I went back to the Arhuaco Indians to read them the book I had written, *Indianerliv* (Elsass 1977). As I have mentioned, I had written there that they lived in a pact with nature and in harmony with the group. But when the Indians had heard me read, they leaned back from the campfire and said that *Indian Life* was interesting to listen to, but more about me and my dreams than about them and their daily life.

Psychological research shows how we project our own understanding onto what we see when we experience other people's behavior, in order to put meaning into the meaningless, to create order out of chaos.

The psychologist Franz From has made studies which included showing a film with actors moving around, arbitrarily and aimlessly. Nonetheless, all the viewers experienced the behavior as having a purpose and a meaning (From 1965). In the same way, Indians have experienced being assigned intentions that they have never had. Therefore, it can be necessary when observing foreign peoples to start with the presupposition that everything is meaningless in order to keep one's Euro-American projections in check.

It can be difficult to accept meaninglessness when one initiates fieldwork among foreign peoples, but it is a prerequisite for being able to understand.

From my own clinical practice I know that as a therapist I must endure long periods during which I feel ignorant and helpless. Therapy is based on openness toward the unknown in any individual, and the more I appear to know, the less the patient will open up for new understanding. As a therapist I must train myself in restraining "immature comprehension." It serves no other purpose than as "a defense against the discomfort of knowing that there is something one does not know" (Casement 1987, 13).

The same conditions prevail in relation to a foreign culture. A prerequisite for successful fieldwork is that one starts by shedding "the protective layer of indisputable truths" (Sjorslev 1988, 163). One "must consciously and critically keep trying out the suppositions one had already arrived at" in order to reach an understanding of the particular (Knudsen 1988, 169).

Decolonization It is nothing new to say that every foreign phenomenon is judged and described on the basis of one's own personal assumptions. Researchers have known this for a long time. However, it is interesting to see how researchers at different times have tried to avoid letting science indirectly become a description of their own biases. Since they could neither negate nor brainwash themselves, one of the possibilities was to become a deserter who ran off to the natives all the time and risked losing his or her identity. By turning their backs on Europe and settling among natives, they could repress the colonialism that gave rise to their projections.

Research thereby became a cultural criticism of colonialism that quickly spread from science to the cultural sphere. It started in the form of movements and isms, in which the artist's personal reactions to the demands of his times—for normalcy, oversocialization, and hypermasculinity—were chaos, individuation, and "pathological" answers (Gay 1984).

In England people like Oscar Wilde, E. M. Forster, Somerset Maugham, W. H. Auden, and Virginia Woolf turned against the colonial consciousness that manifested itself in India. At the same time, the universities in Oxford and Cambridge began to liberate themselves from the dominating, imperial train of thought.

In France, surrealism and dadaism arose, and people like Artaud and Gauguin distanced themselves from the oppressive conditions in Africa and Oceania, settling as they did among the natives. At the same time, a new intellectual leadership took over the Sorbonne.

In Latin America, the same development took place. In the big cities, writers like Vargas Llosa, Fortes, Cortázar, Carpentier, and Asturias, all children of the well-to-do middle class, began to write against colonialism. At the same time, the radical intellectuals built up universities in Buenos Aires, Bogotá, and Montevideo.

Europe between the wars was still flirting with the idea of wildness, and among writers like Conrad and Yeats, fascination was intact. They left a chaotic Europe, journeyed out to meet the noble savage, and came back filled with nostalgia and longing for the true, original human being they had met in the wild.

In his dadaist period, Apollinaire once said on the way home from a party, "One goes home on foot to sleep among fetishes from Oceania and Guinea. They are all Christian, but in another form and a better faith" (Apollinaire 1971, 117).

Thus researchers and artists began to believe that their only possibility for survival was to go native—to live among the natives.

Psychoanalysis was encompassed by this reaction as well. Freud, with his interest in anthropology, described the preoccupation many native peoples had with their history, using magical rituals to relive and reexperience it (Freud 1961). Freud found parallels to these anthropological observations in psychoanalysis, which also provided a method for individuals to rediscover and relive their own histories. Since modern individuals do not necessarily know their own history, and often experience time as irreversible, psychoanalysis became a way of reestablishing the past, both in the present and future. The self shed its skin, and in a reaction against the colonial point of view, which insisted that the self win control over the material world, it was now seen as a matter of gaining self-knowledge. The individual's maturity was contingent on an understanding of the subconscious and its social and biological history. Freudian self-realization came closer and closer to the conception shared by many of the Indian peoples that the more the self knew about itself, the more it would understand how it reflected universal ecological laws.

In art and science, the 1930s formed a reaction, a cultural decolonization, in which intellectuals and artists tried to break the circle of terror (Nandy 1983).

Later however, this counterculture became too ambiguous, intellectual, and chaotic. The journeys back and forth between native societies and our own civilization became a cultural seesaw, a swingboat of the identity. Many solved the dilemma by harboring a one-dimensional political point of view: we went out in solidarity with the suppressed.

Our own disappointed expectations from the sixties and seventies made us seek shelter among peoples like the Indians and slaves. We assigned them all the promises and utopias our own existence denied us. The revolutionary hope that had suffered defeat in the industrial countries got pushed further and further away, first to Russia, then China, and then to the Third World and the Fourth World. "Liberation was relegated to others," Enzensberger said (1987, 28).

Thus cognitive development has moved in a spiral. In the thirties, going native was the way to achieve personal liberation, and in the seventies, solidarity with the same peoples was the path to political liberation. The structure in the development has been the same, though the end result leads to another level each time.

Understanding as a Shamanistic Ritual Today the development from personal and political liberation has reached what could be called a change in paradigm, in which unpredictability and the subjective part of history have become essential elements in a new understanding. Postmodernism has become the slogan, and the new scientific mode of thought bespeaks interpretations of meanings, and contextual relativism, instead of unambiguous truth. Chaos and disorder—irrationalism—has come into focus, and psychoanalysis is of interest again, because in its description of the unconscious, it uses psychological processes that are non-linear and unite incommensurable differences. One of the requirements of this new science is to have the capability of quickly changing perspective and to be ironically self-conscious about its own assumptions.

Many examples can be given of how researchers are departing from earlier cognitive modes:

Rosaldo writes that the traditional anthropological description is like a book of "etiquettes of good behavior" (Rosaldo 1984, 138).

Sass says that "the consistent descriptive mode with its strict methodological demands has made the Indians disappear under the carpets in the corners of the universities, senior rooms" (Sass 1986, 55).

And Wolf: "The church of anthropology has gotten into trouble. Its sacraments have been stolen. People have peeked behind the altar and have found nothing there" (Wolf 1982).

Taussig: "A new understanding must be built on a distrust of coherent explanations, a recognition that scientific facts are not facts at all,

Mamankana, November 10, 1983

Salvador and I are good friends, but the contact between us always deteriorates when one of us begins to ask too many questions about the other's daily life.

For example, a few times it has happened that I asked him about the Arhuaco Indians' funeral rites, or how they celebrate weddings and births. After listening to my questions for a while, he usually turns the situation around and begins to ask me about the most peculiar things. What does a plane ticket from Mamankana to Copenhagen cost? What time is it in Denmark when it is noon in his country? How big is my house and how many cars do I have? What are the names of my mother and father? At first I attempt to answer dutifully, but after a while he gets cantankerous, and I answer his questions with increasing brevity. As, by the way, he does with regard to my questions.

Our friendship is situated smack in-between his and my reality, and if one of us gets too curious about the other's reality, the contact between us evaporates.

but when it comes right down to it, interpretations of interpretations" (Taussig 1987, 445).

Geertz: "The clear-cut realistic tradition in research has become doubtful, because it is dependent on being able to hide the fact that science cannot exist without being written outside the representational mode. Style is no longer decorative; style is substance" (Geertz 1986, 35).

These examples can be summed up as a reaction against a science that all too often has had as its goal to make the world predictable.

The old modes of understanding were but disguised repetitions of the old prevailing ideas. Thesis and antithesis comprised the same understanding, and partners and opponents were part of the same structure. The forms for understanding victimizer and victim, Western civilization and Indians, became a mutual support system. This structure insured the continual repetition of violence and terror.

Therefore, science had to present a challenge, a constant provocation that broke the pattern of repetition. However, this so-called change in paradigm was not only to be a rejection of old ideas and an introduction of new concepts, which were useful for the time being until better ones were found; it was also to be a continuation of the common quest and an insistence on liberation as a central theme.

One example is the shamanism of the Indians. Even though there are many studies of healers, modern anthropologists like Taussig have criticized them for not offering any understanding of why Indians are able to find their survival in magic. Generally speaking, one of the purposes of magic is to create chaos and disorder and add the element of unpredictability to the seeable (Taussig 1980, 1987).

Shamanism is one of the most important elements in the survival of the Indians. It was the basis upon which the Indians were able to organize and throw out the missionaries, as happened among the Arhuaco Indians. Moreover, shamanism has been used by Indians in an attempt at dealing with depression, allowing them momentarily to see it as a symptom of poverty and decolonization, as was the case in Chemescua.

It is characteristic of the shamanistic process that the knowledge it produces does not have a continuous, logical structure that slowly but surely emerges at some predictable point in time. The Arhuacos did not know that they would take over the mission station and throw the missionaries out until a few minutes before it happened. Some mamus had stepped aside and gone into a shamanistic ritual, suddenly revealing some pictures, which had made it necessary to gather everyone together and then take over the mission. In Chemescua the healer drove his patient into strange stories which no one could really believe in, but which nevertheless got the patient to combat the neighbor's "evil eyes" or the mountains' "bad winds" or whatever was put forth as the cause of the symptoms. Shamanism consists of a montage of unpredictable pictures, with the shaman himself becoming wild and uncontrolled in his rituals. The aim is to create pictures that repossess the wildness the Indians had owned prior to colonization, thereby creating disorder in Western thinking.

Similarly, it can be said that the new paradigm within science has the power of bringing disorder into the traditional way of perceiving reality as an objective and continuous entity.

Many advocates of the new science express themselves in ways that characterize shamanistic rituals as well. Foucault says, "we must learn to accept that the effects of truth are produced within a discourse that is in itself neither true nor false" (Foucault 1980, 118). A parallel to this statement can be found in a Mexican shaman, Miguel de la Cruz, who says, "We can no longer contribute with anything original, but at most put things into a false context" (Michael 1973, 9).

Science begins to resemble the shamanistic process, which Lizot described as a theater in which the Indians could gain insight into our world and "how its objects, words and actions have lost their original meaning and have been replaced" (Lizot 1978, 123).

Or as Artaud wrote after going through a shamanistic ritual: "If confusion is the sign of the times, then I see the cause of this confusion in the break that has arisen between objects and words, things and ideas and signs they represent" (Artaud 1981, 56).

Words begin to flow together, and much of the phraseology fits the new science as well as it does shamanism. It is as if anthropology and psychology, for the sake of survival, have begun to resemble the shamanistic rituals to which the Indians resort when they are ill or have to get rid of the old missionaries. We have been possessed by the same magic.

Order and Wildness In summary, it can be said that Indians and slaves have become metaphors in a psychology of survival. With their implicit demand for a change in paradigm in our own sciences, they give a reflection of an original culture in our modern technological society, but they afford us the grounds for another understanding, because their mode of thought is different from ours.

By starting with a perception of "the earth is our mother" as their matrix for survival, we gain other conceptions of the self; it becomes an ecological psyche that breaks down old relations and stretches over earlier divisions in time and space.

With the Indians as metaphors for survival, political classifications break down. Their organizational forms like Indianidad give no possibility for maintaining the old distinctions between right and left, liberal and conservative, revolutionary and reformist, progressive and reactionary. The plurality of the many different Indian groups has to be contained in a unified movement, if they are to survive. The result is not necessarily a single manifesto on liberation. On the contrary, each culture can have a totally different answer to the questions of technology, ecology, exploitation, and repression. The struggle for Indian survival is often an unstructured process in which the different peoples mirror themselves in each other, and instead of trying to find a common goal, they try to find a common footstep.

With the slaves as metaphors, the question of who has power and who commits violence loses validity. When we attempted to penetrate into the slave's relation to the master, the victim-victimizer dyad kept turning around, casting doubt on whether our dynamic psychology could foster an understanding. Unconscious processes made both parties suffer from the very thing they were fighting against in others, just as Jonestown took its own life to avoid being eradicated by the enemy.

If all the fragments are to be gathered into a psychology of survival, it would have to involve a consciousness that our civilization cannot get by without the Indians and slaves, and yet we must suppress and exterminate them. This paradoxical contradiction between life and death stems from our narcissistic need to define ourselves as the last survivors. If the Indian people and the descendants of slaves are to survive our civilization's crisis, they will have to define themselves as a counterculture. They will have to be capable of clearly delimiting their individuality in the face of the larger society, and able to be separate without becoming isolated. They will have to be constantly alert to the next move of their opponent.

The most essential characteristic of an adversary is that it keeps on defining itself in relation to the dominating culture. However, in contrast to the Jews and their reactions to the death camps, Indians and slaves are characterized by another kind of resistance and struggle, as the cultures with which the conquerors arrived were qualitatively different from their own. The Jews, in contrast, were to a larger degree part of the culture that imprisoned and ghettoized them, with the intention, finally, of exterminating them. Indians are marked by difference and therefore can define themselves, to a greater degree than the surviving Jews in our society, as opponents.

However, a counterculture involves more than just survival. It must also have its own cultural content for nourishment. The paradox again is that if it only feeds on itself, it will eventually become incestuous and cultureless. Culture lies in communication, where the partner in dialogue is the larger society. But knowledge is power, and if the smaller community gives away too much of its knowledge, it loses power; if it gives away too little, it becomes incestuous. Or as the Maroons say, "There are a few songs about which it is said that if you sing them, you will die; and yet people still have to sing them."

There is a Latin American expression that characterizes the Indian countercultures as "the cockroaches of our civilization." They are nourished by our filth, and even if all efforts are made to exterminate them, they turn up in the most unexpected places and at the most inconvenient times.

In the same way, one can say that the more our Western culture has attempted to extend itself out into the world, replacing exoticism, the more plurality has crept into our own society. It is as if the more the Indian peoples get eradicated, the more they turn up as metaphors among us, as minorities, subcultures, and as political and religious sects. Either they come from outside, disguised as refugees and foreign workers, or we produce them ourselves in the form of deviants—psychic, cultural, and moral dropouts. We need deviants in order to confront ourselves with counter-images of our own culture, without which we would lose our grip on ourselves.

Durameina, November 15, 1983

The Arhuaco Indians of Durameina were very isolated. They were full of skepticism toward me and offered me nothing. But when I had packed my backpack and was about to go on to the next village, two Indians came over and invited me for coffee.

One of them said offhandedly that some foreigners like me had once come by offering them help. Wanting nothing to do with them, the Indians told them they would be better off helping their own society. There was more use for them there.

When they finished telling the story they added that the cost of the coffee and the night's stay was 450 pesos.

Our journey to the last surviving Indians and slaves is over. As time has gone by, it has demanded greater courage to return from the journey than to start out on it.

On the way back, certain concepts have been turned around. It is no longer the Indians who are wild, but us. From the perspective of the Indians and slaves, it is our Western culture that appears to be the "wild" one; attempting with power and terror to keep out turbulence, discordance, and confusion.

But every one of our demands for order and uniformity loses meaning in the absence of the contrasting forces, wildness and plurality. The Indians and slaves are metaphors for this wildness and plurality; our survival depends on their voice being heard.

2. *Advocacy*

With Kirsten Hastrup

I am always a little ambivalent about advocacy. I always want to advocate; but I also think that they (the people I've studied) could speak better for themselves than I could for them. And, further, to make myself as advocate would provide the other side—government, officials etc.—with an excuse for not talking to the people themselves. . . . I have to distinguish between the local community's need for my advocacy and my emotional and intellectual need/inclination to sympathize with them. I decided long ago that my advocacy—such as it is—had to lie in my ethnography: in presenting them and the complexity of their lives in a way that they would feel did them justice—Cohen in Paine 1985b, 258

On our travels back and forth among the Indians and slaves, my wife and I have rethought our presence in the field. We have used our background in anthropology and psychology, respectively, to consider the role of science for our work among other peoples. Thus we have reconsidered the concept of advocacy in relation to our concern about the survival of the Indians with respect to two concrete experiences from our practice among the Arhuacos—making a film and promoting a project (Hastrup and Elsass 1990; Elsass 1991).

In order to supplement the preceding conclusions, an appendix has been added which takes its point of departure in the academic fields of anthropology and psychology instead of the chaotic field of the Indians and slaves.

As implied in the above quotation by Cohen, "anthropological advocacy" is an ambiguous term. It relates to a praxis which ranges from the writing of ethnography to our active engagement in pleading a particular cause. In the first instance, anthropological advocacy is an inherent feature of anthropological practice in general. It is part of the profession, while in the second we get dangerously close to a self-contradiction.

Our intention here is to discuss the notion of advocacy in order to approach the question of whether it can ever be "anthropological" at all. It is an attempt to meet the challenge formulated by Robert Paine and others, to make a professional statement about the kinds of things we do or should do as anthropologists (Paine 1985b, 257). It is also an attempt to sort out the complex problems raised by the Arhuaco Indians of Colombia, who asked us to promote particular interests. Given our different backgrounds in anthropology and psychology, respectively, we soon found ourselves engaged in a vivid dialogue on the subject of advocacy and we realized how important it was to raise professional awareness of the subject. It is even more pertinent for its bearing on the discussion of anthropological practice in general.

A preliminary conclusion to our discussion is that advocacy, as such, is incompatible with anthropology as a distinct kind of scholarship. To become advocates, anthropologists have to step out of their profession, because no "cause" can be legitimated in anthropological terms per se. Ethnographic knowledge may provide an extremely important background for engaging in individual advocacy for a particular people, but the rationale for advocacy is never ethnographic; it remains essentially moral. Even anthropologists have moral responsibilities, however, and a discussion of the relationship between anthropology and advocacy is badly needed.

Through the following exposition of our own experience with the Arhuacos we approach this relationship from various angles. At each stage of the process we attempt to show how difficult it is to reconcile the role of advocate with that of the anthropologist. The range of the difficulties often impedes action, but sometimes advocacy is no option but an inherent demand in the social relationship established between the anthropologist and the local people.

Applied Anthropology The concept of advocacy immediately acknowledges the position of the anthropologist as intermediary. While this position has now been recognized as theoretically inevitable, it used to be reserved for *applied anthropology.* Set apart from anthropology in general, applied anthropology was unprestigious and seen as an endeavour of the half-baked anthropologist: "Malinowski sent me to study social change because, he said, I didn't know enough anthropology for fieldwork of the standard type" (Mair 1969, 8) The implicit message, that applied anthropology dealt with change, while "real" anthropology dealt with the reproduction of social structure and other sophisticated matters, is not accidental. British anthropology, at least, explicitly linked applied anthropology to studies of social change (Mair 1969, 3); more specifically, it dealt with social change that was externally induced and made the anthropologist cooperate with the government (Grillo 1985, 6). This, of course, is highly debatable since applicability covers much more than cooperation with external authorities in the interest of local development (Gulliver 1985, 38).

The distinction between studies of structure and studies of change cannot be maintained either. With the general historicization of anthropology came the insight that even the reproduction of a social system may contain its own transformation (Sahlins 1981). Social change is not solely induced from outside.

Another point is that, although the detached involvement implied by fieldwork (Agar 1980) can be more or less detached or involved, and will often be a matter of both personal choice and ethnographic circumstances, no anthropologist can escape involvement. The discussion of applicability, therefore, is pertinent to any kind of anthropology; theory is no shield that protects the anthropologist from the use of results. The very *presence* of the ethnographer in a world that contains its own problems, forces us to rethink the role of the scientist vis-à-vis the people under study, whether the actual intent is development or not (cf. Hastrup 1990c).

Insofar as anthropologists now realize that their subject matter always implies a degree of involvement, which of itself contributes to local change, we need a renewed theoretical debate on the actual position of the participant-observer in the course of development. There are few well-established canons about the practical role of the anthropologist, apart from the old ones of remaining objective and staying away from native women (cf. Wallman 1985). Although perhaps ideal in the scientific world, such requirements are impossible in the real world; fieldwork is now openly recognized as a personal encounter, and ethnography seen as an intersubjective reality (cf. Hastrup 1987, 1990a, 1990b). From the current perspective on anthropology there is no way in which the anthropologist can claim to be outside the material; subject and object merge in a world of "betweenness" (Tedlock 1983, 323–24). This is the source of applicability and, indeed, the starting point of advocacy.

Just as the maker of anthropological films must admit that even the apparently neutral method of self-presentation to some degree reflects the filmmaker's presence (Elsass 1991), no anthropological monograph can hide the fact that cultures are essentially "written" (cf. Clifford 1986). But in spite of the fact that the implicit scope of the anthropological endeavour is to make a fieldworker the author of a book (Sansom 1985, 6), even the role of the author in the writing of other cultures has largely been ignored until recently. Small wonder, then, that the hidden role as an agent of change—whether willed or not—has been completely neglected.

Although the founding fathers had purely scientific intentions, their effects were certainly applied (Whisson 1985, 132). If, in the present postmodern position, theory and application merge on the one hand, subject and object on the other, we are forced to consider the practical implications. These are further complicated by the fact that the peoples we study are increasingly articulate about their own opinions and rightfully expect something in return for their information. Which position should the anthropologist choose as a position for exchange, if anthropology as such no longer fulfills the requirements?

One possible position is that of the advocate.

Advocates and Clients An advocate is one who pleads the cause of another, and the role presupposes active engagement (Henriksen 1985, 121). Even this is ambiguous in anthropology however, because there is no sharp division between *self* and *other* in the anthropological discourse; they are categories of thought rather than objective entities. The anthropological advocate, therefore, cannot claim to plead the cause of the other in any straightforward manner; we believe that this point is implicit also in Anthony Cohen's statement about advocacy.

Cohen also implies that there are different *kinds* of advocacy inherent in the anthropological practice, qualified as either "speaking for" or "presenting" the people. A first consideration suggests that these modes of advocacy are but different *degrees* of what is essentially one coherent practice. There is a continuum of anthropological interest, from countering (Western, colonial) ethnocentrism by providing systematic knowledge about other cultures, to actively pleading the cause of a particular ethnic group vis-à-vis a government (cf. Van Esterik 1985, 60ff.). In principle this continuum leaves no anthropologist untouched by the problem of advocacy. Even a purely academic interest in other worlds ultimately leads to a kind of representation. When academic interest turns into active advocacy, the problem of representation becomes a problem of "speaking for," but these modes are not opposites, just different degrees of practical involvement. Theoretically, however, these modes differ in their baseline of legitimization. Ethnography is legitimized by established canons of scholarship and *creation* of knowledge, while advocacy rests on moral commitment and *use* of knowledge.

When anthropologists turn into advocates they have been criticized for furthering "the colonial processes still at work by stealing crucial decisions and political initiatives from indigenous peoples" (Henriksen 1985, 124–25). This is owed to the fact that speaking for somebody often implies the making of clients. Advocates and clients are seen here as complementary roles, qualified as active and passive, respectively. Client making in anthropology must of course be met with skepticism as one more instance of paternalism, but passivity need not be the final outcome on the client's side, even if advocacy initially suggests that the professional takes over the initiative. It may be part of the professional strategy to raise the client's consciousness about the situation so that the client may resume responsibility for his own actions, irrespective of the advocate's personal opinion. Structurally, the two positions are complementary, but even within a relatively short time perspective, the dynamics of the interrelationship may shift the active and passive roles around, just as namer and named may constantly change place in the fieldwork dialogue (Parkin 1982, xxxiv). Drawing a parallel to psychotherapeutic work, where a vast number of different kinds of therapeutical relationships reflect as many theoretical stands, we can see how the relationship embedded in advocacy also has a myriad of expressions—reflecting all possible anthropological stands and a multiplicity of local situations.

In the following we shall discuss two particular cases of advocacy, thereby demonstrating how the complexity of the relationship increases with a deepening understanding of the local—ethnographic and political—situation.

The Film Project

The Advocacy Effect of Two Films An analysis of the effect upon the audience of films about ethnic minorities may provide an important basis for discussing the filmmaker's role in advocacy.

In some films the subjects can more easily be advocates for themselves, whereas others give better possibilities for the filmmaker to act as advocate for the filmed subjects. The first kind are films where the subjects are placed in front of the camera speaking directly to the audience without commentary; these are the so-called observational films and are based on the method of self-presentation. The other kind are films where the method is more self-reflective, in that the context of the production is part of the film, as for example when the director reveals his personal views through a narration. In a way all films are both self-presentative and self-reflective, because both the filmmaker and the filmed subjects are influencing the final product, but the emphasis may be different.

Of course many factors contribute to the final result, such as the control of the camera, selection of the shot, and the editing, but in this section we will focus on the position of the filmed subjects.

Concretely, this will be done by describing and analyzing the reactions of different audiences to two films about the same ethnic minority, the Arhuaco Indians in Colombia. One of the films was made by the method of self-presentation, and the other was based on the self-reflective method. The two films were shown both to Western audiences and to the Indians themselves.

Although both films had the possibilities of being shown to Western audiences, it was the self-reflective film which gained priority and was repeatedly shown. *The Earth Is Our Mother* has often been shown at meetings held by grass-roots movements in support of the Third and Fourth Worlds. The explicit intention has been to stimulate the debate on how our part of the world has been responsible for the suppression of minorities and how a political and moral action could be arranged. For such audiences it has been important that the film is discussed after the screening; the scenes where the Indians react directly to the presence of the film crew have been especially debated.

Although the Arhuacos generally like to discuss and reflect a great deal, they did not have the same interest in discussing either *The Magical Universe* or *The Earth Is Our Mother*. They had the possibility of seeing both films as often as they liked, but most of them viewed the films only once or twice.

Only when directly questioned did the Indians offer any comments. They never commented on any of the scenes which reflected the presence of the film crew. The scenes they mentioned were the ones where they explained their daily life, their cosmology, and their relationship to the environment. They complained that the subjects in *The Earth Is Our Mother* were far too briefly presented to give a coherent explanation and to reveal the logic of their proper way of thinking.

During the filmmaking the Indians had insisted that they were to be shown neither drunk nor poor, but these two conditions were so common that it was virtually impossible to avoid them in the films. In *The Earth Is Our Mother* there was one scene in which an Arhuaco leader spoke directly to the camera while quite drunk, and in another, two Indians were digging in poor soil for something to eat. Although the scenes were intended to reveal the Indians' political situation and their relationship to the earth, they might also have been read as a message of drunkenness and poverty. But directly questioned, the Indians did not have bad feelings about them. As one of them said, "As long as the scenes gave a primary message which was right, the second message was of less importance."

This differentiation between a primary and secondary message is in accordance with the way in which the Arhuacos responded to the general intention of the films. They were often more willing to engage in general reflection and to relate the films to an abstract codex, in contrast to the Western audience who mostly reviewed the film scene by scene.

For the Indians, the director's advocacy in *The Earth Is Our Mother,* of fighting for the Indians' right to self-determination and land, was of secondary importance. One of them stated, "The most important message the film should deliver is that we, the Arhuaco Indians, represent a vision for a better and more meaningful life. The film should portray our way of thinking and living to the white people; the political struggle for preserving our land is of secondary importance."

However, the general result that the Indians preferred the film based on their self-presentation, and the Western society chose the film based on the director's self-reflection, can be attributed to other differences than the choice of methods.

There were differences in the settings of the two films; the Western audiences were not the same and the two films were produced by different directors and companies and had different aesthetic and technical styles. But these differences are presumed to have minor importance: both films were independently reviewed by critics as excellent and of a high professional and technical standard. Thus, the differences between the two films cannot change the general conclusion that the two audiences preferred the versions that were closest to their own cultural context.

Self-Reflection or Self-Presentation The film based on the subjects' self-presentations is the method closest to the informants' unsolicited visualizations of themselves. However, since the foundation of *cinema direct,* the filmmaker's status as an interpreter has changed into a self-reflective position. In the pioneering work of Jean Rouch, film was openly recognized as an interpretation of reality, and the camera was named a *participant camera* or a *living camera* (Rouch 1975, 86). MacDougall in particular has introduced the self-reflective method; his point was that not to interfere with the situation to be filmed is a "curiously irrelevant ambition for an anthropological filmmaker" (MacDougall 1975).

When making a film the subjects are always in some ways transformed, in a process which involves both the method of self-presentation and self-reflection.

A. First, the filmmaker must let the people themselves talk, so their self-presentation can be clues to understanding.
B. Thereafter, the filmmaker has to acknowledge that as soon he has taken life out of its context to capture it and mediate it to an audience, it is the filmmaker himself who presents it, not the people. He has to create their reality against the background of his insight within the rules of the drama.
C. Finally, the filmmaker must understand that the presentation is always a representation.

Although the method of self-presentation emphasizes the first step, and the method of self-reflection the last steps of this process, both methods have the possibility of showing the anthropologist's subjective and interfering interpretations. Therefore, the two methods cannot be distinguished on the basis of the filmmaker's involvement. The distinctive difference between self-presentation and self-reflection is in their views on the status of the subject.

In the method of self-presentation, the Indians are the subjects; they address themselves directly to the audience on the basis of their own culture. By using the method of self-reflection, it is the filmmaker who becomes the subject, and he shows the audience the situation of the Indians from his own context. The two films speak from two different subject positions and, consequently, they have different potentials for advocacy.

Authenticity In the analysis of the audiences' reactions to the two films, the concept of authenticity is essential. The polymorphous language of film has a perceived "closeness" to its subject, and a degree of authenticity which is not immediately established in a written text. In comparison to a text, film and photography pass for incontrovertible proof that a given thing actually happened. As Susan Sontag writes, "The picture may distort; but there is always a presumption that something exists, or did exist, which is like what's on the picture" (Sontag 1977, 5).

For the Indians, their self-presentation in *The Magical Universe of the Arhuaco Indians* resulted in a stronger experience of authenticity, whereas the film did not have the same potential among Western audiences. The Westerners experienced the strongest authenticity in the second film, where one purpose was to acknowledge the filmmaker's entry upon the world of his subjects.

One immediate solution to the problem of authenticity and advocacy is to place the filmmaking in the hands of the people themselves, because this procedure gets closest to the ethics of self-determination and legislation. Since the pioneering work of Worth and Adair (1972) among the Navajo Indians, there have been many examples of indigenous people making excellent films themselves. Thus, MacDougall reports that in a film about the Australian Aborigines, self-presentation had provided an opportunity for expressing the community's opposition to government and landowners' interests (MacDougall 1978). Also some of the Inuit people have successfully taken over media productions (Brisebois 1983).

The situation for indigenous people in Colombia is so acute, however, that it is an unrealistic solution to hand over the filmmaking to the Indians. The Arhuacos cannot wait for the possibilities to create their own media production; they need support now, before their land and culture disappear. In this respect, the self-reflective film is more powerful in gaining the attention of a Western audience, but the method also implies some risks. With reference to the Arhuaco case, we can see how easily a self-reflective film and the alleged advocacy of the director may manipulate the Indians into the role of clients.

Filmmaking about the Fourth World is especially problematic in this respect. There is a strong tendency in a Western audience to interpret a film about the Fourth World with reference to a preconceived notion of the suppression of the self-determination of the people, and to transform it into moral and political stands. This transformation may prevent the audiences from making discoveries which might reduce their ignorance about the culture of these people. In this connection it should be remembered that the Arhuacos' primary criticism of *The Earth Is Our Mother* was the lack of information about the ideational aspects and uniqueness of their culture.

A problem in using the self-reflective film is that the ethnic minority has to create a distance from the film at the outset, because they are a minority. To be an ethnic minority requires sociocultural contrast for its validation, and the ethnic peoples sometimes have to create this contrast in order to maintain their identity (Berreman 1983, 290). Although the director was loyal to the Arhuaco Indians in the self-reflective film, he created a drama according to the rules of his own culture. That may be the reason why some of the Arhuacos had to create a distance to become actors in a Western drama, simply to maintain their ethnic identity.

Another problem in using the self-reflective method is that the one-sided version of the director may be experienced as single-minded. One study has shown that a one-sided version in a media presentation contributed more to the raising of consciousness in a Western audience than a two-sided version (Henny 1981). The reason was supposedly that "the one-sided version led to a higher level of controversy, which is partly due to the fact that audiences in the West are conditioned to expect pluriform information" and "a one-sided film tends to lead automatically to the integrity of the filmmaker" (Henny 1981, 155).

When showing *The Earth Is Our Mother* in Western cinemas, the audience often demanded time after the screening for discussing the film with each other. For the Arhuaco Indians, it was not important to go into such discussion. The one-sided version was single-minded in the Indians' view, and not very important to discuss. For the Western audience the one-sided version was taken as an expression of an engagement and concern which also required that they take a standpoint.

But even if a Western audience is better prepared for a one-sided media presentation, it does not guarantee that the filmmaker's message is transmitted. An audience will sometimes learn something which is unintended and perhaps "wrong" from the filmmaker's point of view. Experiments within the field of psychology of perception have shown that even when the intention of behavior is very consciously made up, the audience can perceive it in another way in accordance with their needs and inner drives (Jensen 1978). The mental process which transforms the stream of events into impressions and moulds them into cognition is mainly an unconscious process, generating a vast number of alternative interpretations. Even a film which presents a situation without any purpose, and with actors moving about according to a script calling for randomized behavior, can be experienced as having a purpose (From 1965). There is therefore a latent risk that the advocacy of the filmmaker may prevent his message from coming through in the way he intended, or as the indigenous people would accept.

The general conclusion must be that the choice between using self-reflection or self-presentation depends on which audience the filmmaker wants to address. The self-presentative film implies fewer risks for the adequacy of the filmmaker's advocacy, but it may not have much effect on a Western audience. The self-reflection film contains risks for an erroneous advocacy, but has larger potential for gaining support in Western society.

As a filmmaker, one has to include the indigenous people in the decision about which method to use. The solution is not always to let the people do the work themselves. For some ethnic minorities, their situation is so acute that the filmmaker has to take the responsibility and do the directing on his own account.

The indigenous peoples are divided in their level of self-reflection. Some are familiar with the international political language, and the style of pressure groups, while other are not; some are familiar with the film media and others are not.

In both films on the Arhuacos, it was mostly the younger generation, who spoke Spanish and had some education, who were able to argue about the fight for survival in a language that was in accordance with Western logic and indignation. The traditionalists were older people who had difficulties in speaking Spanish and often used formulations which seemed too vague, abstract, and complicated to fit into a film suited for public broadcasting.

Possibly, both the self-reflective and the self-presentative film aggravated the division between the modernists and the traditionalists. For instance, it was agreed between the Indians and the filmmakers that the money earned by the films should go back to the Indian community. It was only *The Earth Is Our Mother* that made a profit, but it soon became an object of dispute between the traditionalists and modernists as to how to use this profit. The modernists argued that the money should be used for solving health and educational problems, that is, to buy medicine and schoolbooks. The traditionalists opposed this, because the money then would be administered by the younger people. Although it had the purpose of raising consciousness, traditionalists maintained that the profit so used would create a distance from the original values of the community where all health and education had been in the hands of the older people.

The problem about internal disagreement or unity is reflected in filmmaking. The method of self-presentation depends on a high degree of accord among the individual members of the community, while the self-reflective method more easily can incorporate comments about internal disagreements, as in the narration. The one-sided method requires a high degree of responsibility on the part of the filmmaker to understand the uniqueness of the culture. His advocacy depends on how successfully he can solve the paradox of making a one-sided approach when the cultural reality is pluralistic.

There is no method of filmmaking which is better suited to the Fourth World than others. The choice of method must depend on the audience to which the film is addressed. If the audience is local, the film should be based on self-presentation, but if it is meant for a Western audience the film should be self-reflective. The ethnic peoples themselves have to make the choice of method, but before that the filmmaker has to decide, together with the people, if they can be represented at all. This question determines if a film should or should not be made.

The Horticulture Project

A "Development" Program In 1988 we both visited most parts of the Arhuaco reservation, conducted extensive interviews, and heard their own elaborate views on their current problems within the Colombian state. Toward the end of our stay, they stated their explicit wish that we help them promote a particular "development" program, which allegedly would strengthen their autonomy in Colombian society. Very briefly, they suggested that in a particular region attempts should be made to reintroduce intensive horticulture with irrigation, which would then serve as a model for other regions. The region was a fairly well-defined valley area, embracing some eighty households. The prime movers were the women of the region, who had recently organized themselves, in an attempt to reclaim their position as "defenders of the Earth." The project thus had both highly ecological and cosmological overtones, and, further, it would support the women who appeared to be the principal losers in the process of acculturation. On these scores, we became rather convinced about the basic soundness of the project, even though we had little natural scientific background to evaluate the ecological side of it.

When the women's informal leader asked us to promote this project, she forced us to consider the question of what kind of intermediary position we were actually supposed to take: on the one hand, the Arhuacos stressed their position as an ethnic minority suppressed by the state, and without political means to defend themselves; on the other hand, we knew that there were many well-educated Arhuacos who had previously been perfectly capable of formulating applications and making demands to the government. A number of Arhuacos were currently being trained for professions as lawyers, linguists, and anthropologists. Also, in some of the semiprivate or official bureaus of Indian affairs, they had managed to achieve powerful influence through their lobbying efforts. While there is no doubt, then, that the Arhuacos are structurally dominated by the Colombian state, they are not actually so very "muted" in political matters. We wondered why they wanted us to intervene. Did they, in fact, just want us to do the dirty paperwork and the fighting with bureaucracy, so that it was our money and time that were wasted?

Previously, we had had good relations with the Colombian Bureau of Indigenous Affairs, Asuntos Indigenas, and had been allowed to travel extensively in the area and do research; but how would they react to our shift from the more passive role of spectators to a direct involvement as advocates for a particular cause? Also, were we not as ill-equipped as any other social scientist to deal with state bureaucracy? (Cheater 1985, 68ff.). We proceeded hesitantly.

At the bureau we learned that all economical support from outside had to be channeled through the government, or at least that all projects had to be coordinated with their own initiatives. This apparently paternalistic attitude covered a complex reality. On the one hand, the bureau was actually very interested in our supporting the Arhuacos by means of foreign aid, especially if it could enlarge their own budget for projects in the area. On the other hand, they were conscious that our work for the Indians might eventually turn out to be subversive to the government bureau. They explained how the bureau had to provide a stable link to the Indians amidst a very unstable and complex political situation. The shifting and often violent political scene was ultimately the determinant of the bureau's existence, and if we threw our project onto the scene without having an alliance with the bureau, we might unintentionally jeopardize the necessary continuity of their work for the survival of the Indians.

Being familiar with the rumors about corruption and big pockets among Colombian officials, we were uncertain whether the bureau's demand that we subordinate our activities to their initiative was but a smart way of laying their hands upon any possible outside funds. They were right, nevertheless, that the political situation was so complex that it was impossible for us to orient ourselves without local guidance. Apparently all the powerful elements of the Colombian scene—Indians, bureaucrats, politicians, *guerilleros*—had a vested interest in funds, whatever the actual project in the name of which it was donated.

In spite of our focus on the Arhuacos, it would be grossly naive to forget the crucial role of government bureaucracy in native affairs (cf. La Rusic 1985, 25). It is part of the historical context, just like the surrounding peasant populations are. Most of these are actually as marginalized and dispossessed as the Indians, and no less alienated from government bureaucracy. This realization led us toward new reflections about our position vis-à-vis the Arhuacos.

The Problem of Land We knew that the position of the Arhuacos in the Colombian context was very complex and that, therefore, there was no simple solution to their problems, let alone a simple recipe for our intervention, but we also knew that the Arhuacos had one major, unambiguous and very acute problem—the problem of land. From inside, soil erosion rapidly diminishes the tillable area, and from outside *colonos* ("colonists") infringe upon the reservation.

Land is often mentioned as the key to cultural and even physical survival of indigenous groups (Maybury-Lewis 1985, 137ff.; Bodley 1982). This also applies to the Arhuacos, whose territory has shrunk considerably although its boundaries are now fixed by law. The project was related to this aggravating scarcity of land, being an attempt to establish an intensive horticulture on irrigated fields—not an uncommon idea in local development these days. Immediately sympathetic because it would lessen the local dependence upon outside merchandise, and hence upon cash, the project had further appeal.

The view that native peoples have a dubious claim to land because other groups can make more productive use of it is not uncommon (Maybury-Lewis 1985, 139), and it is of general validity in Colombia, where the various Indian groups are in the minority. The intensification of agriculture within the Arhuaco area would counterbalance the force of this claim. What is more, it would also reestablish the historical link with the ancestral Tairona culture in the area, which was based on terraced fields and irrigation. Due to external pressure in the first centuries of colonialism, the descendants of the Taironas had changed to a more extensive agriculture. The project was thought, therefore, to strengthen the "original" Indian identity vis-à-vis the outside colonial regime. As part of a local strategy for organizing the women in particular, the project would be a clear message about "re-Indianization" of a people who were in a process of being overrun by the state society (cf. Varese 1982, 36).

This all seemed perfectly sensible at first sight, and is probably "right" from all sorts of perspectives; at least it seemed to agree with our own ideological scheme for the right things to support: fighting for the minority's right to their own land, re-Indianization, women's liberation, and so forth. On closer inspection, however, a whole range of new problems arose, suggesting how easy it is to become victims of unconscious notions of good and bad, and to become seduced by "them" into accepting one-sided and to some extent unqualified views of "us" and representatives from "our" world at face value.

First of all, why should we, who claimed to work in support of the suppressed, accept the Indian view of the colonos as enemies without further qualification? Were we in fact replacing one kind of ethnocentrism with another (cf. Wallman 1985, 18), and interpreting the colonos according to preconceived notions of unquestionable evil? Although there is probably a certain truth in Maybury-Lewis's general statement that "settler societies are everywhere unscrupulous about the rights of the autochthonous people whom they dispossess" (Maybury-Lewis 1985, 146), we should not overrate this point.

Evidently, there are unscrupulous settlers, but many colonos are probably poor, alienated peasants trying to survive, and dishonesty is not unheard of in the Indian communities either (cf. Jaramillo 1983). Both groups face problems of extinction that are generated by a complex society with immense economic problems and a remarkable incapability of enforcing its own legal rules—of land protection, for instance. In the antagonistic situation that resulted from this in the region of Sierra Nevada it was easy to resort to the anthropological gut reaction of wanting to protect the islands of culture rather than the apparently cultureless colonos, people of mixed and dubious origin in the marginal areas of the modern state.

The islands of culture, of course, deserve protection to the extent they want it; but this should not conceal the fact that other human groups may also be worthy of consideration. In our own first enthusiasm—which we are still prepared to defend—we were perhaps trapped by the romantic notions indelibly associated with the European vision of the Indian as the ultimate Other. It is worth considering the extent to which such gut reactions actually are extensions of the colonial order itself, because they lock the Indians within a set of Western metaphors and prevent us from a true apprehension of the particularity of their own views (cf. Varese 1982; Taussig 1987).

These questions boiled down to a rather complex problem: Were we prepared to be advocates for the Arhuacos, and in what sense could we speak for them at all, without possibly inflicting postcolonial romantic views upon them to the exclusion of a thorough understanding of the complex Colombian context? This required much more thorough reflection than the immediate and rather facile agreement to promote a particular project, and it was further complicated by considerations of representativity.

Anthropological Advocacy

Representativity Speaking for somebody presupposes that you know who they are. Earlier, anthropologists had an idea of the natives as if they spoke with one voice, their culture having been boiled down to the smallest common denominator. This no longer passes for truth in anthropology. Our "objects" are active subjects, speaking with as many voices as we. Furthermore, what informants speak are not cultural truths but circumstantial responses to the presence of the anthropologist (Clifford 1986). The group of individual Arhuacos who made their plea for intervention might neither be representative of the entire group, nor might their question be anything but an instantaneous attempt to take advantage of our presence. At least, we would be wrong in assuming that our intervention would unquestionably be for the good of the whole group, let alone for Arhuaco culture as such.

The problem of intervention is closely linked with the problem of interpretation, which turns out "to be an essential component of what [has] to be interpreted" (Taussig 1987, 128). Interpretation, in this sense, is inherently violent because it makes an effective counter-representation impossible.

Among the Arhuacos, the effect has been an adoption of a kind of inverse evolutionist model, which is actually a kind of ethnic chauvinism; as such it may be a necessary stage in the process of reconstructing the indigenous history (cf. Varese 1982, 31–32). The Arhuacos regard their white neighbors as a lower kind of people, and speak of them as younger siblings who still have to learn and to be looked after, because they know nothing. In that respect they are like their neighbors, the Kogis, who also claim that the white culture derives from their own (Reichel-Dolmatoff 1985). For instance, they contend that the white people stole the local name *Xusikungui* and transformed it into the name of Jesus Christ (Reichel-Dolmatoff 1985, 355). Thus, the Arhuacos have reversed Western notions of cultural hierarchy—and if we really wanted to speak for them, we would have to adopt this model, which is no more satisfactory than its inverse.

The enemy mirror always shows two faces, the enemy's and your own. For the Arhuacos this is related to the entire power structure in which they are embedded: their strategy for survival has largely been one of defining themselves as a counterculture (cf. Clastres 1977; Elsass 1987). In order to survive they have had to resort to social forms which *we* have determined as underdeveloped, but which were actually sophisticated forms of adaptation to the postcolonial context. One example is the shift from the previous intensive horticulture to extensive farming. The forefathers of the Arhuacos were part of the Tairona civilization, based on intensive agriculture on irrigated and terraced fields. When the conquistadors started to exert their pressure on the land, the local people initiated a more extensive pattern of agriculture, thus making their need for land more visible. Eventually, this efficient strategy made the Colombian government believe that the Arhuacos were in need of development aid, which the Arhuacos gladly received. But even that turned against them, when the new cattle breeding proved to contribute heavily to the grave problems of soil erosion.

The Arhuaco culture is not an unambiguous entity, then, and even if the counterculture could be seen as the effect of a particular powerstructure, it was impossible to overcome the acknowledged fact that cultures as such materialize in contrast to one another (Boon 1982). At the level of ethnicity, we know that "ethnic identity requires socio-cultural contrast for its validation, where the ethnic people have sometimes to create this contrast in order to maintain their identity" (Berreman 1983, 290).

Advocating a particular view on the "good" of Arhuaco culture implied a contrast to the Colombian (and Western) notions of the world and the necessary development. Even more importantly, it implied a choice between "good" and "bad" Arhuaco visions. We knew perfectly well that the community was divided among themselves on important issues. With a simplification we may speak of "traditionalists" and "modernists"—even if the distinction is far from clear-cut.

Briefly, the traditionalists suggest isolation and a return to the exclusive authority of the mamus as the only strategy for survival. The mamus were (and are) the traditional leaders, who had both secular and religious functions. Their authority has not been acknowledged as "power," a concept which has always had a Western (normative) bias and thus failed to include traditional (native) forms of power (Rubinstein and Tax 1985, 304). The modernists have largely accepted the normative view of power and have adapted to the Western power game. They have also changed their dress, cut their hair, and learned to speak Spanish.

We were immediately confronted with the well-known fact that the traditionalists are the most spectacular and the modernists the most articulate—at least in Spanish (Bodley 1982). Accordingly, the Arhuaco modernists became our prime informants. Like other anthropologists we knew little about internal politics in advance (Maybury-Lewis 1985, 143), and during previous visits the Arhuacos (the modernists, as it turned out) had explicitly stressed their unity. As proof of their unity they often referred to their joint venture with the traditionalists in 1982, when an impressive communal meeting followed by advice from their mamus resulted in the aforementioned exile of the mission from Arhuaco territory. When the Arhuacos were still able to identify an external enemy, like the mission, they could engage in joint action. Once the declared enemy had left the reservation, unity seemed to break apart; the communal meetings which had previously been held every year were abandoned, and strategies for survival diversified. At least in 1988, when we were there, closer inspection revealed little consensus and that the 'enemy' was creeping back in. Sometimes it was even brought in by the Arhuacos themselves.

It is a common feature that the new Indian intelligentsia, which is acquiring greater weight in Latin American nationalisms of various kinds, has its origin in what might be termed the Indian petty bourgoisie. They are typically the teachers educated in missionary schools, and are in general bilingual and almost bicultural (Varese 1982, 38). This also appertains to the Arhuaco spokesmen. In their jeans and sombreros, they were the ones to advocate support of "traditional" Arhuaco values, and ask representatives of the outside colonial context for help. In that sense, they were modernists. The "real" traditionalists, on the other hand, would have nothing of that; in their traditional white dresses and coca bags they would look to the mamus for guidance. The authority to manage communal resources had always been in the hands of the older people, and when we began discussing external economic support with the younger generation it was a breach of the elders' cultural code. Although the modernists verbally supported tradition, and sometimes claimed to be even more traditional than the traditionalists, our communication contradicted this claim.

We had to realize that our own work among them might actually split Arhuaco society further apart. Advocacy was difficult under these circumstances, and *anthropological* advocacy seemed impossible. Which part of the ethnography was most worthy of support?

The Need for Unity Quite apart from the anthropologist's problems of choosing whom to speak for, when presentation revealed at least two antagonistic groups within the community, the Arhuacos themselves faced a much more serious problem of cultural survival. We are not talking of survival in the sense of conservation, but in the sense of an inherent capability to define the future from the center of culture itself (cf. Maybury-Lewis 1985). To us it appeared that strategies of both traditionalism and modernism would raise serious problems in the Arhuacos' cultural survival and make them losers in the battle between different world-views.

The traditionalist strategy implied isolation vis-à-vis the external world. Historically this had proved a faint measure against external infringements. We are not only thinking of the colonos who want their land, and social scientists who want to expropriate traditional wisdom, but also of the many subtle ways in which the state and the bureaucracy encroach upon all minorities. Although anthropologists in general are theoretically ill-equipped in matters concerning the penetration of the state into the rural peripheries, we do know that one aspect of the penetration concerns the symbolic structure of policy formulation (Cheater 1985, 68). Isolation and lack of dialogue will eventually and inevitably entail a view of the necessity of outside policymaking. Someone will have to make decisions, and the traditional structure of decision-making will not be evaluated as anything but powerlessness. Even to concerned academics the traditional Indian movements often appear vague and romantic, and essentially useless in a concrete political discourse on Indian self-determination (Varese 1982).

A modernist strategy of biculturalism, on the other hand, may make the Indians victims of an externally defined development. By accepting the power game, they may get overruled by it, and by accepting a double cultural standard for their own negotiations with the outer world, they lay the foundations of a hierarchy of cultures—which may eventually subsume their own.

In this schizophrenic situation the Arhuaco modernists sought support from outside. They had made their own attempts to convince the government officials about the need to enforce their claims to land, and to improve farming conditions. The government was lenient, and the Asuntos Indigenas declared that they could do nothing until the Arhuacos became reunited in their views. In principle, the bureau could negotiate only with the traditional leader, the properly elected spokesman for all Arhuacos. In actual practice, he was a shadow of authority however, and the young educated people propagated their own views. They were the ones to ask us to promote their case elsewhere.

In short, we were facing almost classical problems of representativity in a divided community. Whose interests would we be representing if we advocated one particular strategy for cultural survival at the expense of another? Could we undertake a project in collaboration with people, if the internal political situation was not clarified? For the organization Cultural Survival, the answer clearly would be no (Maybury-Lewis 1985, 144).

If this attitude is taken too rigidly it may become a (false) justification for never intervening. Non-intervention may be right in many particular cases, but it cannot be a matter of principle. To demand unity of other peoples is unwarranted when our own society and institutions are split into multiple factions. Even within an international culture of bureaucracy the institutional split may lead to breakdown of communication and cooperation. For instance, the Danish Red Cross became interested in contributing to a health project among the Arhuacos, but could not proceed without the consent of the Colombian Red Cross. Funds were raised, project descriptions made, and the Arhuacos became very keen on it, since it would allow a handful of them to receive formal education in healthcare. The project was never realized because the Danish Red Cross claimed that the Colombians never answered their telexes, and on the Colombian side the Red Cross complained that the Danes never informed them. Even we, who were promotors of the project and had talked to both parties, were never appropriately informed about the decision-making process and never obtained answers to our queries. Bureaucacy effectively silenced the advocates in this case.

To demand local unity as a premise for cooperation can easily become an excuse for letting time run out without doing anything at all, apart from leaving the Indians to alleged autonomy and self-determination until more violent forces intrude into their world. This situation obtained for the Arhuacos, who complained that no one was concerned about their problems and felt that the external world was splitting them apart. A few years earlier the Arhuacos had made the written proclamation: "We are being divided between government institutions, between religions, between political parties. If it continues we do not have enough people to supply them all" (*Unidad Indigena* no. 1, 1973). Unintentionally they thereby furnished their would-be advocates with an excuse for delaying their intervention.

The Asuntos Indigenas also faces the demands of the state that society ultimately must be one. Thus, the demand that minority groups speak with one voice reflects the general nationalist trend in Latin American societies. "The cry of 'One nation, indivisible' with perhaps added imprecations hurled against tribalists and separatists is all too often used as an ideological weapon against those who wish to alter the status quo and to share fully and equally the privileges of citizenship" (Maybury-Lewis 1985, 133). To alter the status quo may initially require a multivocal discourse within which even minorities need not be reduced to common denominators. Perhaps this is where the desirability and viability of pluralistic polities could initially be demonstrated (Maybury-Lewis 1985).

Resuming the argument, we see how problems of representativity in advocacy actually turn toward much more general problems in anthropology. When the notion that informants speak cultural truths is given up, we always have to face a problem of representativity. Who are the informants and what are they supposed to represent, anyway? No fieldworker talks extensively with all people, and no "native" knows everything. Fortunately, we have also abandoned the idea that we should search for the typical, or the average, in order to assess the common denominator of culture. Each event, whether of speech or action, must be seen as exemplary rather than representative.

The problems of representativity thus change radically once we realize that culture is not an empirical category but an *analytical implication* (Hastrup 1988, 1990c). The point of doing anthropology is to achieve a level of understanding beyond speech, and identify the context within which even contradictory statements gain meaning. Anthropologically, therefore, a person's "speech" must be a presentation of the entire context rather than the "texts" of a selected group. If it is a matter of presenting specific views, the anthropologist may temporarily step out of his scholarly role, if his moral commitment bids him to do so. The anthropological demand, however, is to raise the context awareness of people themselves, so that they may eventually become better suited to plead their own cause.

Cultural survival, then, is not dependent upon the advocation of a specific view to the outside world, but upon the comprehension of the general context in which the relationship between the inside and the outside worlds is embedded.

Culture and Change Whatever else it implies, advocacy entails an active inducement to change. In the age of applied anthropology change was generally conceived of as externally induced, and the anthropologists who engaged themselves in this were less respectable than the rest. It is a general feature in the history of anthropology that culture has been defined as inherently antagonistic to change in general and more particularly to development.

As experts in culture and cultural difference, anthropologists have often resisted development among the people they studied, at least in the sense advocated by development experts. These, in their turn, have regarded culture as a hindrance to development. In these circumstances "development on its own premises" has been regarded as a contradiction in terms, and cultural dissolution has been seen as the "price of progress" (Bodley 1982, 149ff.). The argument has been made that development inevitably will lead to the destruction of the weaker cultures (Maybury-Lewis 1985, 131–132). Sadly enough, history has to a large extent made this argument into a self-fulfilling prophecy, but there are alternatives to destruction (Bodley 1977, 34–36).

In our view, the relationship between culture and development is not inherently antagonistic (Dahl 1986, 14–15). The two concepts of necessity inform each other, because the concept of culture in modern anthropology implies change, just as the notion of development implies a theory of the world (Hastrup 1990a). Development itself is a cultural concept, masking a particular ideology (Dahl and Hjort 1984, 174ff.). The main question, therefore, is not whether culture and development impede each other, but how they can be combined to the satisfaction of a particular people—under the assumption that development is always cultural.

In present-day anthropology there is no logical contradiction between structure and change, or between system and event. They constitute simultaneities (Ardener 1978). In other words, there is no culture outside the living reality of thought and action. In the social space people are both definers and defined (Ardener 1987, 39; Hastrup 1987). This means that human beings themselves are the agents of the social system and of history (cf. Hollis 1985, 232). Cultural survival, therefore, does not imply conservation of a preconceived identity which once and for all is anchored in an objectively existing, reified culture. It implies that the agents of a particular culture remain in charge of the shaping of local history.

The continuity between system and event also dissolves the opposition between stability and change in anthropological theory. They may serve as analytical tools, but they are not contradictory terms of reality. Any event is simultaneously a realization and a change of the system (cf. Sahlins 1985). No social events are ever exact replicas of previous ones (Ardener 1970). Structure is always at the mercy of actions, and the concept of timeless societies or societies without history is untenable. Change or, if you wish, development is inherent in culture.

At particular points in time, local processes of change may be spurred by a return to earlier images of history, like the Arhuacos' return to Tairona ways of agriculture and organization, or their turning to the mamus to oppose the mission. These returns, perhaps, are instances of "nonsynchronous contradiction" coming to life "where qualitative changes in a society's mode of production animate images of the past in the hope of a better future" (Taussig 1987, 166). But they are certainly also instances of simultaneity between culture and event, structure and change.

This implies that development must be rethought in terms of local history rather than in terms of abstract economy. To engage in a local development project, therefore, requires that the local historical potential is analyzed. This may be read as yet another attempt to conserve local cultures as living museums (cf. Bodley 1977), but it is nothing of the sort. It is an acknowledgment of people's rights to define their own future (cf. Maybury-Lewis 1985, 135). Development without local participation is meaningless, and will logically corrupt the continuity between system and event (see Hastrup 1990a). The so-called inevitable destruction of indigenous culture by development projects can and must now be counterbalanced by a view of several possible futures for indigenous peoples.

The inherent connection between culture and development rephrases the problem of representativity. There is no objectively identifiable culture to represent, and any Arhuaco vision of history and society may generate a future. Thus, facing the two (or more) versions of the history of the Arhuacos, the anthropologist has no choice but to acknowledge them both. It is not possible by means of anthropological analysis to determine which one is right and which one is wrong, although we might identify their different possible consequences. In anthropological terms they are equal—if different. The cultural context established by implication must contain both, and ideas of development must accommodate the local split. The advocate cannot take an internal stance—not on anthropological grounds at least.

The Concept of Advocacy Reconsidered As will be apparent, considerations of advocacy rapidly lead toward considerations of common anthropological problems. "Although work on behalf of tribal peoples and ethnic groups may be a peculiar form of advocacy it is not a very strange kind of anthropology" (Maybury-Lewis 1985, 146–47). Anthropology, so to speak, is born from the cultural encounter and anthropological practice always involves some kind of representation of the "other."

There is an inherent dilemma in anthropological advocacy, however. Anthropology is concerned with context rather than interest, while advocacy means making a choice among interests within the context. When some Arhuacos asked us to plead their particular cause to government and funding agencies, they immediately had our sympathy as well as our professional interest. They still have; but before we can go on we must discuss the complexity of the social reality with them. They are not unaware of the conflicting interests, of course, but it appears that in their relation to the outer world (including ourselves) they still want to present themselves as a united community, and therefore tend to be silent on issues of local conflict. We cannot, however, take this self-presentation at face value; it masks a divided truth. Ultimately, our uncovering this truth may enable the Arhuacos to speak much more convincingly for themselves, thus avoiding the fate of becoming passive clients.

What seemed to be a pretty straightforward case of speaking for a suppressed minority became increasingly complicated once we started to unearth the hidden values. As suggested by Van Esterik, it may be important to understand advocacy as a mode of communication, which is likely to be "over-emotional, over-simplified, rhetorical, over-dramatic, exaggerated, single-minded, without footnotes: in short the exact opposite of our academic writing" (Van Esterik 1985, 81). Particular circumstances may warrant such emotional stands, but the credibility of anthropology should not be jeopardized. Conversely, sound anthropological principles of uncovering complex patterns and suspending judgment until then may pave the way for vital instances of advocacy. Also, we should never forget that a commitment to improving the world is no substitute for understanding it (Baer 1986, 10).

Advocacy in this last sense grows out of anthropology in general, but it cannot of itself be anthropological. It is a position anthropologists may land in more by circumstance than by scholarly plan because of lary to our engagement in the fieldwork dialogue, leaving none of the interlocutors unchanged, and making some degree of advocacy almost inevitable. Active advocacy is also a consequence of our work among deprived populations, of course, and of our having to represent them to somebody else. Perhaps the main issue in the discussion of advocacy in relation to anthropology is not whom we are speaking *for*, but whom we are speaking *to*. The conventions of representation may differ vastly in the two instances, neither of which can be deemed superior in any absolute way.

Presenting indigenous problems in well-established anthropological terms in academic monographs is important, even if they only speak to the academic community. The academic discourse provides a necessarily well-informed point of departure for presenting the reality and the hopes of indigenous peoples, both to themselves and to their governments. Advocacy, on the other hand, has its own discourse because it is directed toward specific goals (Harries-Jones 1985). The pursuit of these goals cannot be legitimized in terms of anthropology, while such goals can certainly be informed by it.

As individuals and as a collectivity, even anthropologists must sometimes leave the canons behind in order to keep their professional integrity. Advocacy may become a personal obligation when the anthropologist becomes increasingly involved in the local social context, even if it does not grow out of the anthropological analysis as such. The question of timing is important; the requirements of any particular instance may demand immediate action, if a particular local culture—that is, a mode of defining a particular history—should not succumb to eternal accidents and infringements. In some acute situations, anthropologists should not suspend judgment too long, if they want to invoke anthropology against the inevitability argument in global development—that is, the argument that development will inevitably destroy local cultures.

It is the duty of anthropology to show that other futures are possible, and it is with a view to this that advocacy may sometimes be seen as an acute implication of anthropology, in which any of its practitioners may land. The anthropological interpretation cannot always be reserved for the scholarly community, important though this remains, but must be given active voice and presented to somebody else who has the power to listen.

While anthropological advocacy seems precluded, *anthropologists'* advocacy may sometimes prove vital to a particular group. Anthropology cannot furnish us with any rules for pleading. In the case of advocacy as in the case of ethnography, the anthropologist must establish his or her own authority. In neither case should the anthropologist be left alone, however, but should be backed by a discipline which cannot afford to neglect "the burden of being civilized," such as it has been imposed upon our traditional subject of study (cf. Baer 1986). The lesson of the anthropological involvement in a multivocal discourse is ultimately moral.

Concluding Remarks We have introduced a distinction between anthropological advocacy and anthropologists' advocacy, and argued that while the latter may often present itself as inevitable the former seems impossible. While individual anthropologists may find themselves in situations where a failure to advocate particular causes would be irresponsible, they still have no collective scientific standards for their advocacy. However, anthropology may be better suited than any other discipline in matters of advocating the causes of others, and this may imply a particular morality.

The all-important question of relativism versus objectivism, which, indeed, is on the hidden agenda in this appendix, does not attribute an *amoral* relativism to our position. We would like to think of relativism as a step—our only possible step—toward anthropological objectivism. The scope of anthropology is not only to represent other cultures (however defined) but also to transcend local knowledge and create a general understanding of things human. The problem is, however, that this scientific procedure is not directly translatable into practice. Wherever value judgments are to be made, objectivity evades. While we may be more or less justified in claiming that standards for the construction of anthropological knowledge exist, it is far less certain that we may ever be able to use these as guidelines for advocacy. Our point is: While advocacy is extremely pertinent in a whole range of situations which anthropology may adequately disentangle, no scientific standards for *intervention* exist.

Whatever the applicability of particular analytical results, anthropology as such possesses no key to particular strategies of advocacy. As human beings and as carriers of our own particular cultural standards, we may feel something to be right or wrong, but we can hardly back it by anthropological argument.

In spite of the efforts made by Paine and others to clarify the issue of advocacy and anthropology (Paine 1985b), it is still impossible to draw any final conclusion about the compatibility. To the best of our knowledge no one has as yet provided evidence that anthropology—as a scholarly discourse—made a particular pleading inevitable. Fieldwork and the involvement with a particular community, simple moral commitment and a sense of justice, political observation, and a feeling of anger on behalf of the community, are all of them parts in the decision to advocate. Advocacy, furthermore, may be informed by anthropological knowledge of context and possible contradictions, but where exactly does anthropology give a clue to a specific course of advocacy? Can anyone provide an example which demonstrates—step by step—how anthropological analysis is transformed to practical pleading?

We wholeheartedly subscribe to the notion that an anthropologist without concern is no anthropologist at all, but concern can be expressed in ethnography as well as in advocacy. The general acknowledgment of the anthropologist as intermediary may facilitate the leap from the first to the second. It is still a leap, however, from the collective standards for scholarship and publication to the individual judgment of particular causes and policymaking.

The important question of audience is entangled in this. While we have well-known forms of address in the scholarly community and—to some extent at least—may control our messages, we are almost completely at a loss in the world of politicking; individual anthropologists may of course be exempted from this. This is why we suggest that the problem of whom we are speaking *to* must be given the same consideration as the problem of whom we are speaking *for*. Eventually, this may contribute to a more comprehensive understanding of the total context of advocacy—including the context of communication.

In some sense, the anthropological discourse is always hierarchically related to its object. In order to speak *about* something one must encircle it in a language of a different order from the thing spoken about (Hastrup 1990b). To speak *for* somebody requires that hierarchy be denied. Here, we believe, lies the ultimate logical obstacle to anthropological advocacy. One cannot speak from two positions at the same time, even if one can oscillate between them.

References

Abrahamson, L. Y., Seligman, M. E. P., and Teasdale, J. P. 1978. Learned helplessness in humans: Critique and reformulation. *Journal of Abnormal Psychology* 87: 49–74.

Agar, M. 1980. *The professional stranger: An informal introduction to ethnography*. London: Academic Press.

Anderson, A. B. 1980. Recent acculturation of bush negroes in Surinam and French Guiana. *Anthropologica* 12: 61–84.

Apollinaire, G. 1971. *Zone: Selected writings*. New York: New Directions.

Arcand, B. 1972. The Cuiva. In *The situation of the Indian in South America*. Geneva: World Council of Churches.

Ardener, E. 1970. Witchcraft, economics, and the continuity of belief. In *Witchcraft confessions and accusations*, ed. M. Dougal. ASA monographs, 9. London: Tavistock.

———. 1978. Some outstanding problems in the analysis of events. *Yearbook of Symbolic Anthropology* 1.

———. 1987. Remote areas: Some theoretical considerations. In *Anthropology at home*, ed. A. Jackson. ASA monographs, 25. London: Tavistock.

Artaud, A. 1981. *Texter i urval*. Stockholm: Almqvist and Wiksell.

Baer, H. A. 1986. The concept of civilization in anthropology: A critical review. In *The burden of being civilized: An anthropological perespective on the discontents of civilization*, ed. M. Richardson and M. C. Webb. Athens: University of Georgia Press.

Barba, E. 1986. *Beyond the floating islands*. New York: PAJ Publications.

Bateson, G. 1972. *Steps to an ecology of mind*. New York: Ballantine.

Bauer, M., and Lunn, S. 1984. Jagten på et meningsfuld liv: om det moderne psykoboom. *Politisk Revy, Kontext* 45.

Benjamin, W. 1979. One way street. In *One way street and other writings*, ed. E. Jephcott and K. Shorter. London: New Left Books.

Berreman, G. D. 1983. Identity definition, assertion and politicisation in the Central Himalayas. In *Identity: Personal and sociocultural*, ed. A. Jacobsen-Widding. Uppsala: Acta Universitatis Uppsalensis.

Bettelheim, B. 1979. *Surviving and other essays*. New York: Vintage.

———. 1986. *The informed heart: A study of the psychological consequences of living under extreme fear and terror.* New York: Peregrine Books.

Bion, W. R. 1961. *Experiences in groups.* London: Tavistock.

Blond, A. 1977. *Knægtelse og krænkelse: En undersøgelse af konstituerings-problemet for Freuds teori og af dens status som socialvidenskab.* Copenhagen: Rhodos.

Bodley, J. H. 1977. Alternatives to ethnocide: Human zoos, living museums, and real people. In *Western expansion and indigenous peoples: The heritage of Las Casas,* ed. E. Sevilla-Casas. The Hague: Mouton.

———. 1982. *Victims of progress.* Los Angeles: Mayfield Publishing.

Bonilla, V. D. 1972. *Servants of God or masters of men? The story of a Capuchin mission in Amazonia.* Harmondsworth: Penguin.

Boon, J. 1982. *Other tribes, other scribes: Symbolic anthropology in the comparative study of cultures, histories, religions, and texts.* Cambridge: Cambridge University Press.

Borofsky, G. L., and Brand, D. J. 1980. Personality organization and psychological functioning of the Nuremberg War Criminals: The Rorschach data. In *Survivors, victims, and perpetrators: Essays on the Nazi holocaust,* ed. J. E. Dimsdale. New York: Hemisphere Publishing.

Brandt, P. Å. 1980. *Den talende krop.* Copenhagen: Rhodos.

Bredsdorff, T. 1986. *Magtspil: europæiske familiestykker.* Copenhagen: Gyldendal.

Brisebois, D. 1983. The Inuit Broadcasting Corporation. *Anthropologia* 1: 25–30.

Bromley, D. G., and Shupe, A. 1989. Public reaction against new religious movements. In *Cults and new religious movement: A report of the American Psychiatric Association,* ed. M. Galanter. New York: American Psychiatric Association.

Brown, G. S., and Harris, T. 1978. *The social origins of depression: A study of psychiatric disorder in women.* New York: Free Press.

Brown, N. O. 1968. *Life against death: The psychoanalytical meaning of history.* London: Sphere Books.

Brückner, P. 1974. *Kapitalismens socialpsykologi.* Copenhagen: Reitzels Forlag.

Casement, P. 1987. *Lyt til patienten: Om det dynamiske forhold terapeut-patient i den psykoanalytiske proces.* Copenhagen: Reitzels Forlag.

Cheater, A. P. 1985. Anthropologists and policy in Zimbabwe: Design at the centre and reaction on the periphery. In *Social anthropology and development policy,* ed. R. Grillo. ASA monographs, 23. London: Tavistock.

Christoffersen, E. E. 1986. *Thebens syv porte: En montage om Odin Teatret.* Århus': Århus Universitetsforlag.

Clastres, P. 1977. *Society against the state.* Oxford: Basil Blackwell.

Clifford, J. 1986. On ethnographic allegory. In *Writing culture: The poetics and politics of ethnography,* ed. J. Clifford and G. E. Marcos. Berkeley: University of California Press.

Cooper, D. 1980. *The language of madness.* Harmondsworth: Penguin.

Corbin, J. 1986. Insurrections in Spain: Casas Viejas 1933 and Madrid 1981. In *The anthropology of violence,* ed. D. Riches. Oxford: Basil Blackwell.

Coser, L. 1974. *Greedy institutions.* New York: Free Press.

Coser, R. L., and Coser, L. 1979. Jonestown as a perverse utopia: A "greedy institution" in the jungle. *Disssent* 26: 158–63.

Costa, P. T., and McCrae, R. R. 1980. Somatic complaints in males as a function of age and neuroticism: A longitudinal analysis. *Journal of Behavioral Medicine* 3: 245–58.

Dahl, G., and Hjort, A. 1984. Development as message and meaning. *Ethnos* 49: 3–4.

Dahl, J. 1986. Udviklingsaspektet i kulturen. *Stofskifte:* 14.

Dalton, G. 1971. *Economic development and social change: The modernization of village communities.* Garden City, N.Y.: Natural History Press.

De Groot, S. W. 1973. The bush negroes' chiefs visit Africa: Diary of an historic trip. In *Maroon societies: Rebel slave communities in the Americas,* ed. R. Price. New York: Anchor, Doubleday.

de Maré, P. 1975. The politics of large groups. In *The large group: Dynamics and therapy,* ed. L. Kreeger. Itaska, IL: Peacock Publishers.

de Pres, T. 1980. The survivor: An anatomy of life in the death camp. In *Survivors, victims, and perpetrators: Essays on the Nazi holocaust,* ed. J. E. Dimsdale. New York: Hemisphere Publishing.

Deutsch, A. 1989. Psychological perspectives on cult leadership. In *Cults and new religious movement: A report of the American Psychiatric Association,* ed. M. Galanther. New York: American Psychiatric Association.

de Vegamian, F. M. 1972. *Los Angeles del Tucuco, 1945–1970. Monografias misionales de sus internados indigenas en los veinticinco años de su fundación.* Maracaibo: Tucuco.

———. 1978. *Diccionario ilustrado: Yupa español—español yupa.* Maracaibo: Tucuco.

Dostal, W., ed. 1972. *The situation of the Indian in South America.* Geneva: World Council of Churches.

Douglas, M. 1984. *Purity and danger: An analysis of the concepts of pollution and taboo.* London: Ark.

DSM III. *Diagnostic and statistical manual of mental disorders.* 1980. New York: American Psychiatric Association.

Echeverry, A. 1982. Comenzó la rebelion de los Arhaucos. *Revista Cromos* (August).

———. 1984. *The magical universe of the Arhuaco-Indians.* Bogota: Audiovisuales.

Eitinger, L. 1964. *Concentration camp survivors in Norway and Israel.* London: Allen and Unwin.

Elsass, P. 1991. Self-reflection or self-presentation: A study of the advocacy effect. *Visual Anthropology* 4: 161–73.

———. 1986. Kultur og tænkemåde: Tankeforstyrrelser som overrelevevesesmekanisme hos et indiansk folk i Latinamerika. In *Sygdomsbilleder. Medicinsk*

antropologi og psykologi, ed. P. Elsass and K. Hastrup. Copenhagen: Gyldendal.
———. 1987. Symbols of survival: A social psychological study of two South American peoples. *Folk* 29: 55–75.
———. 1988 *The earth is our mother: Two Indian tribes in Latin America.* New York: Filmmakers Library.
———. 1977. *Indianerliv: 12 rejser bland undertrykte indianske folk i Latinamerika.* Copenhagen: Gyldendal.
———. 1980. *Emigrantliv: Kolonier, ghettoer og folk på flugt i Latinamerika.* Copenhagen: Gyldendal.
Enzensberger, H. M. 1987. Hvad nu hvis dette helt fremmede slet ikke eksisterer. *Teater 87* 35: 26–28.
Esslin, M. 1968. *Det absurde teater.* Copenhagen: Rhodos.
Fanon, F. 1967. *The wretched of the earth.* Middlesex: Penguin. (Fordømte her på jord. Copenhagen: Rhodos, 1968).
———. 1970. *Black skin, white mask: The experience of a black man in a white world.* Harmondsworth: Penguin.
Feinsod, E. 1981. *Awake in a nightmare: Jonestown. The only eyewitness account. Based on interviews with Odell Rhodes.* New York: W. W. Norton.
Festinger, L. 1957. *A theory of cognitive dissonance.* Stanford: Stanford University Press.
Forge, A. 1972. The golden fleece. *Man* 7: 527–40.
Foster, G. M. 1969. *Applied anthropology.* Boston: Little, Brown.
Foucault, M. 1977. *Overvågning og straf.* Copenhagen: Rhodos.
———. 1980. *Power and knowledge: Selected interviews and writings.* New York: Pantheon.
Frank, L. 1987. Udviklingsspillet, Copenhagen. *Hug!* 49: 41–51.
Frankl, V. E. 1966. Logotherapy and existential analysis: A review. *American Journal of Psychotherapy* 20: 252–89.
———. 1970. *Psykiatri og sjælesorg: Grundlaget for logoterapi og eksistensanalyse.* Copenhagen: Gyldendal.
Frazier, E. F. 1974. *The negro church in America.* New York: Lincoln Press.
Freud, S. 1955. *Beyond the pleasure principle.* London: Hogarth Press and the Institute of Psycho-analysis. *S. E.* vol. 18.
———. 1959. *Group psychology and the analysis of the ego.* New York. W. W. Norton.
———. 1961. *Civilisation and its discontents.* London: Hogarth Press and the Institute of Psycho-analysis. *S. E.* vol. 21.
———. 1964. *Moses and monotheism.* London: Hogarth Press and the Institute of Psycho-analysis. *S. E.* vol. 23.
Friedlander, J. 1975. *Being Indian in Hueyapan: A study of forced identity in contemporary Mexico.* New York: St. Martin's Press.
From, F. 1965. *Oplevelsen af andres adfærd.* Copenhagen: Nyt Nordisk Forlag.
Fromm, E. 1977. *The anatomy of human destructiveness.* London: Penguin.

Gad, T., and Gad, B. 1982. *Eneboeren i Søndermarken: En bog om ensomhed.* Copenhagen: Reitzels Forlag.
Galanter, M., ed. 1989. *Cults and new religious movement: A report of the American Psychiatric Association.* New York: American Psychiatric Association.
Galeano, E. 1977. *Latinamerikas åreladning.* Copenhagen: Suensons Forlag.
Garber, J., and Hollon, S. D. 1980. Universal versus personal helplessness in depression: Belief in uncontrollability or incompetence. *Journal of Abnormal Psychology* 89: 56–66.
Garber, J., and Seligman, M. E. P., eds. 1980. *Human helplessness: Theory and applications.* New York: Academic Press.
Gay, P. 1984. *Education of the senses: The bourgeois experience. Victoria to Freud.* New York: Oxford University Press.
Geertz, C. 1986. Slide show: Evans-Pritchard's African transparencies. *Raritan* 2: 62–80.
Girard, R. 1982. *La violence et le sacré.* Paris: Grasset.
Goffman, E. 1968. *Asylums: Essays on the social situation of mental patients and other inmates.* New York: Pelican.
Goodenough, W. H. 1963. *Cooperation in change.* New York: Wiley.
Goodwin, J. 1982. *Sexual abuse: Incest victims and their families.* Boston: Academic Press.
Grey, A. 1986. Udviklingsdimensioner. *Stofskifte: Tidskrift for antropologi* 14: 87–105.
———. 1987. The Amer-Indian of South America, London. *Minority Right Group,* report no. 15.
Grillo, R. 1985. Applied anthropology in the 1980s: Retrospect and prospect. In *Social anthropology and development policy,* ed. R. Grillo. ASA monographs, 23.
Grotowski, J. 1975. *Towards a poor theatre.* London: Methuen.
Gulliver, P. H. 1985. An applied anthropologist in East Africa during the colonial era. In *Social anthropology and development policy,* ed. R. Grillo. ASA monographs, 23.
Hammen, C., and deMayo, R. 1982. Cognitive correlates of teacher stress and depressive symptoms: Implications for attributional models of depression. *Journal of Abnormal Psychology* 91: 96–101.
Hammen, C. L., Krantz, S., and Cochran, S. 1981. Relationships between depression and causal attributions about stressful life events. *Cognitive Therapy and Research* 5: 351–58.
Harries-Jones, P. 1985. From cultural translator to advocate: Changing circles of interpretation. In *Advocacy and anthropology, first encounters,* ed. R. Paine. Newfoundland: Memorial University of Newfoundland.
Harrower, M. 1976. Rorschach records of the Nazi war criminals: An experimental study after thirty years. *Journal of Personality Assessment* 40: 341–51.

Hastrup, K. 1985. Anthropology and the exaggeration of culture: A review article. *Ethnos* 50: 3–4.

———. 1987. The reality of anthropology. *Ethnos* 52: 23–44.

———. 1988. Kultur som analytisk begreb. In *Kulturbegrebets kulturhistorie,* ed. H. Hauge and Horstbøll. Århus: Århus Universitetsforlag.

———. 1990a. Udvikling eller historie. Antropologiens bidrag til en ny verden. *Den Ny Verden* 23: 21–45.

———. 1990b. Writing ethnography: State of the art. In *Anthropology and autobiography,* ed. H. Callaway, H. and J. Okeley. London: Routledge.

———. 1990c. The ethnographic present: A reinvention. *Cultural Anthropology* 5: 53–72.

Hastrup, K., and Elsass, P. 1988. Incest i tværkulturel belysning. *Nordisk Sexologi* 1: 12–25.

———. 1990. Anthropological advocacy: A contradiction in terms? *Current Anthropology* 3: 301–11.

Hastrup, K., and Ramløv, K. eds. 1988. *Feltarbejde: Oplevelse og metode i etnografien.* Copenhagen: Akademisk Forlag.

Henny, L. M. 1981. Effects of one-sided and two-sided media presentations in social conscientization. In *Methodology in anthropological filmmaking,* ed. N. C. R. Bogaart and W. E. R. Katelaar. Papers of the IAUES-Intercongress. Amsterdam: Edition Herodot.

Henriksen, G. 1985. Anthropologists as advocates: Promoters of pluralism or makers of clients? In *Advocacy and anthropology, first encounters,* ed. R. Paine. Newfoundland: Memorial University of Newfoundland.

Héritier, F. 1982. The symbolics of incest and its prohibition. In *Between belief and transgression,* ed. M. Izard and P. Smith. Chicago: University of Chicago Press.

Herman, J. L. 1985. *Father-daughter incest.* Cambridge: Harvard University Press.

Herskovits, M. J. 1934. *Rebel destiny among bush negroes of Dutch Guiana.* New York: McGraw-Hill.

Herzog, W. 1984. The screenplay. In *Burden of dreams,* ed. L. Blank and J. Bogan. Berkeley: North Atlantic Books.

Hilberg, R. 1980. The nature of the process. In *Survivors, Victims, and perpetrators: Essays on the Nazi holocaust,* ed. J. E. Dimsdale. New York: Hemisphere Publishing.

Hinkle, L. E. 1984. The effect of exposure to culture change, social change, and changes in interpersonal relationships on health. In *Stressful life events: Their nature and effects,* ed. B. S. Dohrenwend and B. P. Dohrenwend. New York: Wiley.

Hollis, M. 1985. Of masks and men. In *The category of the person: Anthropology, philosophy, history,* ed. J. Carrithers. Cambridge: Cambridge University Press.

Holmes, T. H., and Masuda, M. 1974. Life changes and illness susceptibility. In

Stressful life events: Their nature and effects, ed. B. S. Dohrenwend. New York: Wiley.

Holmes, T. H., and Rahe, R. H. 1967. The social readjustment rating scale. *Journal of Psychosomatic Research* 11: 213–218.

Huggins, N. I. 1981. *Sort odyssé: Afro-amerikanernes prøvelser under slaveriet.* Copenhagen: Gyldendal.

Hvalkoff, S. 1984. *Antropologiens grønne bagland. Den økologiske antropologis historiske, teoretiske og epistemologiske udvikling med særlig reference til Amazonas.* Ph.D. diss., Copenhagen University.

Isaacs, J. 1983. *Las tribus indigenas del Magdalena.* Bogotá: Ediciones Incunables.

IWGIA. 1971. *Declaration of Barbados.* Copenhagen: International Work Group for Indigenous Affairs, document no. 1.

Jaramillo, O. 1983. Algunos elementos culturales de la vida del colono en el catatumbo. *Cuardernos de Agroindustria y Economia Rural* 10: 12–24.

Jaulin, R. 1973. *La paz blanca: Introduccion al etnocidio.* Buenos Aires: Tiempo Contemporanea.

Jensen, J. P. 1978. *De forfulgtes psykologi: Om psykologisk tortur og Ulrike Marie Meinhof i statens varetægt.* Copenhagen: Bo Cavefors Bogforlag.

Kilduff, M., and Javers, R. 1979. *The suicide cult: The inside story of the Peoples Temple Sect and the massacre in Guyana.* New York: Bantam.

Kleinman, A. 1980. *Patients and healers in the context of culture.* Berkeley: University of California Press.

———. 1986. Anthropology and psychiatry: The role of culture in cross-cultural research on illness and care. In *Psychiatry and its related disciplines—The next 25 years,* ed. R. Rosenberg, F. Schulsinger, and E. Strömgren. Copenhagen: World Psychiatric Association.

Kleinman, A., and Good, B., ed. 1985. *Culture and depression: Studies in the anthropology and cross-cultural psychiatry of affect and disorder.* Berkeley: University of California Press.

Knudsen, A. 1988. Når verden er anderledes: Korsikanske utroligheder. In *Feltarbejde: Oplevelse og metode i etnografien,* ed. K. Hastrup and K. Ramløv. Copenhagen: Akademisk Forlag.

Kobasa, S. C. 1979. Stressful events, personality, and health: An inquiry into hardiness. *Journal of Personality and Social Psychology* 37: 1–11.

Kobasa, S. C., Maddi, S. R., and Kahn, S. 1982. Hardiness and health: A prospective study. *Journal of Personality and Social Psychology* 45: 839–50.

Kohut, H. 1977. *The restoration of the self.* New York: International Universities Press.

Kovel, J. 1970. *White racism: A psychohistory.* New York: Vintage.

Küng, A. 1981. *Bruce Olson: Missionary or colonizer?* New York: Christian Heralds Books.

Lacan, J. 1981. *Speech and language in psychoanalysis.* Baltimore: Johns Hopkins University Press.

Laing, R. 1970. *Sanity, madness, and the families of schizophrenics.* Harmondsworth: Penguin.

Lane, M. 1980. *The strongest poison.* New York: Hawthorn.

La Rusic, I. 1985. Reinventing the advocacy wheel? In *Advocacy and anthropology, first encounters,* ed. R. Paine. Newfoundland: Memorial University of Newfoundland.

Lasch, C. 1979. *The culture of narcissism.* New York: W. W. Norton.

———. 1984. *The minimal self: Psychic survival in troubled times.* New York: W. W. Norton.

Lazarus, R. S., and Folkman, S. 1984. *Stress, appraisal, and coping.* New York: Springer.

Lazarus, R. S., Kanner, A. D., and Folkman, S. 1980. Emotions: A cognitive-phenomenological analysis. In *Theories of emotion.* Vol. 1. *Emotion: Theory, research, and experience,* ed. R. Plutchik and R. Kellerman. New York: Academic Press.

Lévi-Strauss, C. 1969. *The elementary structures of kinship.* London: Eyre and Spottiswode.

Lewis, O. 1962. *Five families: Mexican case studies in the culture of poverty.* New York: Science Editions.

Lizarralde, R., and Beckerman, S. 1982. Historia contemporanea de los Bari. *Antropologica* 4: 58–89.

Lizarralde, R., Beckerman, S., and Elsass, P. 1987. *Indigenous survival among the Bari and Arhuaco: Strategies and perspectives.* Copenhagen: International Work Group for Indigenous Affairs, document no. 60.

Lizot, J. 1973. Economy or society ? *Journal de la Societé des Americanistes* 9: 137–75.

———. 1978. *El circulo de los fuegos: Vida y costumbres de los indios Yanomami.* Caracas: Monte Avila Editores.

Loaiza, T. A. 1984. *La organization indigena Arhauca y el proceso de educacion bicultural.* Tesis de grado, Universidad de los Andes, Bogotá.

Lorenz, K. 1966. *On aggression.* London: Methuen.

MacDougall, D. 1975. Beyond observational cinema. In *Principles of visual anthropology,* ed. P. Hockings. The Hague: Mouton.

———. 1978. Ethnographic film: Failure and promise. *Annual review of Anthropology.*

———. 1988. Media friend or media foe? *Visual Anthropology* 2: 54–58.

Mair, L. 1969. *Anthropology and social change.* LSE Monographs on Social Anthropology, 38. London: Athlone Press.

Manuel, G., and Posluns, M. 1978. *Den fjerde verden: En indiansk virkelighed.* Copenhagen: Informations Forlag.

Marcuse, H. 1955. *Eros and civilization.* Boston: Beacon Press.

Marquez, V. T. 1978. *Los Arhuacos y la vida de la civilizacion.* Bogotá: Editorial America Latina.

Marsella, A. J. 1985. Culture, self, and mental disorder. In *Culture and self:*

Asian and western perspectives, ed. A. J. Marsella, G. DeVos, and F. L. K. Hsu. New York: Tavistock.

Marsella, A. J., Sartorius, N., Jablensky, A., and Fenton, F. R. 1985. Cross-cultural studies of depressive disorders: An overview. In *Culture and depression: Studies in the anthropology and cross-cultural psychiatry of affect and disorder,* ed. A. Kleinman and B. Good. Berkeley: University of California Press.

Marvin, H. 1979. *Kanibaler og konger: Om økologiens indflydelse på kulturens udvikling.* Copenhagen: Berlinske Forlag.

Maybury-Lewis, D. 1985. A special sort of pleading: Anthropology at the service of ethnic groups. In *Advocacy and anthropology, first encounters,* ed. R. Paine. Newfoundland: Memorial University of Newfoundland.

Mead, M. 1972. *Blackberry winter: My earlier years.* London: Angus and Robertson.

Meunier, J., and Savarin, A. 1970. *Mord i Amazonas, 500 års indianutrotning.* Stockholm: PAN-Nordstedt.

Michael, I. 1973. *Mayalandet.* Copenhagen: Rhodos.

Milgram, S. 1974. *Obedience to authority: An experimental view.* New York: Harper and Row.

Muntslag, F. H. J. 1979. *Tembe: Surinaamse houtsnijkunst.* Paramaribo: VACO.

Naipaul, S. 1981. *Journey to nowhere: A new world tragedy.* New York: Simon & Schuster.

Nandy, A. 1983. *The intimate enemy: Loss and recovery of self under colonialism.* Oxford: Oxford University Press.

Obeyesekere, G. 1985. Depression, Buddhism, and the work of culture in Sri Lanka. In *Culture and depression: Studies in the anthropology and cross-cultural psychiatry of affect and disorder,* ed. A. Kleinman and B. Good. Berkeley: University of California Press.

Olsen, P. 1978. *Historie og psykologi.* Copenhagen: Dansk Psykologisk Forlag.

Olson, B. 1973. *Por esta cruz te mataré.* Miami, FL: Vida.

Overmeier, J. B., and Seligman, M. E. P. 1967. Effects of inescapable shock upon subsequent escape and avoidance responding. *Journal of Comparative and Physiological Psychology* 63: 28.

Paine, R. 1985a. Overview. In *Advocacy and anthropology, first encounters,* ed. R. Paine. Newfoundland: Memorial University of Newfoundland.

———, ed. 1985b. *Advocacy and anthropology, first encounters.* Newfoundland: Memorial University of Newfoundland.

Parkin, D. 1982. Introduction. In *Semantic anthropology.* ASA Monographs, 22. London: Academic Press.

Parsons, T. 1958. Definitions of health and illness in the light of American values and social structures. In *Patients, physicians, and illness,* ed. E. G. Jaco. New York: Free Press.

Patterson, O. 1973. Slave and slave revolts: A sociohistorical analysis of the first Maroon War, 1665–1740. In *Maroon societies: Rebel slave communities in the Americas,* ed. R. Price. New York: Anchor, Doubleday.

Persson, L. 1971. *Flodkildernes folk*. Copenhagen: Rhodos.

———. 1972a. *De dødsdømte indianere: De sydamerikanske indianeres situation idag*. Copenhagen: Rhodos.

———. 1972b. *Motilonernes berg: Vandringer og meditationer i Colombias djungler*. Stockholm: Nordstedt.

Pinton, S. 1965. Les Bari. *Journal de la Société de Americanistes* 54: 247–333.

Price, R. 1973. Maroons and their communities. In *Maroon societies: Rebel slave communities in the Americas,* ed. R. Price. New York: Anchor, Doubleday.

———. 1983. *First-time: The historical vision of an Afro-American people*. Baltimore: Johns Hopkins University Press.

Price, S., and Price, R.: 1980. *Afro-American arts of the Suriname rain forest*. Los Angeles: Museum of Cultural History, University of California.

Reich, W. 1972. *Fascismens massepsykologi*. Copenhagen: Rhodos.

Reichel-Dolmatoff, G. 1978. The loom of life: A Kogi principle of integration. *Latina Americana* 4: 5–27.

———. 1984. The Kogi Indians and the environment impending disaster. *Akwesasne Notes:* 22–23.

———. 1985. *Los Kogi: Una tribu de la Sierra Nevada de Santa Marta, 1 and* 2. Bogotá: Procultura.

———. 1991. *Los Fka, Sierra Nevada de Santa Marta, Colombia,* Notas etnograficas, 1946–1966. Bogotá: Universidad Nacional de Colombia.

Reichel-Dolmatoff, G., and Reichel-Dolmatoff, A. 1961. *The people of Aritama: The cultural personality of a Colombian mestizo village*. Chicago: University of Chicago Press.

———. 1977. *Estudios antropologicos: El misionero ante las culturas indigenas*. Bogotá: Instituto Colombiano de Cultura Impresso en Editorial Andes.

Reiterman, T. 1982. *Raven: The untold story of the Rev. Jim Jones and his people*. New York: E. P. Dutton.

Riches, D. 1986. The phenomenon of violence. In *The anthropology of violence,* ed. D. Riches. Oxford: Basil Blackwell.

Rosaldo, M. 1984. Towards an anthropology of self and feeling. In *Culture theory,* ed. R. A. Schweder and R. A. Le Vine. Cambridge: Cambridge University Press.

Rouch, J. 1975. The camera and man. In *Principles of visual anthropology,* ed. P. Hockings. The Hague: Mouton.

Rubinstein, R. A., and Tax, S. 1985. Power, powerlessness, and the failure of "political realism." In *Native power,* ed. J. Brøsted. Oslo: Universitetsforlaget.

Rumualdo, A. 1987. Hace veinticinco anos. *Revista de Animacion Missionera* 527: 151–63.

Sahlins, M. D. 1981. Historical metaphors and mythical realities: Structure in the early history of the Sandwich Island Kingdom. Ann Arbor: The University of Michigan Press. 1981.

———. 1985. *Islands of history*. Chicago: University of Chicago Press.
Sanders, D. E. 1977. *The formation of the World Council of Indigenous Peoples*. Copenhagen: International Work Group for Indigenous People, document no. 29.
Sansom, B. 1985. Canons of anthropology? In *Advocacy and anthropology, first encounters,* ed. R. Paine. Newfoundland: Memorial University of Newfoundland.
Sass, L. A. 1986. Anthropology's native problems, revisionism in the field. *Harpers Magazine* (May): 49–57.
Seligman, M. E. P. 1974. Depression and learned helplessness. In *The psychology of depression: Contemporary theory and research,* ed. R. J. Friedman and M. M. Katz. New York: Wiley.
———. 1975. *Helplessness*. San Francisco: Freeman.
Shupe, A. D., and Bromley, D. G. 1982. Shaping the public response to Jonestown: The People's Temple and the anti-cult movement. In *Violence and religious commitment,* ed. K. Levy. Philadelphia: University of Pennsylvania Press.
Sjørslev, I. 1988. Deltagelsens dilemma: Et brasiliansk offer. In *Feltarbejde: Oplevelse og metode i etnografien,* ed. K. Hastrup and K. Ramløv. Copenhagen: Akademisk Forlag.
Skinningsrud, T. 1987. Anthropological films and the myth of scientific truth. *Visual Anthropology* 1: 47–70.
Slater, P. 1963. Libidinal diffusion in big organizations. *American Sociological Review,* no. 1.
Smith, R. C. 1985. A search for unity within diversity. In *Native peoples and economic development: Sex case studies from Latin America,* ed. T. Macdonald. Cambridge, MA: Cultural Survival.
Sontag, S. 1977. *On photography*. New York: Farrar, Straus and Giroux.
Stedman, J. G. 1966. *Narrative of a five-years' expedition against the revolted negroes of Surinam from the year 1772 to 1777*. London: J. Johnson and J. Edwards.
Storr, A. 1988. *Solitude*. New York: Free Press.
Tarp, E. 1984. Socialisme i Nicaragua. Planlagt kollekitivitet eller kollektiv bevidsthed: Om Miskito-indianerne i Østnicaragua. *Stofskifte: Tidskrift for antropologi* 10: 93–115.
Taussig, M. T. 1980. *The devil and commodity fetishism in South America*. Chapel Hill: University of North Carolina Press.
———. 1987. *Shamanism, colonialism, and the wild man: A study in terror and healing*. Chicago: University of Chicago Press.
Tedlock, D. 1983. *The spoken word and the work of interpretation*. Philadelphia: University of Pennsylvania Press.
Timerman, J. 1982. *Fange uden navn, celle uden nummer*. Copenhagen: Gyldendal.
Toits, P. A. 1983. Dimensions of life events as influences upon the genesis of psychological distress and associated conditions: An evaluation and synthesis

of literature. In *Psychosocial stress: Trends in theory and research,* ed. H. B. Kaplan. New York: Academic Press.

Tversky, A., and Kahneman, D. 1971. Belief in the law of small numbers. *Psychological Bulletin* 76: 105–10.

———. 1981. The framing of decision and the psychology of choice. *Science* 211: 453–58.

Van Esterik, P. 1985. Confronting advocacy confronting anthropology. In *Advocacy and anthropology, first encounters,* ed. R. Paine. Newfoundland: Memorial University of Newfoundland.

Varese, S. 1982. Restoring multiplicity: Indianities and the civilizing project in Latin America. *Latin American Perspectives* 9: 29–41.

Veber, H. 1984. Indfødte folk i politisk bevægelse. *Stofskifte: Tidskrift for Antropology* 10: 31–63.

Wallman, S. 1985. Rules of thumb. In *Advocacy and anthropology, first encounters,* ed. R. Paine. Newfoundland: Memorial University of Newfoundland.

Weightman, J. M. 1983. *Making sense of the Jonestown suicides.* New York: Edwin Mellen Press.

Whisson, M. G. 1985. Advocates, brokers and collaborators: Anthropologists in the real world. In *Social anthropology and development policy,* ed. R. Grillo. ASA monographs, 23. London: Tavistock.

Wilbert, J. 1961. Identificacion etno-linguistica de las tribus indigenas del occidente de Venezuela. *Naturales La Salle 21* 58: 5–27.

Wilden, A. 1972. *System and structure: Essays in communication and exchange.* London: Tavistock.

Wolf, E. R. 1982. *Europe and the people without history.* Berkeley: University of California Press.

Woodburn, J. C. 1979. Minimal politics: The political organization of the Hadza of North Tanzania. In *Politics in leadership: A comparative perspective,* ed. P. S. Cohen and W. A. Schack. London: Clarendon Press.

———. 1982. Egalitarian societies. *Man* 17: 431–51.

Woods, M. J. 1981. *Psycho-social perspectives of the Jonestown phenomenon.* Santa Cruz: University of California.

Worth, S., and Adair, J. 1972. *Through Navajo eyes: An exploration in film communication and anthropology.* Bloomington: Indiana University Press.

Yee, M. S., and Layton, T. N. 1982. *In my father's house: The story of the Layton family and the Rev. Jim Jones.* New York: Holt, Rinehart and Winston.

Zimbardo, P. G., and Hartley, C. 1987. Who gets recruited during the initial contact phase of cult recruitment? *Cultic Studies Journal* 2: 91–147.

Index